CONCEPTS AND APPLICATIONS

SUPPLEMENTAL PRACTICE PROBLEMS
STUDENT EDITION

 **Glencoe
McGraw-Hill**

New York, New York   Columbus, Ohio   Woodland Hills, California   Peoria, Illinois

Chemistry
Concepts and Applications

Student Edition

Teacher Wraparound Edition

Teacher Classroom Resources:
- Laboratory Manual SE and TE
- Study Guide SE and TE
- Problems and Solutions Manual
- Supplemental Practice Problems SE and TE
- Chapter Review and Assessment
- Section Focus Transparency Package
- Basic Concepts Transparency Package
- Problem Solving Transparency Package
- ChemLab and MiniLab Worksheets
- Critical Thinking/Problem Solving
- Chemistry and Industry
- Consumer Chemistry
- Tech Prep Applications
- Applying Scientific Methods in Chemistry
- Spanish Resources
- Lesson Plans
- Calculator-based Labs

Technology
- Computer Test Bank: Windows and Macintosh
- CD-ROM Multimedia System: Windows and Macintosh Versions
- Videodisc Program
- Chapter Summaries, English and Spanish Audiocassettes
- MindJogger Videoquizzes
- Mastering Concepts in Chemistry—Software

The Glencoe Science Professional Development Series
- Cooperative Learning in the Science Classroom
- Alternate Assessment in the Science Classroom
- Lab and Safety Skills in the Science Classroom
- Performance Assessment in the Science Classroom
- Using the Internet in the Science Classroom

Glencoe/McGraw-Hill

A Division of The McGraw·Hill Companies

Copyright © by The McGraw-Hill Companies, Inc. All rights reserved. Permission is granted to reproduce the material contained herein on the condition that such material be reproduced only for classroom use; be provided to students, teachers, and families without charge; and be used solely in conjunction with the *Chemistry: Concepts and Applications* program. Any other reproduction, for use or sale, is prohibited without prior written permission of the publisher.

Send all inquiries to:
Glencoe/McGraw-Hill
8787 Orion Place
Columbus, Ohio 43240-4027

ISBN 0-02-825553-4
Printed in the United States of America.

13 HES 13 12

Contents

	Introduction	1
Chapter 1	Chemistry: The Science of Matter	7
Chapter 2	Matter Is Made up of Atoms	13
Chapter 3	Introduction to the Periodic Table	19
Chapter 4	Formation of Compounds	23
Chapter 5	Types of Compounds	25
Chapter 6	Chemical Reactions and Equations	37
Chapter 7	Completing the Model of the Atom	51
Chapter 8	Periodic Properties of the Elements	55
Chapter 9	Chemical Bonding	59
Chapter 10	The Kinetic Theory of Matter	67
Chapter 11	Behavior of Gases	71
Chapter 12	Chemical Quantities	83
Chapter 13	Water and Its Solutions	107
Chapter 14	Acids, Bases, and pH	113
Chapter 15	Acid and Base Reactions	117
Chapter 16	Oxidation-Reduction Reactions	125
Chapter 17	Electrochemistry	131
Chapter 18	Organic Chemistry	139
Chapter 19	The Chemistry of Life	155
Chapter 20	Chemical Reactions and Energy	157
Chapter 21	Nuclear Chemistry	163
Appendix A	Supplement to Chemistry Skill Handbook, Appendix A, of the Student Book	169
Appendix B	Data Tables	181

To the Student

The Supplemental Practice Problems book will help reinforce your chemistry knowledge and problem-solving skills. After an introduction of how to read chemistry, it includes brief summaries of key points for each chapter, as well as example problems. The summaries and example problems will help you to answer the questions and problems that are presented throughout the book. These questions and problems are designed to reinforce what you have already learned in your student edition of **Chemistry: Concepts and Applications,** in addition to supplying more practice and some challenges.

Read each summary, study the example problems, and answer the questions and problems that follow. Reading the summaries and doing the exercises in this book will also help you study for a test.

Introduction

The factual style of writing in science textbooks is different from the narrative style of most other books you read. Thus, reading science requires special skills. In order to be successful in chemistry, you must adjust to the amount of factual information presented. You must read critically and sense relationships among ideas, as well as build on previous knowledge. You must master a new, technical vocabulary. Skills are needed to use supplementary materials, like this problems book, to enhance understanding. You must learn to interpret information presented in tables, graphs, and diagrams. Laboratory experimentation also requires special skills to interpret and apply scientific knowledge. In this section you will learn some techniques that can help you master these skills.

READING SCIENTIFIC MATERIALS

Reading for meaning, or comprehension, is one of the most important skills to master. Once the foundation is laid for strong comprehension the other skill areas will be facilitated. For example, if you have a basic understanding of the concepts presented in a particular chapter, new vocabulary words will be grasped more quickly from context clues. Problems and laboratory activities will also gain perspective.

When previewing or reading you should identify the main ideas in the material. The **main idea** is the most important concept described in a passage. The main idea can be located at any point in a paragraph and may be more than a single sentence. The main ideas in a sequence of paragraphs can serve as a summary of the material.

You should always try to understand what you read and avoid rote memorization. One way to broaden your understanding is to look for statements that support the main idea. Some of these statements may be real world examples of the main idea; others may be conclusive research data. Supporting statements often explain the "how" or "why" questions you may have about the main idea. You should associate these supporting statements with the main idea. These associations will help you increase your knowledge from factual repetition of main ideas to broader understanding of the concept described.

One additional type of statement you should look for as you read is linking sentences. Linking sentences provide perspective on the material. The linking sentences tie the main idea to previously learned material or to material to be presented later. Use linking sentences to determine where to store new information in your mind. As you add new information to various compartments of information your knowledge base will expand. You will also avoid trying to remember lots of unrelated concepts.

Let's practice some of these suggestions with a paragraph from your textbook.

An interesting third category of solution is called **supersaturated solution.** Such solutions contain more solute than the usual maximum amount and are unstable. They cannot permanently hold the excess solute in solution and may release it suddenly. Supersaturated solutions, as you might imagine, have to be prepared carefully. Generally, this is done by dissolving a solute in the solution at an elevated temperature, at which solubility is higher than at room temperature, and then slowly cooling the solution. Fudge making involves preparation of a supersaturated solution.

The main idea is that supersaturated solutions contain more solute than the usual maximum amount and are unstable. This information alone is not very helpful to our general understanding of supersaturated solutions. We would have a better understanding if a "how" question was answered. The fifth sentence does this by telling us how a supersaturated solution is made. The first sentence serves as a link with previous information, categories of solutions. The last sentence provides a real world application of the main idea.

DRAWING CONCLUSIONS

You may be asked to draw conclusions concerning a passage you have read. The answer to the question may not be stated directly in the passage. However, by understanding the main idea and some supporting details you can make an educated guess. For example, you know that pressure is caused by the collisions of particles with the walls of their container. You also know that temperature increases the speed of particles. You conclude that pressure increases with an increase in temperature because the particles would have more collisions.

When you make conclusions you may use inductive reasoning. **Inductive reasoning** involves applying specific concepts to general situations to form a conclusion. For example, consider the following.

> Hans Geiger and Ernest Marsden subjected a very thin sheet of gold foil to a stream of subatomic particles. They found that most of the particles passed right through the sheet. From this observation Rutherford concluded that the atom is mostly empty space. They also found that a few particles (about 1 in 8000) bounced back in almost the opposite direction from which they started. Rutherford explained this observation as meaning that there was a very small "core" to the atom. The core contained all the positive charge and almost all the mass of the atom. This core is now called the nucleus.

Rutherford used inductive reasoning to develop this theory of atomic structure. He used specific data from the Geiger-Marsden experiment to develop a general description of atomic structure.

Deductive reasoning involves applying general concepts to answer specific problems. The following is an example of how deductive reasoning is used.

> Reactivity of alkali metals increases as you move down the column on the periodic table. This means rubidium is more reactive than potassium, and cesium is more reactive than rubidium.

General information about reactivity is used to find specific answers about the relative reactivity of metals.

PROBLEMS

Read the following paragraph and answer the questions that follow.

The density of gases and vapors is most often expressed in grams per liter. We express it in these units because the usual density units, g/mL, lead to very small numbers for gases. It is possible to calculate the density of a gas at any temperature and pressure from data collected at any other temperature and pressure. Assuming that the number of particles remains the same, a decrease in temperature would decrease the volume and increase the density. An increase of pressure would decrease the volume and increase the density. The following problem illustrates this calculation. (Remember 1000 mL equals 1 L.)

1. The purpose of this passage is to describe _____.
   a. how many mL are in 1 L
   b. the units used for gas density
   c. typical density units
   d. the effects of temperature and pressure on gas density

2. In what units is gas density measured?
   a. g/mL
   b. 1000 mL
   c. g/L
   d. 1 L

3. What value must remain constant in order to determine gas density?
   a. number of particles
   b. temperature
   c. pressure
   d. volume

4. Which of the following is not mentioned in the paragraph?
   a. effects of temperature decrease
   b. effects of pressure decrease
   c. usual density units
   d. gas density units

5. What can you expect to learn in the text that would follow this paragraph?
   a. effects of temperature on volume
   b. effects of pressure on volume
   c. how to calculate gas density
   d. conversion units for density

6. Compare gas density units with usual density units. You would conclude that _____.
   a. gases are less dense than other forms of matter
   b. gases are more dense than other forms of matter
   c. gases have the same density as other forms of matter

7. In order to answer question 6 you must use _____.
   a. deductive reasoning
   b. inductive reasoning

8. If the temperature of a sample of gas changed from 52°C to 23°C, the volume of the gas would _____.
   a. increase   b. decrease   c. remain the same

9. In order to answer question 8 you must use _____.
   a. deductive reasoning   b. inductive reasoning

SECTION REVIEW

Read the following paragraph and answer the questions that follow.

An immediate application of electrochemistry is its use in quantitative analysis. For example, suppose that it is necessary for you to determine the percentage of copper in a given water soluble copper compound. A sample of the compound of known mass could be dissolved in water and inert electrodes inserted. The mass of the cathode should be measured before the current is applied. As the current is passed through the cell, metallic copper plates onto the electrode of known mass. When the action is complete and current no longer flows, all the copper is plated. The mass of the electrode is again measured. The difference in mass (due to the copper) is compared to the mass of the sample to find the percentage of copper in the sample. Electroanalysis is a useful tool of the chemist.

1. The best title for this passage is _____.
   a. Electroanalysis   c. Copper Analysis
   b. Electrochemistry   d. Chemistry Tools

2. All the copper has been plated when _____.
   a. the copper compound dissolves in water
   b. the percentage of copper in the sample is determined
   c. current no longer flows
   d. the mass of the electrode is measured

3. Which of the following is not mentioned as a step in plating copper?
   a. a sample of copper compound is dissolved in water
   b. the electrodes are attached to a power source
   c. the mass of the cathode is measured
   d. electrodes are inserted into the copper solution

4. With what topic is this passage most closely associated?
   a. finding mass of substances   c. electrochemistry
   b. electricity   d. chemistry of copper

5. Electroanalysis is _____.
   a. an application of electrochemistry
   b. a useful tool of the chemist
   c. a form of quantitative analysis
   d. all of the above

6. You should conclude that the mass of the cathode _____.
   a. increases with plating
   b. decreases with plating
   c. remains the same with plating

7. In order to answer question 6 you must use _____.
   a. deductive reasoning
   b. inductive reasoning

Chemistry: The Science of Matter

1.1 THE PUZZLE OF MATTER

Matter is anything that has mass and takes up space. Matter can be classified in a variety of ways. When matter is classified according to physical state, it can be solid, liquid, or gas. We may also classify matter according to composition as homogeneous or heterogeneous, substance or mixture, element or compound.

HETEROGENEOUS AND HOMOGENEOUS MATERIALS

Most of the things around us contain two or more different materials. Concrete, for example, contains sand, gravel, lime, and clay. Air is a mixture of oxygen, nitrogen, carbon dioxide, and other gases. If we look closely at a piece of concrete, we see it has different compositions depending on where we look. It is not uniform throughout. Such nonuniform materials are called **heterogeneous mixtures.** The physically separate parts, such as sand, gravel, lime, and clay, are called phases. A **phase** is any region of a material with a uniform set of properties.

Materials such as air, which consist of only one phase, are **homogeneous.** Homogeneous means the same throughout. Within these materials there is a uniform distribution of particles. Homogeneous mixtures are also called **solutions.** They contain a dissolved material called a **solute,** and a dissolving material called a **solvent.** As in all mixtures, the components of a solution may be present in varying amounts or concentrations.

ELEMENTS AND COMPOUNDS

Homogeneous materials that contain one kind of matter are called substances. All matter is composed of substances. A **substance** is a material with definite composition and properties. A type of substance that cannot be broken down into a simpler substance is called an **element.** A substance that can be broken down into simpler substances is called a **compound.** Another way to define a compound is a chemical combination of two or more elements.

PROBLEM

1. Indicate which of the following is an element, compound, heterogeneous mixture, or solution.

   a. ocean water
   b. calcium
   c. vitamin C
   d. dry ice (solid CO_2)
   e. copper
   f. grain alcohol
   g. after-shave lotion
   h. hamburger
   i. aluminum foil
   j. milk
   k. table salt
   l. iron nail

SYMBOLS

The chemical name for an element can be abbreviated to form a **chemical symbol**. Usually the chemical symbol contains the first letter of the element's name. If the names of two elements begin with the same letter, another letter from one name is added. For instance, B is boron, Br is bromine. The first letter is always uppercase, the second letter is always lowercase: Na is sodium, O is oxygen, and He is helium.

The use of upper and lowercase letters is important. For instance, the following elements and compounds are represented by the same letters.

Element	Compound
Co, cobalt	CO, carbon monoxide

For elements with atomic numbers greater than 109, the chemical symbols contain three letters. See the table of atomic masses, **Table B-14** in Appendix B, for names and symbols for the elements.

CHEMICAL FORMULAS

A **chemical formula** provides the clearest and simplest method of designating compounds. It is a combination of chemical symbols that indicates the number and kinds of elements in a compound. The chemical formula for vitamin A is $C_{20}H_{30}O$. Thus, there are twenty carbon atoms, thirty hydrogen atoms, and one oxygen atom.

Compounds that consist of two elements are called binary compounds (HCl, H_2O, C_2H_6). The formula of a compound composed of a metal and a nonmetal is written with the symbol of the metal first, as in NaCl and Al_2S_3. Generally, you can determine whether an element is a metal or a nonmetal by its position in the periodic table. Metals are listed at the left and center in the standard periodic table. Nonmetals are listed at the extreme right.

PROBLEMS

2. Which symbol would be written first in the formula for the compound formed from each of the following pairs of elements? Use the periodic table.
   a. S and Cu
   b. Bi and S
   c. N and Nb
   d. C and Mg
   e. Ta and Cl
   f. Al and As

3. Which element would be placed first in the formula for the compound formed from each of the following pairs of elements?
   a. oxygen (O), copper (Cu)
   b. sulfur (S), potassium (K)
   c. lithium (Li), fluorine (F)
   d. calcium (Ca), nitrogen (N)
   e. sodium (Na), chlorine (Cl)
   f. magnesium (Mg), bromine (Br)

1.2 PROPERTIES AND CHANGES OF MATTER

PHYSICAL PROPERTIES AND CHANGES

Physical properties are those that do not involve changes in composition. Physical properties are divided into two types, extensive and intensive. **Extensive properties** depend upon the amount of matter present. Mass, length, and volume are examples. **Intensive properties** do not depend upon the amount, but upon the nature of the substance. Density, solubility, boiling point, and conductivity are examples.

When a material changes form, but not chemical composition, a **physical change** has occurred. Grinding into powder, melting, boiling, and dissolving are examples. Physical changes are often used to separate mixtures. Salt may be separated from a saltwater solution by boiling off the water. Distillation, fractional crystallization, filtration, and precipitation are laboratory techniques that are used to separate the components of mixtures.

DENSITY

One quantity used to characterize substances is density. **Density*** is the amount of matter (mass) contained in a unit of volume. The density of solids and liquids is expressed in g/mL. Gases are much less dense than solids or liquids. Their densities are usually given in g/L.

TABLE 1-1

Densities of Some Materials at 25°C (g/mL)

aluminum	2.70
carbon (diamond)	3.614
gold	19.3
iron	7.874
lead	11.34
magnesium	1.738
mercury	13.534
platinum	21.410
potassium	0.856
sodium	0.968
water	1.00

*Density varies with temperature. For convenience, we will assume that the density of solids and liquids does not vary significantly.

EXAMPLE

What is the density of a hydrochloric acid solution that has a mass of 17.84 g and occupies 15.00 mL?

Solving Process:

$$\text{density} = \frac{\text{mass}}{\text{volume}}$$

$$= \frac{17.84 \text{ g}}{15.00 \text{ mL}}$$

$$= 1.189 \text{ g/mL}$$

The equation for density may be solved for volume or mass as well.

$$\text{volume} = \frac{\text{mass}}{\text{density}} \qquad \text{mass} = \text{volume} \times \text{density}$$

PROBLEMS

Calculate the density of the following materials.

1. 35.0 g of a substance that occupies 25.0 mL

2. 2750 g of a substance that occupies 250 mL

3. 2.80 g of a substance that occupies 2.00 L

4. Determine the volume that 35.2 g of carbon tetrachloride will occupy if it has a density of 1.60 g/mL.

5. The density of ethanol is 0.789 g/mL at 20°C. What is the mass of 150 mL of this alcohol?

6. A block of lead displaces a volume of 27.00 mL. Calculate the mass of this block, if the density of lead is 11.34 g/mL.

CHEMICAL PROPERTIES AND CHANGES

A familiar chemical reaction is burning. The color, density, and other characteristics of the ashes are different from the material before it was burned. A **chemical change** occurs when a substance burns because new substances with different properties are formed. **Chemical properties** are those that can be observed only when there is a change in the composition of the substance. A chemical property always relates to a chemical change, the change of one or more substances into other substances. For example, does it burn? Does it react with acids? Such questions help to determine the chemical properties of a substance.

PROBLEMS

7. Classify each of the following as a chemical or physical property.
   a. reacts with H₂O
   b. is red
   c. conducts electricity
   d. resists corrosion
   e. boils at 88°C
   f. dissolves in gasoline
   g. is ductile
   h. is flammable
   i. is 1.5 m long
   j. is malleable
   k. is corrosive
   l. freezes at −17°C

8. Classify each of the following as a chemical or physical change.
   a. alcohol evaporating
   b. a firefly lighting up
   c. a battery charging
   d. ice melting
   e. an explosion
   f. salt dissolving in H₂O
   g. digesting food
   h. hammering hot iron into a sheet

SECTION REVIEW

1. 30.0 g of each of the following acids are needed. What volume of each should be measured out?

Acid	Density (g/mL)
a. hydrochloric acid, HCl	1.1639
b. sulfuric acid, H₂SO₄	1.834
c. nitric acid, HNO₃	1.251

2. Use the densities given in **Table 1-1** to determine which would be heavier—a ball of lead that displaces a volume of 4.19 mL or a cylinder of iron that displaces a volume of 56.5 mL.

Matter Is Made up of Atoms

2.1 ATOMS AND THEIR STRUCTURE

EARLY ATOMIC THEORIES

Scientists use models to explain atomic structure, because atoms cannot be seen directly. Models help provide mental images for concepts such as atomic structure. The research and theories described in this section will help you develop a mental model for what scientists believe atoms would look like if individual atoms could be seen.

In 1799, Joseph Proust developed his theory that atoms have fixed masses. An atom of one element has the same mass no matter what other elements it combines with. In a given chemical compound, the elements are always combined in the same proportion by mass. This statement is the **law of definite proportions.**

In the 1800's John Dalton proposed an atomic theory of matter. His theory had three main points: (1) all matter is made up of atoms; (2) atoms are indestructible and cannot be divided into smaller particles (atoms are indivisible); (3) all atoms of one element are exactly alike, but they are different from atoms of other elements. Dalton's theory was modified when subatomic particles and isotopes were discovered.

Since the late 1800's there has been a great deal of scientific research to determine the actual structure of atoms. In 1897, J. J. Thompson used cathode ray tubes in a magnetic field to determine the charge to mass ratio for an electron. A few years later, Robert Millikan designed his "oil drop" experiment to determine the charge on an electron. This information provided the data needed to calculate the mass of the electron from Thompson's charge to mass ratio for an electron. In 1913, Henry Moseley used X rays to find the relationship between wavelength and atomic number. Based on his work we know that the number of protons determines the identity of the element.

Niels Bohr and Ernest Rutherford used spectroscopy to expand their knowledge of atomic structure. They viewed the atom as a central nucleus of positive charge surrounded by electrons after Rutherford's gold foil experiment in 1909. Today we know that absorption and emission spectra are like fingerprints for the elements. Bohr pictured the hydrogen atom as an electron circling a nucleus. The electron moves from its ground state or normal state if it absorbs a photon, energy of a certain frequency. When an electron drops from a larger orbit to a smaller one, a definite amount of energy, a quanta, is radiated.

ISOTOPES AND ATOMIC NUMBER

The **atomic number** of an element is represented by the symbol Z. The atomic number is the number of protons in the nucleus of an atom. Because an atom is electrically neutral, the number of electrons must equal the number of protons.

The number of protons determines the identity of the element. The atomic number can be found in the table of atomic masses, **Table B-14,** in Appendix B.

Isotopes are atoms of an element that are exactly alike chemically but slightly different in mass. Isotopes have the same number of protons but a different number of neutrons. The different number of neutrons is what accounts for the differences in mass of isotopes of an element. The number of neutrons determines the particular isotope of the element.

The particles that make up an atomic nucleus are called **nucleons.** The total number of nucleons, protons plus neutrons, in an atom is called the **mass number,** A. Thus, the number of neutrons = $A - Z$. Isotopes are often symbolized by placing the atomic number and mass number to the left of the chemical symbol. The mass number is a superscript, the atomic number a subscript. The isotope of radon, an indoor air pollutant, is shown as follows.

$$\text{mass number (protons + neutrons)} \quad ^{222}_{86}\text{Rn}$$
$$\text{atomic number (protons)}$$

The name of this isotope is radon-222.

EXAMPLE

Compute the number of electrons, protons, and neutrons in the atom of carbon with $A = 14$, and write its nuclear symbol.

Solving Process:
The atomic number, Z, is read from the table of atomic masses. The atomic number (number of protons) of carbon is 6. Because the atom is electrically neutral, the number of electrons equals the atomic number. The mass number, A, is the total number of nucleons. This particular isotope of carbon has a mass number of 14.

$$\text{number of neutrons} = A - Z = 14 - 6 = 8$$

In carbon-14, there are 6 protons, 8 neutrons, and 6 electrons. Its nuclear symbol is $^{14}_{6}\text{C}$.

PROBLEMS

1. Use the table of atomic masses, **Table B-14,** in Appendix B to compute the number of electrons, neutrons, and protons in the following isotopes. Write the symbol for each isotope.

   a. Cr $A = 50$
   b. Cl $A = 37$
   c. Mg $A = 26$
   d. Ir $A = 193$
   e. Si $A = 29$
   f. Ne $A = 22$

2. Moseley used X rays to determine the atomic numbers of the elements. Identify each of the following elements by name.

   a. 1 proton
   b. 4 protons
   c. 8 protons
   d. 12 protons
   e. 20 protons
   f. 30 protons

ATOMIC MASS

The actual mass of an atom is extremely small. One isotope of hydrogen has a mass of $1.67 = 10^{-24}$ g and one isotope of oxygen has a mass of $2.66 = 10^{-23}$ g. Because these masses are impractical to use, chemists have defined an average **atomic mass scale** based on the mass of a carbon-12 atom. **Atomic mass** is the relative mass of an average atom of an element with carbon-12 atoms used as reference. For convenience, the carbon-12 atom has been arbitrarily assigned the atomic mass of 12 atomic mass units (u). An atomic mass unit is defined as 1/12 the mass of a carbon-12 atom. The mass of an average hydrogen atom is approximately 1/12 the mass of a carbon-12 atom. See the table of atomic masses, **Table B-14,** in Appendix B.

AVERAGE ATOMIC MASS

The atomic mass unit, u, is used to measure atomic mass. The carbon-12 atom is the standard for the atomic mass scale. One carbon-12 atom has a mass of 12 atomic mass units. The subatomic particles that we have studied have the following atomic masses.

$$\text{electron} = 9.11 \times 10^{-28} \text{ g} = 0.000\ 55 \text{ u}$$
$$\text{proton} = 1.67 \times 10^{-24} \text{ g} = 1.01 \text{ u}$$
$$\text{neutron} = 1.67 \times 10^{-24} \text{ g} = 1.01 \text{ u}$$

As you can see, the masses of the protons and neutrons in an atom make up nearly all of the atom's mass.

The **average atomic mass** of an element can be determined from relative amounts of each isotope. In a naturally occurring element, the fractional abundance is the fraction of a particular isotope in the total sample of atoms. The atomic masses in the atomic mass table and the periodic table are based on the weighted average of the masses of all isotopes of an element. The average atomic mass of the element is used in most chemical calculations.

EXAMPLE

Chlorine has two isotopes. Chlorine-35 has an actual mass of 34.9689 u and chlorine-37 has a mass of 36.9659 u. In any sample of chlorine atoms, 75.771% will be chlorine-35 and 24.229% will be chlorine-37. Calculate the average atomic mass of chlorine.

Solving Process:
Each of the isotopic masses is multiplied by its fractional abundance. Then the products are added.

$$(34.9689)(0.75771) + (36.9659)(0.24229) = 35.453 \text{ u}$$

PROBLEMS

3. Calculate the average atomic mass of magnesium using the following data for three magnesium isotopes.

isotope	mass (u)	fractional abundance
Mg-24	23.985	0.7870
Mg-25	24.986	0.1013
Mg-26	25.983	0.1117

4. Calculate the average atomic mass of iridium using the following data for two iridium isotopes.

isotope	mass (u)	fractional abundance
Ir-191	191.0	0.3758
Ir-193	193.0	0.6242

SECTION REVIEW

Indicate whether each of the following statements is true or false. Correct the false statements.

1. Dalton's atomic theory includes a statement that says atoms of the same element are identical.

2. Proust's theory states that atoms have variable masses.

3. J. J. Thompson is credited with the "oil drop" experiment.

4. The mass of an electron is equal to the mass of a proton.

5. The mass of a proton is approximately equal to the mass of a neutron.

6. Millikan devised an experiment to determine the charge on an electron.

7. The atomic number represents the number of protons in a nucleus and is represented by the symbol Na.

8. The proton has a mass of approximately 1 u.

9. The difference in mass of isotopes of the same element is due to the different number of protons in the nucleus.

10. The isotope carbon-12 is used as the relative mass standard for the atomic mass scale.

11. Calculate the average atomic mass of chromium.

isotope	mass (u)	fractional abundance
Cr-50	49.946	0.043 500
Cr-52	51.941	0.838 00
Cr-53	52.941	0.095 000
Cr-54	53.939	0.023 500

12. How many protons are in the nucleus of each of the following elements?
    a. uranium
    b. selenium
    c. helium
    d. bohrium

13. Give the number of neutrons in each of the following isotopes.
    a. titanium-46
    b. nitrogen-15
    c. $^{34}_{16}S$
    d. $^{65}_{29}Cu$

14. Fill in the blanks in the table below for neutral atoms. Use only the information given in the table.

	Atomic Number	Mass Number	Number of Protons	Number of Neutrons	Number of Electrons
calcium-43			20		
lead-211				129	
plutonium-242	94				
chromium-50					24

Chemistry: Concepts and Applications

Introduction to the Periodic Table

3.1 DEVELOPMENT OF THE PERIODIC TABLE

MODERN PERIODIC TABLE

In 1869 Dmitri Mendeleev, a Russian chemist, prepared a periodic table of the elements. The elements were arranged in order of their atomic masses in horizontal rows so that the elements in any vertical column had similar properties. In 1914, Moseley determined the atomic numbers of the elements from their X-ray spectra. He then reordered the elements in the periodic table according to increasing atomic number. Observation of this arrangement gave rise to our modern **periodic law.** It states that *the properties of the elements are a periodic function of their atomic numbers.*

SECTION REVIEW

1. What Russian scientist designed the first periodic table?

3.2 USING THE PERIODIC TABLE

ELECTRON DOT DIAGRAMS

The Lewis electron dot diagram is useful when showing how atoms bond together. In these diagrams the outer energy level electrons (valence electrons) are represented by dots placed around the letter symbol of the element.

The symbol of the element represents the nucleus and all the electrons except the valence electrons in the outer energy level. To write a Lewis electron dot diagram, determine the number of valence electrons that each element in that group has. Remember that the elements in the same group all have the same number of valence electrons (except helium, which has two valence electrons instead of eight like the rest of the noble gases). This does not apply to the transition elements, however.

Each "side" (above, below, left, right) of the symbol represents placements for the valence electrons. Draw dots on the sides to represent the valence electrons. For one to four valence electrons, only one electron will go on a side. The exception to this rule is helium. Helium is written with its two dots on the same side of the symbol because it has only one energy level, which can only contain two electrons. If there are five to eight valence electrons, then go around the symbol again, and pair them up. (I.e., if there are five valence electrons, then only one side will have two dots, and the remaining three sides will have one each.)

EXAMPLE

Write the Lewis electron dot diagram for selenium (Z = 34).

Solving Process:
Step 1. Find the group number of selenium on the periodic table.

Group 16—the same group as oxygen

Step 2. Members of group sixteen have six valence electrons. Since there are more than four valence electrons, you will go around the element twice. Go around once, placing one dot on each side of the symbol. Then, since there are two more valence electrons, go around again until they are used up.

PROBLEM

1. Using the periodic table as a reference, draw Lewis electron dot diagrams for the following elements.
   a. Li   b. N   c. Be   d. O   e. B   f. F   g. C   h. Ne

METALS AND NONMETALS

Many of the columns in the table have family names. Group 1, except hydrogen, is called the **alkali metal family.** Group 2 is called the **alkaline earth metal family.** Groups 1 and 2 of the periodic table contain the most active metals.

On the other side of the table are the nonmetals. Group 16 is called the **chalcogen** (KAL kuh juhn) **family.** Group 17 is known as the **halogen family.** The elements of Group 18 are called the **noble gases.**

The majority of elements are **metals.** We are all familiar with typical metallic properties. Metals have a luster and are malleable. They conduct heat and electricity well. **Nonmetals** are generally gases or brittle solids at room temperature. They are usually poor conductors of heat and electricity. Exceptions are types of carbon: diamond, an excellent conductor of heat, and graphite, an electrical conductor. There are some elements that have properties of both metals and nonmetals. These elements are called **metalloids.** These elements lie to the right and left of the stairstep line on the periodic table. Aluminum is usually considered to be a metal.

The elements in Groups 3 through 12 are called **transition elements.** They all show metallic properties. The elements 58 through 71, the **lanthanides,** and 90 through 103, the **actinides,** are metals.

PROBLEMS

2. Classify the following elements as metal, metalloid, or nonmetal.
   a. cadmium   c. californium   e. calcium
   b. fluorine   d. carbon   f. germanium

3. Are the transition elements metals or nonmetals?

*Match each of the following terms with a letter from the periodic table in **Figure 3-1**.*

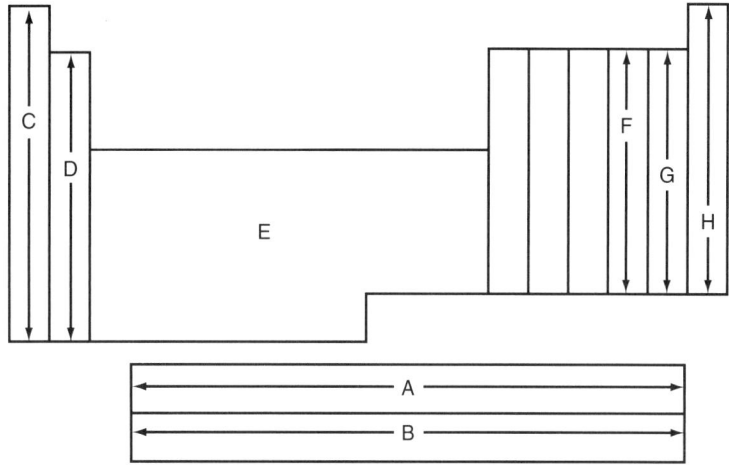

FIGURE 3-1

4. alkali metals

5. alkaline earth metals

6. lanthanides

7. actinides

8. chalcogens

9. halogens

10. noble gases

11. transition metals

SECTION REVIEW

1. How are substances that are gases or brittle solids at room temperature classified?

2. Which group of elements contains the most active metals?

3. Which group of elements is unreactive?

4. The Lewis electron dot diagram is used to represent only which electrons in an atom?

5. Draw the Lewis electron dot diagram for the following elements.
   a. rubidium
   b. barium
   c. phosphorus
   d. krypton
   e. tin
   f. aluminum

6. Classify the following elements as metals, metalloids, or nonmetals.
   a. chlorine ($Z = 17$)
   b. tungsten ($Z = 74$)
   c. radium ($Z = 88$)
   d. arsenic ($Z = 33$)
   e. promethium ($Z = 61$)
   f. uranium ($Z = 92$)

Formation of Compounds

4.2 HOW ELEMENTS FORM COMPOUNDS

IONIC BONDING

When elements come together with enough energy to form compounds, an interaction between electrons occurs. The electrons rearrange themselves to form a stable octet of electrons—a noble gas configuration. This rearrangement occurs by two processes: transferring electrons and sharing electrons.

Recall the compound sodium chloride, also known as common table salt. In the formation of this compound, electron transfer, or ionization, occurs. The sodium atom gives up one of its electrons to the chlorine atom. As a result, the sodium ion has a positive charge, and the chlorine ion has a negative charge. The opposite charges attract each other, and a compound is formed.

Notice that when sodium gave up its one electron, its outer electron arrangement became the same as neon's. When chlorine gained one electron, its outer electron arrangement became the same as argon's. Both atoms achieved a stable noble gas configuration through ionization.

When a compound like sodium chloride is formed through ionization and the transfer of electrons, the compound is an **ionic compound.** The bond that is formed between the two ions as a result of opposing charges is called an **ionic bond.**

COVALENT BONDING

Sometimes elements do not have enough attraction for another element's valence electrons to completely steal them away, and an ionic bond cannot form. Instead the two atoms end up sharing the electron(s). This is called a **covalent bond** and compounds formed in this way are **covalent compounds.** A good example of a covalent compound is water. Oxygen and hydrogen share electrons to obtain a stable noble gas outer electron level configuration.

INTERPARTICLE FORCES

The physical states of ionic and covalent compounds can be explained by the **interparticle forces.** These forces are the forces between particles that make up a substance. In an ionic compound, the interparticle forces are strong, and the ions are held rigidly. Almost all ionic compounds are solids at room temperature. Covalent compounds, on the other hand, are mostly liquids or gases at room temperature. This is because the interparticle forces are weak and do not hold the particles rigidly in place. The particles have some flex to their position.

SECTION REVIEW

1. When elements come together to form compounds, why do the electrons rearrange themselves?

2. What type of compound is mostly found in the solid state?

3. Interparticle forces are weaker in which type of compound?

4. What prevents an element in a covalent compound from taking away another element's valence electrons?

Types of Compounds

5.1 IONIC COMPOUNDS

NAMING COMPOUNDS

There is a systematic method of naming practically all ionic compounds and binary covalent compounds. The names of only a few compounds, particularly acids, will not be included in our discussion of this system.

Compounds containing only two elements are called binary compounds. To name a binary compound, first write the name of the element having a positive charge. Then add the name of the negative element. The name of the negative element must be modified to end in -ide.

EXAMPLE

Name the compound with the formula ZnO.

Solving Process:
The compound is formed by zinc and oxygen. It is named zinc oxide.

The binary compounds containing hydrogen and a nonmetal, called hydrides, often have common names, such as ammonia, NH_3; methane, CH_4; and water. These compounds will be discussed later.

TABLE 5-1
Names for Nonmetals in Binary Compounds

B	C	N	O	F
boride	carbide	nitride	oxide	fluoride
Si		P	S	Cl
silicide		phosphide	sulfide	chloride
		As	Se	Br
		arsenide	selenide	bromide
		Sb	Te	I
		antimonide	telluride	iodide
				At
				astatide

PROBLEM

1. Name the following compounds.
   - **a.** Na_2S
   - **b.** Li_2O
   - **c.** $MgBr_2$
   - **d.** AlN
   - **e.** CaF_2
   - **f.** KI
   - **g.** $ZnCl_2$
   - **h.** Na_3P
   - **i.** K_2Se

OXIDATION NUMBER

An atom or group of atoms that is positively or negatively charged is known as an **ion**. The charge on the ion is known as the **oxidation number** of the atom. For example, Mg represents the metallic element magnesium, while Mg^{2+} represents the magnesium ion. The oxidation number of the magnesium atom is 2+. The nonmetallic element fluorine is represented by the symbol F, while F^- represents the fluoride ion. The oxidation number of fluorine is 1−.

Some metals have the same positive charge in all compounds. The elements in Group 1, such as lithium, sodium, and potassium, always have an oxidation number of 1+. Group 2 metals, such as magnesium, calcium, strontium, and barium, always have an oxidation number of 2+. Aluminum always has an oxidation number of 3+.

In ionic compounds, the total positive charge is equal to the total negative charge. One Mg^{2+} ion with a charge of 2+ will combine with two Cl^- ions to form $MgCl_2$. For $MgCl_2$ the total positive charge is 2+ and the total negative charge is 2(1−) or 2−. In a correctly written formula, the sum of the total positive charge and total negative charge is zero.

PREDICTING OXIDATION NUMBERS

The outer, high energy electrons are involved in the reaction of atoms with each other. Recall that the noble gas configuration of eight valence electrons is stable. Oxidation numbers for most elements can be predicted from their position on the periodic table.

Consider the metals in Group 1. Each atom has one valence electron. The loss of this one electron will give these metals the same configuration as a noble gas. Group 1 metals have an oxidation number of 1+. In Group 2 we would expect the loss of two electrons for the atom to achieve the same configuration as the prior noble gas. That loss leads to a prediction of 2+ oxidation number for the alkaline earth metals.

In groups 3 through 12, the transition elements, predicting the oxidation number can be difficult. The transition elements often have more than one oxidation number. These oxidation numbers typically range from 2+ to 8+, although some transition elements, such as copper, can have an oxidation number of 1+.

Group 13 elements lose three electrons and have an oxidation number of 3+. Group 14 may have a 2+ or 4+ oxidation number.

In Groups 15, 16, and 17, there is a general tendency to gain electrons to complete the octet. The outside level is already more than half-filled. These elements show oxidation numbers of 3−, 2−, and 1− respectively. It is also possible for these elements to lose electrons and have positive oxidation numbers. The tendency to lose electrons increases as we move down a column.

PROBLEM

2. Predict the oxidation numbers for the following elements.
   - **a.** Al
   - **b.** N
   - **c.** Cl
   - **d.** Mg
   - **e.** S
   - **f.** Na
   - **g.** K
   - **h.** O
   - **i.** Ga
   - **j.** P
   - **k.** Se
   - **l.** Br

WRITING CHEMICAL FORMULAS

Knowing the oxidation numbers for elements allows us to write chemical formulas. The key to writing chemical formulas is to have the oxidation numbers add to zero, because a compound should be neutral. For example, calcium, Ca, has an oxidation number of 2+. We know this because it is located in the second column in the periodic table. Also from the periodic table, we know that fluorine, F, in Group 17, has an oxidation number of 1−. The formula would be written using the chemical symbols for calcium and fluorine as follows.

$$Ca^{2+}F^-$$
$$1(2+) + 1(1-) \neq 0$$

But notice that the oxidation numbers do not add to zero. We have positive two and negative one. If we have two fluorine ions though, we then have two negative ions which gives us a total of zero for the formula. To indicate the chemical formula, we need two fluorine ions, so we write a 2 after the symbol for fluorine.

$$CaF_2$$
$$1(2+) + 2(1-) = 0$$

PROBLEM

3. Write formulas for the following compounds.
   - **a.** sodium fluoride
   - **b.** potassium chloride
   - **c.** rubidium bromide
   - **d.** sodium selenide
   - **e.** potassium oxide
   - **f.** lithium sulfide
   - **g.** strontium fluoride
   - **h.** calcium chloride
   - **i.** magnesium bromide
   - **j.** barium iodide
   - **k.** beryllium oxide
   - **l.** calcium sulfide

POLYATOMIC IONS

The term **polyatomic ion** is an ion that has two or more different elements. The term is used to designate a group of atoms that act as a unit in a wide variety of chemical reactions. A common positive polyatomic ion is NH_4^+, the ammonium ion. A common negative polyatomic ion is hydroxide, OH^-.

Prefixes and suffixes are used in the name of some ions to indicate the oxygen content in relation to other ions in a series of similar ions. Examples of this can be seen in the following and in **Table 5-2**.

	Prefix	Suffix	Example
Increasing oxygen content ↑	per-	-ate	ClO_4^- perchlorate
		-ate	ClO_3^- chlorate
		-ite	ClO_2^- chlorite
	hypo-	-ite	ClO^- hypochlorite

TABLE 5-2
Some Common Polyatomic Ions Containing Oxygen

BrO_3^- bromate	IO_6^{5-} periodate	SO_4^{2-} sulfate	NO_3^- nitrate
	IO_3^- iodate	SO_3^{2-} sulfite	NO_2^- nitrite
BrO^- hypobromite	IO^- hypoiodite		

Compounds containing the ammonium ion are named by using the name "ammonium" followed by the appropriate name for the negative ion.

ammonium bromide	ammonium sulfide	ammonium nitride
NH_4Br	$(NH_4)_2S$	$(NH_4)_3N$

To name a compound containing a negative polyatomic ion, the appropriate positive ion name is followed by the name of the polyatomic ion.

sodium sulfate	magnesium carbonate	aluminum nitrate
Na_2SO_4	$MgCO_3$	$Al(NO_3)_3$

Notice the formula for aluminum nitrate has parenthesis around the polyatomic ion. When more than one polyatomic ion is included in a chemical formula, the ion must be enclosed in parentheses to avoid confusion. For example, $Ca(OH)_2$ is not the same thing as $CaOH_2$. The subscript located to the right of the parenthesis indicates the number of polyatomic ions present. The formula for magnesium hydroxide, $Mg(OH)_2$, contains two hydroxide ions. There are three ammonium ions in $(NH_4)_3N$.

In more complex compounds the metallic ions are still written first. Hydrogen is indicated by adding the word "hydrogen" immediately in front of the name of the negative ion. For example, $NaHCO_3$ is sodium hydrogen carbonate. (**Table B-7** in Appendix B lists additional polyatomic ions.)

EXAMPLE

Write the formula for the compound made from calcium and the phosphate ion.

Solving Process:
Using **Tables B-6** and **B-7** in Appendix B, we see the oxidation states of calcium and the phosphate ion are as follows

$$Ca^2 \quad PO_4^{3-}$$

It is necessary to have three Ca^{2+} and two PO_4^{3-} in the compound to maintain neutrality. Writing calcium ions in the formula is simple, Ca_3. For the phosphate ion, the entire polyatomic ion must be placed in parentheses to indicate that two phosphate ions are required.

$$Ca_3(PO_4)_2$$
$$3(2+) + 2(3-) = 0$$

PROBLEMS

4. Write formulas for the following compounds.
   a. sodium cyanide
   b. sodium hydroxide
   c. sodium bromate
   d. sodium acetate
   e. barium cyanide
   f. barium hydroxide
   g. barium oxide
   h. barium sulfate

5. Write formulas for the following compounds.
   a. barium azide
   b. zinc molybdate
   c. cesium perchlorate
   d. aluminum silicate
   e. boron phosphide
   f. silver nitride
   g. cadmium oxalate
   h. potassium thiocyanate
   i. calcium hypophosphite
   j. aluminum hexafluorosilicate

6. Write formulas for the following compounds.
   a. calcium sulfate
   b. sodium nitrate
   c. potassium perchlorate
   d. aluminum sulfate
   e. potassium chlorate
   f. magnesium sulfite
   g. lithium nitrite
   h. sodium chlorite
   i. ammonium dichromate
   j. sodium nitrite

7. Name the following compounds.
   a. $Mg(OH)_2$
   b. CaO
   c. $LiCH_3COO$
   d. $MgSO_4$
   e. $Ca(ClO)_2$
   f. $Ba(NO_2)_2$
   g. NH_4MgPO_4
   h. KNO_2
   i. $KNaCO_3$

8. Name the following compounds.
   a. Na_2SO_4
   b. $AgNO_3$
   c. $ZnCr_2O_7$
   d. NH_4CH_3COO
   e. $KClO_4$
   f. NH_4ClO_3
   g. CaC_2O_4
   h. $BaCO_3$
   i. NaH_2PO_4

COMPOUNDS OF TRANSITION ELEMENTS

A number of metallic elements can form compounds in which the metal ions have different charges. For example, iron forms one series of compounds in which the iron is Fe^{2+}, and another series in which iron is Fe^{3+}. In naming these compounds, the charge (or oxidation number) of the metal is written in Roman numerals enclosed in parentheses following the metal. The Roman numeral system is thus used to differentiate between ions that have two or more possible charges. For example, FeBr$_2$ is iron(II) bromide, and FeBr$_3$ is iron(III) bromide. To name these compounds we must know the oxidation number of iron.

The following rules will enable you to determine the oxidation numbers of metal ions from the formulas of their compounds.

1. *In metallic halides and other binary metallic compounds, the halogen (F, Cl, Br, and I) always has an oxidation number of 1−.* AuCl$_3$ is gold(III) chloride (read as "gold three chloride"). The three Cl atoms have a combined oxidation number of 3−. Since the compound has no charge, the oxidation number of the gold atom must be 3+.

2. *In binary compounds that contain oxygen combined with a metal, the oxygen can usually be assumed to have an oxidation number of 2−.* FeO is iron(II) oxide.

3. *The sum of the charges of the atoms composing a polyatomic ion is the charge on the ion.* This charge is indicated as a superscript. The perchlorate ion, ClO$_4^-$, has a charge of 1− (the sum of the charges of one Cl atom and four O atoms). Since the sum of all the oxidation numbers in a compound is zero, in Fe(ClO$_4$)$_2$ the Fe must have an oxidation number of 2+. This compound is named iron(II) perchlorate.

EXAMPLE

Write the names of the compounds Cu$_2$O and CuO.

Solving Process:
From Rule 2 we know that O in these compounds has a 2− charge. Since the sum of all the oxidation numbers in a compound is zero, in Cu$_2$O the Cu must have a charge of 1+. In CuO, the charge on Cu must be 2+. The compounds are named

Cu$_2$O	CuO
copper(I) oxide	Copper(II) oxide
2(1+) + 1(2−) = 0	1(2+) + 1(2−) = 0

Some binary compounds composed of nonmetals form a series of two or more compounds such as CO and CO$_2$. The number of atoms of a given kind is indicated by the use of a Greek prefix preceding the name of the element to which it refers. The prefixes are *mono-*(1), *di-*(2), *tri-*(3), *tetra-*(4), *penta-*(5), *hexa-*(6), *hepta-*(7), and *octa-*(8). The prefix mono- is usually omitted except when it is used for emphasis, as in carbon monoxide. Common usage omits the double vowel. That is, CO is named carbon monoxide, not mono-oxide. CO$_2$ is carbon dioxide.

The names of the common acids do not follow the rules for naming other compounds. The rules for naming acids will be presented in Chapter 14. **Table 5-3** lists names and formulas of acids commonly used in the laboratory. They should be memorized.

TABLE 5-3
Common Acids

Formula	Name	Formula	Name
CH_3COOH	acetic acid	HNO_3	nitric acid
H_2CO_3	carbonic acid	H_3PO_4	phosphoric acid
HCl	hydrochloric acid	H_2SO_4	sulfuric acid

PROBLEMS

9. Write formulas for the following compounds.
   a. manganese(III) chloride
   b. iron(III) bromide
   c. chromium(III) bromide
   d. tin(IV) chloride
   e. manganese(II) bromide
   f. tin(IV) oxide
   g. chromium(III) oxide
   h. lead(II) oxide
   i. manganese(VII) oxide
   j. mercury(I) oxide

10. Name the following compounds. (Roman numeral system)
    a. $TiCl_2$
    b. $TiBr_4$
    c. CuCl
    d. PbI_2
    e. $SnCl_4$
    f. Sb_2O_5
    g. CrO_3
    h. Mn_3O_4
    i. TiO_2
    j. PbO
    k. BiF_5
    l. $NiBr_2$
    m. $CuBr_2$
    n. $PbCl_2$
    o. CrF_3

11. Name the following compounds. (Roman numeral system)
    a. $Fe_2(SO_4)_3$
    b. $Cr(OH)_2$
    c. $Hg_2(ClO_3)_2$*
    d. $Fe(ClO_4)_2$
    e. $MnSO_4$
    f. $Hg(IO_3)_2$
    g. $Pb(ClO_2)_2$
    h. $Cu(CH_3COO)_2$
    i. Cu_2SO_4
    j. $CoSO_4$

12. Write formulas for the following compounds.
    a. copper(II) chlorate
    b. bismuth(III) telluride
    c. manganese(III) sulfate
    d. iron(III) nitrate
    e. tin(IV) nitrate
    f. chromium(III) sulfate
    g. iron(II) hydroxide
    h. copper(II) phosphate
    i. mercury(I) nitrite
    j. lead(II) nitrate

13. Write formulas for the following compounds.
    a. dichlorine oxide
    b. chlorine dioxide
    c. carbon disulfide
    d. chlorine trifluoride
    e. dichlorine heptoxide
    f. sulfur hexafluoride

*Mercury exists as Hg_2^{2+}, mercury(I), in which two mercury atoms are bound together. It also exists as Hg^{2+}, mercury(II).

14. Name the following compounds. (Greek prefixes)
    a. CO$_2$ b. NO$_2$ c. SO$_3$ d. PCl$_3$ e. NO f. P$_2$O$_5$

HYDRATES

A number of compounds called **hydrates** attract and hold water molecules in their crystal structure. The compound has a specific ratio of water to ionic compound. The water is called **water of hydration** and may be removed by heating. The solid residue remaining after the water is removed is called the anhydrous material. **Anhydrous** means "without water."

In the formula of a hydrated compound, the number of water molecules involved is indicated by placing a raised dot after the anhydrous formula followed by the number of water molecules per formula unit of compound. For example, CuSO$_4$ · 5H$_2$O is copper(II) sulfate pentahydrate. *Hydrate* means "water" and the Greek prefix *penta-* indicates the number of water molecules per formula unit of compound. For example:

Na$_2$CO$_3$	sodium carbonate
Na$_2$CO$_3$ · H$_2$O	sodium carbonate monohydrate
Na$_2$CO$_3$ · 7H$_2$O	sodium carbonate heptahydrate
Na$_2$CO$_3$ · 10H$_2$O	sodium carbonate decahydrate

The ions of some anhydrous substances have such a strong attraction for water molecules that the dehydrated crystal will recapture and hold water molecules from the air. Such a substance is called a hygroscopic (hi gruh SKAHP ihk) substance. Some substances are so **hygroscopic** that they take up enough water from the air to dissolve and form a liquid solution. These substances are said to be **deliquescent** (del ih KWES uhnt). The opposite process can also occur. Water of hydration may be spontaneously released to the air. A substance that releases water molecules to the air from the crystal is said to be **efflorescent** (ef luh RES uhnt).

PROBLEMS

15. Name each of the following compounds.
    a. MgCO$_3$
    b. MgCO$_3$ · 3H$_2$O
    c. MgCO$_3$ · 5H$_2$O
    d. Nd(CH$_3$COO)$_3$ · H$_2$O
    e. Ni(CN)$_2$ · 4H$_2$O
    f. Pr$_2$(CO$_3$)$_3$ · 8H$_2$O

16. Write formulas for each of the following compounds.
    a. calcium oxalate monohydrate
    b. cerium(III) bromate nonahydrate
    c. hydrogen bromide hexahydrate
    d. iron(II) oxalate dihydrate
    e. iron(III) oxalate pentahydrate
    f. lithium iodide trihydrate

SECTION REVIEW

Predict the oxidation number of the following elements.

1. a. Li   d. C   g. F
   b. Be   e. P   h. Ar
   c. B   f. O   i. K

2. a. Rb   b. I   c. Al   d. S   e. Cs   f. Ba

Write the formula for each of the following compounds.

3. a. sodium nitrite
   b. sodium carbonate
   c. sodium sulfate
   d. potassium hydroxide
   e. potassium nitrate
   f. potassium sulfite
   g. potassium phosphate
   h. calcium oxalate
   i. calcium carbonate
   j. calcium sulfate
   k. calcium phosphate
   l. aluminum bromide
   m. aluminum nitrate
   n. aluminum sulfide

4. a. magnesium nitrate
   b. magnesium sulfate
   c. magnesium carbonate
   d. barium bromide
   e. barium nitrate
   f. barium sulfate
   g. iron(II) oxide
   h. iron(II) hydroxide
   i. iron(II) carbonate
   j. iron(II) sulfate
   k. iron(III) phosphate
   l. iron(III) bromide

5. a. strontium chloride
   b. strontium hydroxide
   c. strontium nitrate
   d. strontium sulfite
   e. strontium sulfide
   f. iron(III) sulfate
   g. iron(III) arsenate
   h. mercury(II) bromide
   i. mercury(II) carbonate
   j. mercury(II) sulfide

6. a. sodium hydroxide
   b. mercury(II) sulfate
   c. calcium hypochlorite
   d. lead(II) phosphate
   e. aluminum chlorate
   f. ammonium sulfide
   g. copper(I) carbonate
   h. mercury(I) sulfide
   i. lead(II) acetate
   j. manganese(IV) oxide
   k. manganese(II) sulfate
   l. potassium oxide
   m. magnesium nitrate
   n. chromium(III) sulfite
   o. ammonium dichromate
   p. iron(III) oxide

Write the formula for each of the following compounds.

7. a. magnesium nitrite
   b. sodium acetate
   c. barium perchlorate
   d. potassium nitrite
   e. ammonium sulfate
   f. ammonium silicate
   g. barium molybdate
   h. lithium thiocyanate

8. a. calcium hexafluorosilicate
   b. antimony(V) sulfide
   c. bismuth(III) telluride
   d. titanium(IV) iodide
   e. nickel(II) fluoride
   f. manganese(IV) oxide
   g. lead(IV) oxide
   h. calcium tartrate
   i. mercury(II) oxide
   j. cobalt(III) oxide

Write the name for each of the following compounds.

9. a. $NaNO_3$
   b. Na_2SO_3
   c. Na_3PO_4
   d. KNO_2
   e. K_2CO_3
   f. K_2SO_4
   g. $CdBr_2$
   h. $Cd(NO_3)_2$
   i. $CdSO_3$
   j. CdS
   k. $AlCl_3$
   l. $Al(OH)_3$

10. a. $Mg(NO_2)_2$
    b. $MgSO_3$
    c. $Mg_3(PO_4)_2$
    d. $Ba(NO_2)_2$
    e. $BaSO_3$
    f. $BaCO_3$
    g. $Al_2(SO_4)_3$
    h. $AlPO_4$
    i. $FeBr_2$
    j. $Fe(NO_3)_2$
    k. $FeSO_3$
    l. FeS

11. a. $Ba_3(PO_4)_2$
    b. $SrBr_2$
    c. $Sr(NO_3)_2$
    d. $SrCO_3$
    e. $SrSO_4$
    f. $Sr_3(PO_4)_2$
    g. $FeCl_3$
    h. $Fe(NO_3)_3$
    i. Fe_2S_3
    j. $HgCl_2$
    k. $Hg(NO_3)_2$
    l. $HgSO_4$

12. a. $NaCH_3COO$
    b. $Ni(NO_3)_2$
    c. Hg_2Cl_2
    d. $Sn_3(PO_4)_2$
    e. $Cr(OH)_2$
    f. $Zn(ClO_3)_2$
    g. $MgBr_2$
    h. CuN_3
    i. CaH_2
    j. $Ba(NO_2)_2$
    k. MnS
    l. $Sn(NO_3)_4$
    m. $(NH_4)_2SO_4$
    n. PbO
    o. KCN

13. a. $FeSO_4$
    b. NH_4ClO_3
    c. $Fe(CH_3COO)_2$
    d. $CuCrO_4$
    e. $Mg(NO_3)_2$
    f. $AlPO_4$
    g. Na_2SO_3
    h. $Ca(ClO_2)_2$
    i. $(NH_4)_2CO_3$
    j. Ag_2CrO_4
    k. $Ba_3(PO_4)_2$
    l. $KClO_4$

14. a. $Zn(SCN)_2$
    b. Sb_2O_5
    c. TiO
    d. InP
    e. Mn_2O_3
    f. $Cr(CH_3COO)_3$

15. Water molecules may be incorporated into the crystal structure. What do we call these crystals?

16. What is a substance called after the water of hydration has been removed?

17. Some crystals will recapture and hold water molecules from the air. What is such a substance called?

18. Some substances will absorb enough water from the air to dissolve and form a solution. What term is applied to these substances?

19. What term is used to describe a substance that releases water molecules to the air from the crystal?

20. Name the following compounds.
    a. $NiCl_2 \cdot 6H_2O$
    b. $Mg(ClO_4)_2 \cdot 6H_2O$
    c. $Mg_3(PO_4)_2 \cdot 4H_2O$
    d. $Ca(NO_3)_2 \cdot 3H_2O$

21. Write the formula for the following hydrates.
    a. cobalt(II) chloride hexahydrate
    b. barium hydroxide octahydrate
    c. gallium(III) oxide monohydrate
    d. magnesium hydrogen arsenate heptahydrate

Chemical Reactions and Equations

6.1 CHEMICAL EQUATIONS

REPRESENTING CHEMICAL CHANGES

Scientists rely on a variety of shorthand methods for expressing chemical information. You have already seen how chemical symbols are used for the names of elements and chemical formulas for the names of compounds. A **chemical equation** is a shorthand expression that represents a chemical reaction. A **chemical reaction** is the process by which one or more substances are changed into one or more new substances. A chemical equation shows the relative amount of each substance taking place in a chemical reaction.

The starting substances in a chemical reaction are called **reactants.** The substances that are formed are called **products.** The general format for a chemical equation is as follows.

$$CO_2(g) + H_2O(l) \longrightarrow H_2CO_3(aq)$$
$$\text{reactants} \quad \text{yield} \quad \text{products}$$

Reactants are generally written on the left side of chemical equations; products are written on the right side.

The letters in parentheses indicate the physical state of each substance involved in the reaction. The following symbols should be used in your work.

(g) gas   (s) solid   (l) liquid   (aq) water solution

COEFFICIENTS

The formula of a compound represents a definite amount of that compound. This amount is called a formula unit. It may be one molecule or the smallest number of particles giving the true proportions of the elements in the compound.

When we wish to represent two molecules of water we write $2H_2O$. The number prefixed as a multiplier is called the **coefficient.** For example, when the coefficient 3 is written before the formula unit Fe_2O_3, it means three times everything in the formula. In $3Fe_2O_3$ there are 6 iron atoms and 9 oxygen atoms.

PROBLEMS

1. Write the number of formula units represented by the following.
   a. 5NaCl
   b. H_2O
   c. $6MgCl_2$
   d. $ZnSO_4$
   e. $2CuSO_4$
   f. $12Pb(NO_3)_2$

2. Determine the number of atoms of each element in the following.
   a. $7H_2O$ b. $2(NH_4)_3PO_4$ c. $4Al_2O_3$ d. $3CuSO_4$

BALANCING EQUATIONS

The first step in writing a chemical equation is writing a word equation. It is composed of the names of the substances that are involved in a chemical reaction.

copper(I) chloride + hydrogen sulfide → copper(I) sulfide + hydrochloric acid

The second step is writing a skeleton equation. This equation includes the chemical symbols and formulas for all the reactants and products identified in the word equation.

$$CuCl(aq) + H_2S(g) \rightarrow Cu_2S(s) + HCl(aq)$$

The third step in writing a chemical equation is balancing the equation. The balanced equation includes the coefficients, numbers placed directly in front of the chemical formulas and symbols. The coefficients indicate the relative proportions of each substance involved in the chemical reaction.

$$2CuCl(aq) + H_2S(g) \rightarrow Cu_2S(s) + 2HCl(aq)$$

This equation states that two units of CuCl(aq) react with one unit of $H_2S(g)$ producing one unit of $Cu_2S(s)$ and two units HCl(aq).

The fourth step is to check and make sure that it is balanced.

	Reactants	Products
Cu	2	2
Cl	2	2
H	2	2
S	1	1

EXAMPLE

Sodium reacts with water to produce a metallic hydroxide and hydrogen gas. Write a balanced equation for the reaction.

Solving Process:
Step 1. Write the word equation. Determine the products and reactants.

sodium + water → sodium hydroxide + hydrogen

Step 2. Write a skeleton equation. Since hydrogen is a diatomic gas, its formula is H_2. The formula for water may be written as HOH; this may make it easier to balance the equation.

$$Na + HOH \rightarrow NaOH + H_2$$

Step 3. Balance the equation. The metallic element sodium is balanced. One atom of sodium is on each side of the equation. There is one hydrogen atom on the reactant side (the H in OH has been accounted for) and 2 hydrogen atoms on the product side. Place a 2 in front of the HOH to balance the hydrogen atoms.

$$Na + 2HOH \rightarrow NaOH + H_2$$

There are now 2OH on the left and 1 on the right. Place a 2 in front of the NaOH to give the same number of OH on each side.

$$Na + 2HOH \rightarrow 2NaOH + H_2$$

Put a 2 in front of the sodium metal. The balanced equation reads

$$2Na(s) + 2HOH(l) \rightarrow 2NaOH(aq) + H_2(g)$$

Step 4. Check to see if the equation is balanced.

	Reactants	Products
Na	2	2
H	4	4
O	2	2

PROBLEMS

Balance each of the following chemical reactions.

3. $Mg(s) + O_2(g) \rightarrow MgO(s)$

4. $Fe(s) + O_2(g) \rightarrow Fe_2O_3(s)$

5. $H_2O(l) + N_2O_3(g) \rightarrow HNO_2(aq)$

6. $Na_2O(s) + H_2O(l) \rightarrow NaOH(aq)$

7. $Fe(s) + H_2O(l) \rightarrow Fe_3O_4(s) + H_2(g)$

Write balanced equations for the following chemical reactions.

8. magnesium bromide(aq) + chlorine(g) →
   magnesium chloride(aq) + bromine(g)

9. chlorine(g) + sodium iodide(s) → sodium chloride(s) + iodine(g)

10. potassium nitrate(s) → potassium nitrite(s) + oxygen(g)

11. zinc(s) + hydrochloric acid(aq) → zinc chloride(aq) + hydrogen(g)

12. calcium oxide(s) + hydrochloric acid(aq) → calcium chloride(aq) + water(l)

SECTION REVIEW

1. Write the number of formula units expressed by each of the following.
   a. $5H_2O$
   b. $9O_2$
   c. $3(NH_4)_2SO_4$
   d. $6NF_3$
   e. $C_{12}H_{22}O_{11}$
   f. $4Fe_2O_3$

Balance the following reactions.

2. $HgO(s) \rightarrow Hg(l) + O_2(g)$

3. $H_2O(l) \rightarrow H_2(g) + O_2(g)$

4. $Al(s) + Pb(NO_3)_2(aq) \rightarrow Al(NO_3)_3(aq) + Pb(s)$

5. $Cu(s) + AgNO_3(aq) \rightarrow Cu(NO_3)_2(aq) + Ag(s)$

6. $K(s) + H_2O(l) \rightarrow KOH(aq) + H_2(g)$

7. $MnO_2(s) + HCl(aq) \rightarrow MnCl_2(aq) + Cl_2(g) + H_2O(l)$

8. $Cl_2(g) + LiI(aq) \rightarrow LiCl(aq) + I_2(g)$

9. $F_2(g) + H_2O(l) \rightarrow HF(aq) + O_3(g)$

10. $AgNO_3(aq) + K_2SO_4(aq) \rightarrow Ag_2SO_4(aq) + KNO_3(aq)$

11. $NH_3(g) + O_2(g) \rightarrow N_2O_4(g) + H_2O(g)$

6.2 TYPES OF REACTIONS

CLASSIFYING CHEMICAL CHANGES

The products of a chemical reaction may often be predicted by applying known facts about common reaction types. While there are hundreds of different "kinds" of chemical reactions, only five general types of reactions will be considered: synthesis, decomposition, single displacement, double displacement, and combustion.

Synthesis. In a synthesis reaction two or more substances are combined to form one new and more complex substance. The general form is as follows.

element/compound + element/compound → compound

$$a + b \rightarrow ab$$

The following are some general types of synthesis reactions.

1. Two or more elements combine to form a compound.

$$Fe(s) + S(l) \rightarrow FeS(s)$$

2. An acid anhydride, nonmetallic oxide, combines with water to give an acid.

$$SO_2(g) + H_2O(l) \rightarrow H_2SO_3(aq)$$

3. A basic anhydride, metallic oxide, combines with water to form a base.

$$Na_2O(s) + H_2O(l) \rightarrow 2NaOH(aq)$$

4. A basic oxide combines with a nonmetallic oxide to form a salt.

$$CO_2(g) + Na_2O(s) \rightarrow Na_2CO_3(s)$$

PROBLEMS

Balance the following equations.

1. $Na(s) + Cl_2(g) \rightarrow NaCl(s)$

2. $Br_2(g) + H_2O(l) + SO_2(g) \rightarrow HBr(aq) + H_2SO_4(aq)$

3. $CaO(s) + H_2O(l) \rightarrow Ca(OH)_2(aq)$

4. $P_2O_5(s) + BaO(s) \rightarrow Ba_3(PO_4)_2(s)$

Balance each of the following reactions after predicting the products.

5. barium oxide(s) + water(l) →

6. sulfur(IV) oxide(g) + magnesium oxide(s) →

7. carbon dioxide(g) + water(l) →

8. magnesium(s) + fluorine(g) →

9. nitrogen(III) oxide(g) + water(l) →

Decomposition. When energy in the form of heat, electricity, light, or mechanical shock is supplied, a compound may decompose to form simpler substances. The general form for this type of reaction is as follows.

compound → two or more elements/compounds

$$ab \rightarrow a + b$$

The following are some general types of decomposition reactions.

1. When some acids are heated, they decompose to form water and an acidic oxide.

$$H_2CO_3(aq) \rightarrow CO_2(g) + H_2O(l)$$

2. When some metallic hydroxides are heated, they decompose to form a metallic oxide and water.

$$Ca(OH)_2(s) \rightarrow CaO(s) + H_2O(g)$$

3. When some metallic carbonates are heated, they decompose to form a metallic oxide and carbon dioxide.

$$Li_2CO_3(s) \rightarrow Li_2O(s) + CO_2(g)$$

4. When metallic chlorates are heated, they decompose to form metallic chlorides and oxygen.

$$2KClO_3(s) \rightarrow 2KCl(s) + 3O_2(g)$$

5. Most metallic oxides are stable, but a few decompose when heated.

$$2HgO(s) \rightarrow 2Hg(l) + O_2(g)$$

6. Some compounds cannot be decomposed by heat, but can be decomposed into their elements by electricity.

$$2NaCl(l) \rightarrow 2Na(s) + Cl_2(g)$$

PROBLEMS

Balance the following equations.

10. $KNO_3(s) \rightarrow KNO_2(s) + O_2(g)$

11. $PbO_2(s) \rightarrow PbO(s) + O_2(g)$

12. $NaOH(s) \rightarrow Na_2O(s) + H_2O(l)$

13. $MgCO_3(s) \rightarrow MgO(s) + CO_2(g)$

Balance each of the following reactions after predicting the products.

14. When heated, sulfurous acid, $H_2SO_3 \rightarrow$

15. When heated, calcium carbonate $\rightarrow$

16. When heated, iron(III) hydroxide $\rightarrow$

17. When heated, sodium chlorate $\rightarrow$

18. When heated, silver oxide $\rightarrow$

19. By electricity, water $\rightarrow$

Single Displacement. One element displaces another element in a compound. A single displacement has this general form.

$$\text{element a} + \text{compound bc} \rightarrow \text{element b} + \text{compound ac}$$

$$a + bc \rightarrow b + ac$$

$$\text{element d} + \text{compound bc} \rightarrow \text{element c} + \text{compound bd}$$

$$d + bc \rightarrow c + bd$$

The following are some general types of single displacement reactions.

1. An active metal will displace the metallic ion in a compound of a less active metal.

$$Fe(s) + Cu(NO_3)_2(aq) \rightarrow Fe(NO_3)_2(aq) + Cu(s)$$

2. Some active metals, such as sodium and calcium, will react with water to give a metallic hydroxide and hydrogen gas.

$$Ca(s) + 2H_2O(l) \rightarrow Ca(OH)_2(aq) + H_2(g)$$

3. Active metals, such as zinc, iron, and aluminum, will displace the hydrogen in acids to give a salt and hydrogen gas.

$$Zn(s) + 2HCl(aq) \rightarrow ZnCl_2(aq) + H_2(g)$$

4. An active nonmetal will displace a less active nonmetal.

$$Cl_2(g) + 2NaBr(aq) \rightarrow 2NaCl(aq) + Br_2(aq)$$

PROBLEMS

Balance the following reactions.

20. $Al(s) + Pb(NO_3)_2(aq) \rightarrow Al(NO_3)_3(aq) + Pb(s)$

21. $Cu(s) + AgNO_3(aq) \rightarrow Cu(NO_3)_2(aq) + Ag(s)$

22. $K(s) + H_2O(l) \rightarrow KOH(aq) + H_2(g)$

23. $Cl_2(g) + LiI(aq) \rightarrow LiCl(aq) + I_2(g)$

Balance each of the following reactions after predicting the products.

24. aluminum(s) + hydrochloric acid(aq) →

25. iron(s) + copper(II) sulfate(aq) → (iron(II) compound is formed)

26. zinc(s) + sulfuric acid(aq) →

27. chlorine(g) + magnesium iodide(aq) →

28. sodium(s) + water(l) →

29. magnesium(s) + hydrochloric acid(aq) →

Double Displacement. The positive portions of two ionic compounds are interchanged in a double displacement reaction. The form of these reactions is easy to recognize.

compound ac + compound bd → compound ad + compound bc

ac + bd → ad + bc

The following are some general types of double displacement reactions.

1. A reaction between an acid and a base yields a salt and water. Such a reaction is a neutralization reaction.

$$2KOH(aq) + H_2SO_4(aq) \rightarrow K_2SO_4(aq) + 2H_2O(l)$$

2. Reaction of a salt with an acid forms a salt of the acid and a second acid that is volatile.

$$2KNO_3(aq) + H_2SO_4(aq) \rightarrow K_2SO_4(aq) + 2HNO_3(g)$$

This same reaction of a salt with an acid or base may yield a compound that can be decomposed. H_2CO_3, H_2SO_3, and $NH_3(aq)$ decompose to give a gas and H_2O.

$$CaCO_3(aq) + 2HCl(aq) \rightarrow CaCl_2(aq) + H_2CO_3(aq)$$
$$H_2CO_3(aq) \rightarrow CO_2(g) + H_2O(l)$$

3. Reactions of some soluble salts produce an insoluble salt and a soluble salt.

$$AgNO_3(aq) + NaCl(aq) \rightarrow AgCl(s) + NaNO_3(aq)$$

PROBLEMS

Balance the following equations.

30. $Ca(OH)_2(aq) + HCl(aq) \rightarrow CaCl_2(aq) + H_2O(l)$

31. $KOH(aq) + H_3PO_4(aq) \rightarrow K_3PO_4(aq) + H_2O(l)$

32. $Al(NO_3)_3(aq) + H_2SO_4(aq) \rightarrow Al_2(SO_4)_3(aq) + HNO_3(aq)$

33. $Na_2SO_3(aq) + HCl(aq) \rightarrow NaCl(aq) + H_2O(l) + SO_2(g)$

Balance each of the following reactions after predicting the products.

34. sodium hydroxide(aq) + phosphoric acid(aq) →

35. ammonium sulfate(aq) + calcium hydroxide(aq) →

36. silver nitrate(aq) + potassium chloride(aq) →

37. magnesium hydroxide(aq) + phosphoric acid(aq) →

38. iron(II) sulfide(s) + hydrochloric acid(aq) →

39. ammonium sulfide(aq) + iron(II) nitrate(aq) →

Combustion. A substance combines with oxygen to form one or more oxides. Combustion has this general form.

$$element/compound + oxygen \rightarrow oxide(s)$$

$$a + O \rightarrow aO$$

The following are some general types of combustion reactions.

1. A metal will combine with oxygen to produce a metallic oxide.

$$Mg(s) + O_2(g) \rightarrow MgO(s)$$

2. In a substance containing hydrogen, water is always one of the products.

$$4NH_3(g) + 7O_2(g) \rightarrow 4NO_2(g) + 6H_2O(l)$$

3. Hydrocarbons (compounds made of carbon and hydrogen) will react with oxygen to produce carbon dioxide (oxide of carbon) and water.

$$CH_4(g) + 2O_2(g) \rightarrow CO_2(g) + 2H_2O(l)$$
$$C_6H_{12}O_6(s) + 6O_2(g) \rightarrow 6CO_2(g) + 6H_2O(l)$$

4. Certain non-metals will burn with oxygen.

$$S(s) + O_2(g) \rightarrow SO_2(g)$$

PROBLEMS

Balance the following equations.

40. $C_3H_8(g) + O_2(g) \rightarrow CO_2(g) + H_2O(l)$

41. $Li(s) + O_2(g) \rightarrow Li_2O(s)$

42. $Fe(s) + O_2(g) \rightarrow Fe_2O_3(s)$

43. $H_2(g) + O_2(g) \rightarrow H_2O(l)$

Balance each of the following reactions after predicting the products.

44. methanol(CH$_3$OH)(l) + oxygen(g) →

45. potassium(s) + oxygen(g) →

46. carbon(s) + oxygen(g) →

SECTION REVIEW

Write a balanced equation and indicate the reaction type (single or double displacement, decomposition, synthesis, or combustion) for each of the following reactions.

1. aluminum nitrate(aq) + sodium hydroxide(aq) →
    aluminum hydroxide(s) + sodium nitrate(aq)

2. sulfur trioxide(g) → sulfur dioxide(g) + oxygen(g)

3. phosphoric acid(aq) + magnesium hydroxide(aq) →
    magnesium phosphate(s) + water(l)

4. ammonium nitrite(s) → nitrogen(g) + water(l)

5. ammonia(g) + oxygen(g) → nitrogen(II) oxide(g) + water(g)

6. barium chloride(aq) + sodium sulfate(aq) →
    sodium chloride(aq) + barium sulfate(s)

7. carbon dioxide(g) + water(l) → carbonic acid(aq)

8. magnesium hydroxide(aq) + ammonium phosphate(aq) →
    magnesium phosphate(s) + ammonia(g) + water(l)

9. aluminum(s) + copper(II) chloride(aq) → aluminum chloride(aq) + copper(s)

10. iron(s) + silver acetate(aq) → iron(II) acetate(aq) + silver(s)

Balance each of the following reactions after predicting the products.

11. magnesium hydroxide(aq) + phosphoric acid(aq) →

12. iron(II) sulfide(s) + hydrochloric acid(aq) →

13. ammonium sulfide(aq) + iron(II) nitrate(aq) →

14. sulfuric acid(aq) + potassium hydroxide(aq) →

15. aluminum sulfate(aq) + calcium phosphate(s) →

16. barium carbonate(s) + hydrochloric acid(aq) →

17. silver acetate(aq) + potassium chromate(aq) →

18. ammonium phosphate(aq) + barium hydroxide(aq) →

19. chromium(III) sulfite(aq) + sulfuric acid(aq) →

20. calcium hydroxide(aq) + nitric acid(aq) →

21. One type of fire extinguisher contains concentrated sulfuric acid that reacts with a solution to produce carbon dioxide. What solution, sodium hydrogen carbonate or sodium carbonate, would give the greater amount of carbon dioxide in a reaction with the same amount of acid?

22. If iron pyrite, FeS_2, is not removed from coal, oxygen from the air will combine with both the iron and the sulfur as the coal burns. Write a balanced chemical equation illustrating the formation of iron(III) oxide and sulfur dioxide.

23. Sodium sulfite, Na_2SO_3, can be used for the removal of SO_2 produced as a by-product in manufacturing operations. The SO_2 reacts with a sodium sulfite solution to form sodium hydrogen sulfite. The $NaHSO_3$ solution is heated to regenerate the original sodium sulfite for reuse. Write the equation for this reaction.

6.3 NATURE OF REACTIONS

In the previous chapters we have assumed that the reactions have gone to completion (reacted until at least one of the reactants was completely used up, and then stopped). Reactions tend to go to completion because of the formation of a gas (e.g., CO_2, SO_2), a precipitate (e.g., AgCl, $PbSO_4$), or a slightly ionized substance (e.g., H_2O, HF). Formation of these or similar species causes the elements from the initial reactants to be removed from the reaction.

$$2KClO_3(s) \rightarrow 2KCl(s) 1\ 3O_2(g)$$
(formation of a gas)

$$Na^+(aq) + F^-(aq) + H^+(aq) + Cl^-(aq) \rightarrow Na^+(aq) + Cl^-(aq) + HF(aq)$$
(formation of a slightly ionized substance, hydrofluoric acid)

$$AgNO_3(aq) + NaCl(aq) \rightarrow NaNO_3(aq) + AgCl(s)$$
(formation of a precipitate)

REVERSIBLE REACTIONS

It has been determined experimentally that the conversion of some reactants to products is incomplete, regardless of the reaction time. Initially the reactants are present at a definite concentration. As the reaction proceeds, the reactant concentration decreases as the product is produced. However, a point is reached at which the reactant concentration levels off and becomes constant. The concentration levels for the reactants and products no longer change. A state of **chemical equilibrium** is established.

An example of a reaction that can proceed in either direction is the equilibrium system involving nitrogen, hydrogen, and ammonia gases. The reversible reaction is written as follows.

$$N_2(g) + 3H_2(g) \underset{\text{reverse}}{\overset{\text{forward}}{\rightleftharpoons}} 2NH_3(g) + energy$$

A reversible chemical reaction is in chemical equilibrium when the rates of the opposing reactions are equal and the overall concentrations remain constant. Thus a state of chemical equilibrium is considered to be dynamic.

LE CHATELIER'S PRINCIPLE AND REACTANTS

Sometimes, systems initially at equilibrium are subjected to an outside influence or disturbance. Concentration, pressure, and temperature changes affect equilibrium because they produce a disturbance. **Le Chatelier's principle** states: *If a system in equilibrium is subjected to a disturbance, the equilibrium will shift in an attempt to reduce the disturbance and regain equilibrium.* To see how these variables affect the equilibrium, consider the reaction between nitrogen and hydrogen to form ammonia.

If more reactant is added to the system in equilibrium, the reaction shifts to the right (the product side) and more product is formed. For example, in the ammonia equation

$$N_2(g) + 3H_2(g) \rightleftharpoons 2NH_3(g) + energy$$

the addition of N_2 disturbs the system. The system can relieve this disturbance by consuming N_2. The system shifts to the right to consume N_2, and in the process, produces more NH_3. If a reactant is removed, the reaction shifts to the left. In the ammonia synthesis, if we remove some H_2, the system can relieve the disturbance by producing H_2. When the system shifts left to replace the missing H_2, it also produces more N_2 and consumes NH_3.

Pressure affects only gaseous equilibrium systems. As pressure on the reactant gases is increased, the reaction shifts toward the side with the least volume. In the ammonia synthesis, an increase of pressure would shift the equilibrium to the right. In the process of shifting, four particles ($N_2 + 3H_2$) are converted to two particles ($2NH_3$). The number of particles colliding is thereby reduced, which also reduces the pressure. Lowering the pressure relieves the disturbance.

If temperature is increased, the reaction shifts in such a way that the endothermic reaction is favored. In the ammonia synthesis, the reaction from left to right is exothermic, while the reaction from right to left is endothermic. Consequently, a rise in temperature will shift the reaction to the left.

Catalysts speed up the reaction by lowering the activation energy, but this does not cause the equilibrium to shift. Catalysts do not increase the amount of product being produced. They simply just speed up the production process. In the same way, inhibitors do not shift the equilibrium. They just slow down the reaction. In the end, the same amount of product will be produced with the inhibitor as without the inhibitor.

PROBLEM

1. For the following gaseous equilibrium reactions, indicate what happens to the equilibrium position (shift to right or left) when the indicated disturbance or condition change occurs.

    a. remove NH_3 gas **b.** decrease pressure

    $$N_2 + 3H_2 \rightleftharpoons 2NH_3 + energy$$

    c. decrease temperature **d.** add a catalyst

    $$CO_2 + H_2 + energy \rightleftharpoons CO + H_2O$$

    e. increase SO_2 concentration **f.** increase temperature

    $$2SO_2 + O_2 \rightleftharpoons 2SO_3 + energy$$

    g. increase temperature **h.** increase CO concentration

    $$CO_2 + C + energy \rightleftharpoons 2CO$$

    i. decrease pressure **j.** remove N_2O_4

    $$N_2O_4 + energy \rightleftharpoons 2NO_2$$

    k. increase H_2 concentration **l.** increase pressure

    $$H_2 + Cl_2 \rightleftharpoons 2HCl + energy$$

    m. decrease O_2 concentration **n.** add catalyst

    $$N_2 + O_2 + energy \rightleftharpoons 2NO$$

SECTION REVIEW

1. Ammonia can be converted to the high nitrogen content fertilizer urea, NH_2CONH_2, according to the following equation.

    $$CO_2(aq) + 2NH_3(aq) \rightleftharpoons NH_2CONH_2(aq) + H_2O(l) + energy$$

    Indicate whether the equilibrium shifts left or right when the indicated disturbance or condition change occurs.

    a. remove urea, NH_2CONH_2
    b. increase CO_2 concentration
    c. increase temperature
    d. add catalyst

Completing the Model of the Atom

7

7.2 THE PERIODIC TABLE AND ATOMIC STRUCTURE

ORDER OF FILLING SUBLEVELS

The **electron configuration** of an atom is used to describe the electron distribution in the sublevels. Each sublevel symbol is written following a coefficient that represents the energy level containing the sublevel. Each sublevel symbol has a superscript on the right giving the number of electrons in the sublevel. For example, the electron configuration of the boron atom (atomic number 5) is written $1s^2 2s^2 2p^1$.

The order of filling corresponds to the increasing energy of the sublevels. By filling the sublevels of the lowest energy first, we have a model of an atom in the ground state. The *s* sublevel can hold a maximum of two electrons, the *p* sublevel, six, the *d* sublevel, ten, and the *f* sublevel, fourteen. In many atoms with higher atomic numbers, the sublevels are not regularly filled. There is a rule of thumb that will give a correct configuration for most atoms in the ground state. This rule of thumb is the **arrow diagram** and is shown in **Figure 7-1.** If you follow the arrows from tail to head, listing the orbitals passed as you move from left to right, you can find the electron configuration of most atoms.

FIGURE 7-1

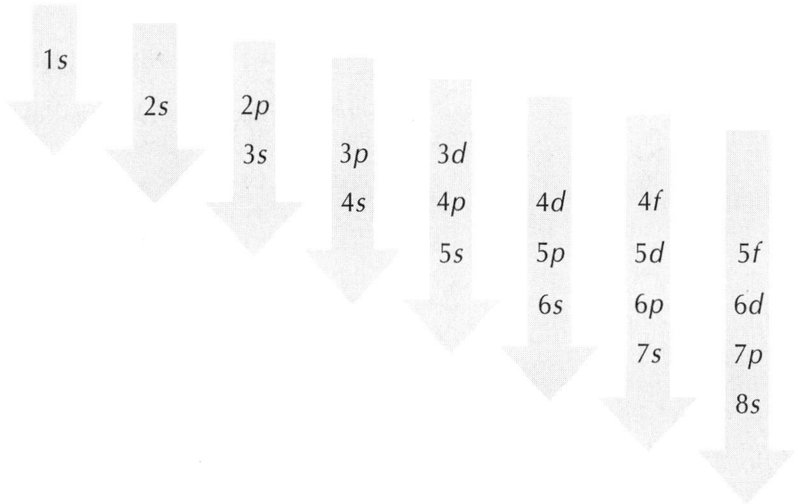

```
1s
2s   2p
3s   3p   3d
     4s   4p   4d   4f
          5s   5p   5d   5f
               6s   6p   6d
                    7s   7p
                         8s
```

EXAMPLE

Write the electron configuration of arsenic (Z = 33).

Solving Process:
The arrow diagram gives us the order 1s, 2s, 2p, 3s, 3p, 4s, 3d, 4p. The sublevels are then filled to capacity with the 33 electrons present in arsenic beginning with 1s, then 2s, and so on. The final 3 electrons are placed in the 4p. The electron configuration is $1s^2 2s^2 2p^6 3s^2 3p^6 4s^2 3d^{10} 4p^3$.

The sum of the superscripts equals the atomic number, 33.

PROBLEMS

1. Which of the following show the correct order of filling?
   a. 1s2s2p
   b. 1s2s2p3s3p
   c. 1s2s3s
   d. 1s2s2p3s3p4s
   e. 1s2s2p3p3d4s
   f. 1s2s2p3s3p4s4p

2. Write the name of the element represented by each of the following configurations.
   a. $1s^2 2s^2 2p^5$
   b. $1s^2 2s^2 2p^6 3s^2$
   c. $1s^2 2s^2 2p^6 3s^2 3p^6 4s^2 3d^{10} 4p^1$
   d. $1s^2 2s^2 2p^6 3s^2 3p^4$

3. Write the electron configuration for each of the following elements using the diagonal rule.
   a. aluminum (Z = 13)
   b. iron (Z = 26)
   c. cadmium (Z = 48)
   d. carbon (Z = 6)
   e. barium (Z = 56)
   f. hafnium (Z = 72)

4. Predict electron configurations using the diagonal rule for atoms of the following elements.
   a. Li   b. N   c. Be   d. O   e. B   f. F   g. C   h. Ne

ELECTRON CONFIGURATION

The periodic table can be used to read the electron configuration of an element. The written configuration of any element in Group 1 will end in s^1. The coefficient of s^1 is easily found from the table because the number of the period indicates the energy level. Group 2 elements end their electron configuration with s^2. The same procedure can be used for Groups 13 through 18. There the endings are p^1 through p^6 preceded by a coefficient that is the same number as the period. For example, arsenic (Z = 33) is in period 4 and Group 15. Its electron configuration will end in $4p^3$.

For Groups 3 through 12 the endings are d^1 through d^{10} preceded by a coefficient that is one less than the period number. For the lanthanides, the endings are f^1 through f^{14} preceded by a coefficient that is two less than the period number.

To understand some of the exceptions to the diagonal rule, it is necessary to know that there is a special stability associated with certain electron configurations in an atom. An atom with eight electrons in the outer level has a special stability. *An atom having a filled or half filled sublevel is also more stable.* For example, chromium is predicted to have two electrons in its 4s sublevel and four electrons in its 3d sublevel. Actually it has only one electron in its 4s sublevel and five electrons in its 3d sublevel. Thus, the atom has two half-full sublevels instead of one full sublevel and one with no special arrangement. Copper is similar. It has one electron in its 4s sublevel and ten electrons in its 3d sublevel. Most of the exceptions from predicted configurations can be explained in this way.

PROBLEMS

5. Give the group number for the elements that have the following electron configurations.
    a. $1s^2 2s^2 2p^1$
    b. $1s^2 2s^2$
    c. $1s^2 2s^2 2p^6 3s^2 3p^5$
    d. $1s^2 2s^2 2p^6 3s^2 3p^4$
    e. $1s^2 2s^2 2p^6 3s^2 3p^6 4s^2 3d^3$
    f. $1s^2 2s^2 2p^6 3s^2 3p^6 4s^2 3d^{10}$

6. Give the names of each of the elements listed in problem 5.

7. Write the electron configurations for the following elements.
    a. potassium ($Z = 19$)
    b. mercury ($Z = 80$)
    c. lithium ($Z = 3$)
    d. phosphorus ($Z = 15$)
    e. calcium ($Z = 20$)
    f. indium ($Z = 49$)

8. In what period would the element with the configuration $1s^2 2s^2 2p^6 3s^2 3p^6 4s^2 3d^{10} 4p^6 5s^1$ be located?

9. Which two elements in the fourth period have configurations that are apparent contradictions to the diagonal rule?

SECTION REVIEW

1. What is the arrow diagram used to predict?

2. Write the electron configuration for each of the following elements.
    a. beryllium ($Z = 4$)
    b. radium ($Z = 88$)
    c. sodium ($Z = 11$)
    d. lead ($Z = 82$)
    e. tin ($Z = 50$)
    f. krypton ($Z = 36$)

3. For the transition elements, as the atomic number increases, to which sublevel are electrons being added?

4. According to the octet rule, how many pairs of outer electrons do the most stable atoms have?

5. In the lanthanide series, as the atomic number increases, to which sublevel are electrons being added?

6. Write the electron configurations of the following elements.
    a. silicon ($Z = 14$)
    b. bromine ($Z = 35$)
    c. copper ($Z = 29$)
    d. cesium ($Z = 55$)

7. Identify the elements whose electron configurations end with the following.
   a. $4s^2 3d^2$
   b. $2s^2 2p^6$
   c. $4s^1 3d^5$
   d. $7s^2 5f^6$
   e. $4s^2 3d^{10} 4p^5$
   f. $3s^1$

8. Write the electron configurations of the following elements.
   a. iodine ($Z = 53$)
   b. oxygen ($Z = 8$)
   c. nickel ($Z = 28$)
   d. strontium ($Z = 38$)

Periodic Properties of the Elements

8.1 MAIN GROUP ELEMENTS

RADII OF ATOMS

The periodic table is a powerful tool of the chemist. Similar properties of the elements occur at predicted intervals. The properties are periodic because both the position and properties arise from the electron configurations of the atoms.

As you look at the periodic table from top to bottom, each period represents a new energy level. *In each new energy level, more electrons get added, and the size of the electron cloud increases.* Chemists discuss the size of atoms by referring to the radii. As you look across the periodic table, the positive charge on the nucleus increases by one proton for each element. This increase in charge results in the outer electron cloud being pulled closer to the nucleus. Thus, *atoms generally decrease slightly in size from left to right across a period.*

PROBLEM

1. From each of the following pairs, use the periodic table to select the atom that is larger in radius.

   a. Sn, Sr   **c.** Na, Rb   **e.** S, P   **g.** B, Al
   b. Cl, I   **d.** Mg, Be   **f.** Ac, U   **h.** Au, Ba

RADII OF IONS

Generally, when atoms unite to form compounds, their structures become more stable. Ionic compounds are formed from atoms that have lost or gained electrons in order to obtain a noble gas configuration. A **noble gas configuration** is particularly stable because the eight outer electrons fill the outer sublevels. Metals, on the left and in the center of the table, tend to lose electrons, forming positive ions. This loss of electrons results in the formation of a smaller metallic ion. Nonmetals are located on the right side of the table. Nonmetallic ions are formed by atoms gaining electrons. The negatively charged nonmetallic ions are larger than the atoms from which they are formed.

PROBLEM

2. From each of the following pairs of particles, select the particle that is larger in radius.

   a. Ca, Ca^{2+} **c.** As^{3-}, P^{3-} **e.** Mg^{2+}, Be^{2+} **g.** C, C^{4-}
   b. F^-, Cl^- **d.** Pb^{4+}, Pb   **f.** Te^{2-}, Te   **h.** Ag, Ag^+

Chemistry: Concepts and Applications

REPRESENTATIVE METALS

Lithium, sodium, and potassium belong to Group 1, the alkali metals. These elements have low densities, are soft, and very reactive, forming 1+ ions. Reactivity increases as the atomic numbers of these metals increase. It becomes easier to knock electrons off the atom because the more electrons you have, the farther away from the nucleus the valence electrons are. Alkali metals form binary compounds with most nonmetals. Lithium is not typical of this group, since its reactions are more like magnesium, a Group 2 element.

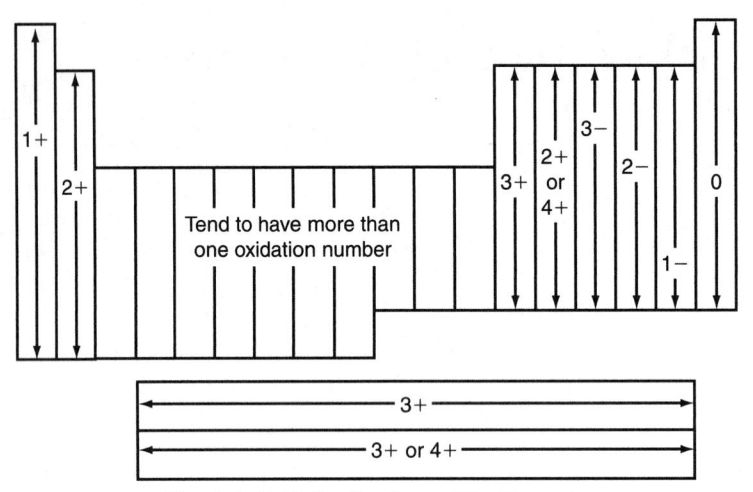

Trends in Oxidation Numbers of the Elements

Group 2 elements are known as alkaline earth metals. These elements are also reactive, and they form 2+ ions. Most compounds of these metals are soluble in water.

Aluminum, one of the Group 13 metals, is the most abundant metal in the earth's crust. It tends to share its three outer electrons, and is less reactive than the metals of Groups 1 and 2.

REPRESENTATIVE NONMETALS

The elements of Group 14 have atoms with four electrons in the outer level. These elements generally react by sharing electrons. Carbon is the first element in this group. The major part of carbon chemistry is classed as organic chemistry. **Catenation** occurs when carbon forms "chains" with other carbon atoms. Generally, compounds that do not contain carbon are called inorganic compounds.

Nitrogen and phosphorus differ greatly even though they are adjacent members of Group 15. Nitrogen occurs in oxidation states ranging from 3− through 5+. Phosphorus shows only 3−, 0, 3+, and 5+ oxidation states. Nitrogen gas, N_2, is very stable but many nitrogen compounds are relatively unstable. TNT, an explosive, is one example. Elemental phosphorus, solid at room temperature, occurs as P_4 molecules. White and red phosphorus are two forms of phosphorus.

Oxygen, Group 16, is the most plentiful element in the earth's crust. It gains two electrons to achieve a stable octet and forms O^{2-} ions. Metallic oxides generally react with water to form basic solutions. Nonmetallic oxides generally form acidic solutions when dissolved in water. Some oxides, called amphoteric oxides, can produce either acidic or basic solutions, depending on the other substances present. Ozone, O_3, is a highly reactive form of oxygen. The chemistry of sulfur is similar to that of oxygen.

Group 17 is the highly reactive halogen (salt forming) family. These elements exist as diatomic molecules. They react either by forming 1− ions or by sharing electrons. Fluorine is the most reactive of all elements, because of its small radius. Electrons are very readily attracted to the nucleus of fluorine. (Remember, fluorine has an oxidation number of 1−.)

In 1962, the first "inert" gas compound was synthesized. Since that time the gases of Group 18 have been called the noble gases. Xenon, krypton, and radon compounds have been made. However, the noble gases are generally considered the most stable elements.

SECTION REVIEW

1. Within a group, does the radii of atoms increase or decrease as the atomic number increases?

2. Does the radii of atoms within a period increase or decrease as the atomic number increases?

3. In each of the following pairs of atoms, pick the one that is larger.
   a. Mg, Na
   b. K, Ca
   c. Al, B
   d. Br, Cl
   e. F, N
   f. Ne, Ar

4. In each of the following pairs of particles, pick the one that is smaller.
   a. Fe, Fe^{3+}
   b. S^{2-}, S
   c. Ac^{3+}, U^{3+}
   d. Br^-, Se^{2-}
   e. Mo^{6+}, Mo
   f. As^{3-}, As

Identify the false statements and correct them.

5. Group 2 elements that form 2+ ions are known as alkali metals.

6. The tendency of carbon atoms to form long chains is called catenation.

7. Organic chemistry is the chemistry of carbon compounds.

8. The family of elements having eight outer electrons, Group 18, is called the halogens.

9. Amphoteric oxides react with water to form either acidic or basic solutions.

10. The most reactive elements on the periodic table are in Groups 2 and 17.

8.2 TRANSITION ELEMENTS

TRANSITION METALS, LANTHANIDES AND ACTINIDES

The transition metals are those elements whose highest energy electrons are in *d* sublevels. The *d* electrons may be lost, one at a time, after the outer *s* electrons have been lost. The fourth period elements, titanium through zinc, are used primarily as structural metals. They can be used alone or as alloys. Chromium is a transition metal. It has multiple oxidation numbers. Because of its $4s^1 3s^5$ outer electron configuration, it is stable and resists corrosion. Zinc's behavior differs slightly from other transition elements due to a full *d* sublevel, $4s^2 3d^{10}$.

All of the lanthanides show 3+ as the most stable state. Neodymium, a soft reactive metal, is a typical example of the elements whose highest energy level electrons are in the 4*f* sublevel. The actinides are those elements whose highest energy level electrons are in the 5*f* sublevel. Curium, a silvery, hard metal of medium density is an example. It is reactive and highly toxic.

SECTION REVIEW

Indicate whether the following statement is true or false. If it is false, correct it to make it true.

1. The transition metals are those elements whose highest energy electrons are in the 4*f* sublevel.

Chemical Bonding

9.1 BONDING OF ATOMS

BOND CHARACTER

The chemical bonds formed between atoms depend on two periodic properties: the electron configurations of the atoms and the attraction the atoms have for electrons. A measure of the ability of an atom in a bond to attract electrons is called **electronegativity.** Examine **Table B-8** in Appendix B. It shows the variation in electronegativity over the periodic table.

When two atoms transfer electrons, ions are produced. The electrostatic force that holds two ions together due to their differing charges is the **ionic bond.** Ionic compounds have high melting points, conduct electricity in the molten state, tend to be soluble in water, and usually crystallize as well-defined crystals.

If two elements combine by sharing electrons, they are said to form a **covalent bond.** The shared pair or pairs of electrons constitute a covalent bond. The resulting particle is called a **molecule.** Covalent compounds typically have low melting points, do not conduct electricity, and are brittle.

In some covalent bonds, the sharing of the electrons is not equal. These bonds are called **polar covalent bonds.** Polar covalent bonds have a significant degree of ionic character. The unequal sharing creates two poles across the bond. One end is negative, and the other is positive. The negative end is created by the electrons spending more time at that end of the bond, and the positive end is where they spend less time. The positive pole is centered on the less electronegative atom. The symbols used to represent the two poles are δ^+ and δ^-. Water is a good example of a polar covalent bond.

Electronegativity differences can be used to determine whether a bond is ionic, covalent, or polar covalent. If the electronegativity difference is 2.0 or greater (up to 3.3), the bond is mostly ionic. If it is between 0.5 and 2.0, the bond is polar covalent. And if the electronegativity difference is 0.0 to 0.5, the bond is mostly covalent.

EXAMPLE

Classify as ionic, covalent, or polar covalent, the bond that forms between calcium and oxygen.

Solving Process:
From **Table B-8** the electronegativity of calcium is found to be 1.0 and oxygen is 3.5.

$$\text{Electronegativity difference} = 3.5 - 1.0 = 2.5$$

The bond is considered to be an ionic bond.

PROBLEMS

1. Classify the bonds between the following pairs of atoms as principally ionic or covalent.
   a. lithium—chlorine
   b. potassium—sulfur
   c. cobalt—carbon
   d. strontium—oxygen
   e. copper—bromine
   f. selenium—iodine

2. For each compound listed below, determine the electronegativity difference, and indicate whether the bond is ionic, covalent, or polar covalent.
   a. NiO   b. BN   c. $CaCl_2$ d. FeSi   e. NaF   f. Zn_3P_2

SECTION REVIEW

1. Use **Table B-8** to predict which of the following bonds will be ionic, covalent, or polar covalent.
   a. Ca—F   b. S—H   c. H—O   d. K—Cl

2. Answer the following questions about trends on the periodic table with "increases" or "decreases."
   a. Within a family of elements, what happens to the atomic radii as the atomic number increases?
   b. Within a family of elements, what happens to the electronegativity as the atomic number increases?
   c. Within a period, what happens to the electronegativity as the atomic number increases?

9.2 MOLECULAR SHAPE AND POLARITY

The structure of a substance determines its properties. It is, therefore, important to be able to predict the structure of molecules. Several theories have been proposed to explain the structure of molecules.

LEWIS ELECTRON DOT STRUCTURES

Being able to draw Lewis structures for polyatomic ions and molecules is very helpful in determining their structures. Guidelines for drawing these structures follow. Methane, CH_4, and the carbonate ion, CO_3^{2-}, are used as examples.

1. The first step is to decide what atoms are bonded together. The formula may suggest how the atoms are to be arranged. For those atoms given, the arrangements are as follows.

$$\begin{array}{c} H \\ H\ C\ H \\ H \end{array} \quad \text{and} \quad \begin{array}{c} O\ \ O \\ C \\ O \end{array}$$

This choice is not always easy. For most binary covalent compounds and polyatomic ions, the central atom will be the atom that occurs once in the formula.

For oxygen-containing acids, the hydrogens that are released from these compounds are bonded to oxygen. When in doubt, choose the most symmetrical atom arrangement.

2. Count the total number of outer level electrons in the ion or molecule. For CH_4, there are eight, four from carbon plus one from each of the four hydrogens. For CO_3^{2-} there are twenty-four, four from carbon, six from each of the three oxygens, plus the two added to give the ion a charge of $2-$.

3. Place a pair of electrons (dots) between the central atom and each of the other atoms.

$$\begin{array}{c} H \\ \cdot\cdot \\ H:C:H \\ \cdot\cdot \\ H \end{array} \qquad \begin{array}{c} O\ \ \ O \\ \ \ C \\ \ \ O \end{array}$$

4. Distribute the remaining outer electrons so that each atom has a filled outer energy level, usually an octet of electrons. Some exceptions are H, which has two, and B, which will have six.

Our structure for CH_4 above is complete. We have used all eight electrons in such a way that carbon has eight and each hydrogen has two. However, we must add electrons to the carbonate unit.

$$\left[\begin{array}{c} :\ddot{O}: \\ \ \ C \\ :\ddot{O}\ \ \ \ddot{O}: \end{array}\right]^{2-} \quad \text{or} \quad \left[\begin{array}{c} :\ddot{O}:C:\ddot{O}: \\ :\ddot{O}: \end{array}\right]^{2-}$$

Neither structure meets the requirement of eight electrons around each atom. This leads to step 5.

5. When there are not enough electrons, make double or triple bonds. When there are extra electrons, place these on the central atom.

To have eight electrons on each atom, we move an additional pair of electrons between C and an O to create a double bond.

$$\left[\begin{array}{c} :\ddot{O}:C::\ddot{O}: \\ :\ddot{O}: \end{array}\right]^{2-} \quad \text{or} \quad \left[\begin{array}{c} :\ddot{O}-C=\ddot{O} \\ \ \ | \\ :\ddot{O}: \end{array}\right]^{2-}$$

Thus, the unit contains 24 electrons arranged so that each atom has 8 electrons.

PROBLEM

1. Draw Lewis structures for each of the following.
   a. H_2S
   b. NH_4^+
   c. NO_3^-
   d. CO
   e. CCl_4
   f. HCOOH (one H bonds to C, one to O)

OUTER LEVEL ELECTRON PAIR REPULSION

One theory of molecular geometry holds that the outer level electron pair charge clouds repel each other. Thus, *the electron pairs, shared or unshared, stay as far apart as possible to minimize repulsion.*

This theory explains why CO_2 is linear, H_2O is bent, or angular, and CH_4 is tetrahedral. See **Table 9-1**.

TABLE 9-1

Molecular Geometry			
Number of Electron Clouds	Electron Geometry	Hybridization at Central Atom (A) and Examples	Shape
2	:—A—: linear	sp (180°) $BeCl_2$ CO_2	
3	trigonal planar	sp^2 (120°) BF_3 BCl_3	
4	tetrahedral	sp^3 (109°28′) CH_4 CCl_4	
5	trigonal bipyramidal	sp^3d or dsp^3 (90°, 120°, 180°) PF_5 $AsCl_5$	
6	octahedral	sp^3d^2 or d^2sp^3 (90°, 180°) SF_6 SeF_6	

EXAMPLE

Predict the molecular structure of water, H_2O.

Solving Process:
Examine the electron dot structure for water.

$$H:\overset{..}{\underset{..}{O}}:$$
$$H$$

There are four electron pairs on oxygen. When these electron pairs are as far apart as possible, their clouds will point to the corners of the tetrahedron. In a regular tetrahedron the bond angles are 109.5° as they are in CH_4 and CCl_4, each of which contains four shared electron pairs. The H-O-H bond angle in water is 104.5°. This angle is caused by the two unshared pairs of electrons that spread their charge clouds over a larger volume. The repulsion between unshared pairs is greater than that between shared pairs. Thus, the two hydrogen atoms form an angular molecule with oxygen, as their electron clouds are bent away from the two unshared electron pairs.

MULTIPLE BOND MOLECULAR SHAPES

Carbon atoms can form four chemical bonds. These can be single bonds in a tetrahedral arrangement having bond angles of 109.5°. The four bonds can also form one double bond and two single bonds having a trigonal planar geometry with a bond angle near 120°. Two double bonds are arranged in a linear molecule with a bond angle of 180°. Carbon can also form one single bond and one triple bond. This bond geometry will be 180°.

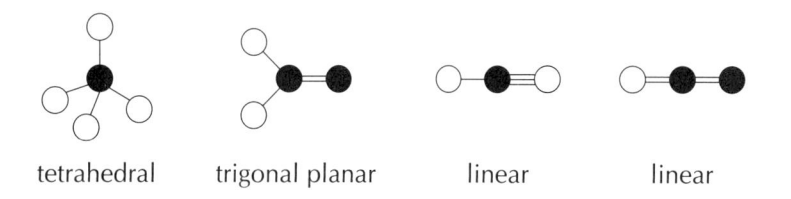

tetrahedral   trigonal planar   linear   linear

CHROMATOGRAPHY

When it is necessary to separate several materials from a mixture, the process used is called **fractionation.** Polarity differences between molecules can be used to effect this separation. When polarities are used the process is called **chromatography** (writing in color). Often the fractions are different colors.

In chromatography there are two phases. The **mobile phase** consists of the mixture to be separated. It is dissolved in a liquid or gas. The **stationary phase** consists of either a solid or a liquid adhering to the surface of a solid. For example, when using paper chromatography to separate black ink, a mixture, the paper is the stationary phase. The polar solvent moves up the paper by capillary action. The solvent and the ink are the mobile phase.

The different substances in a mixture will travel at different rates because of their varying polarity. A polar substance will be attracted by the polar solvent. The stationary phase will also attract some of the substances more strongly than others. The slowest moving substance will have the strongest attraction for the stationary phase. The fastest moving substance will have the greatest attraction for the polar solvent and the least attraction for the stationary phase. As a result, the components of the mixture are separated.

The chemist uses many different types of chromatography to separate and identify components of a mixture. **Paper chromatography** is carried out on paper in which one end is placed in a solvent. A drop of a solution containing the substances to be separated is placed at one end of the strip of paper. As the solvent moves up the paper strip by capillary action, the mixture is separated.

In **column chromatography** a glass or plastic tube, called the column, is filled with a solid material called the packing. The packing is the stationary phase. The packing can be magnesium carbonate, sodium carbonate, activated charcoal, an ion exchange resin, clays, or gels. The material to be separated is placed on the top of the packing in the column. A solvent, the mobile phase, is poured into the top of the column. Fresh solvent is continuously poured onto the top of the packing and allowed to percolate through the column. Each substance in the mixture moves down the column at a rate that depends on its relative attractions for the packing and for the solvent. The liquid can be collected as it leaves the column. The solvent is then evaporated, and each pure, separated substance is collected.

Thin layer chromatography is similar to paper chromatography. A glass or plastic plate is coated with a very thin layer of stationary phase, usually a white powder. A solvent moves up the plate by capillary action to separate the substances in the spot of unknown.

Gas chromatography is used to separate and identify volatile liquids and mixtures of gases or vapors. This method involves a column and a packing similar to that used in column chromatography. An inert gas such as helium is used to flush the mixture through the tubing. An electronic sensor at the end of the column detects varying amounts of electric current conducted through the contaminated gas. The contaminants are the various components of the mixture undergoing analysis. These variations are recorded and analyzed by a computer.

POLARITY

As you have seen, most chemical bonds are neither 100% ionic nor 100% covalent. Atoms have different electron-attracting abilities, as measured electronegativities. This difference results in unequal sharing of the bonding electrons, producing polar covalent bonds and often polar molecules. Remember, a polar covalent bond is one in which there is an uneven charge distribution. In the molecule HCl, for example, chlorine has a partial negative charge (δ^-) and hydrogen a partial positive charge (δ^+).

$$\overset{\delta^+}{H}\!-\!\overset{\delta^-}{Cl} \quad \text{or} \quad H \rightarrow Cl$$

The electronegativity difference is $3.0 - 2.1 = 0.9$. The result is a polar covalent bond, or dipole, and also a polar molecule. An arrow is used to represent a polar bond. The arrow points to the element with higher electronegativity.

Not all molecules having polar covalent bonds are polar. Molecular geometry must be considered. If the polar covalent bonds are arranged symmetrically, the polar effects cancel, as in CO_2, BCl_3, and CCl_4.

Unsymmetrical arrangements occur in H_2O and NH_3, producing polar molecules.

Many physical properties of molecules, such as melting and boiling points and solubility are affected by the degree of polarity of molecules.

EXAMPLE

Determine the polarity of HCN and $SOCl_2$.

Solving Process:
Determine the molecular geometry by drawing Lewis structures and using the electron pair repulsion theory.

$$H:C:::N:$$
linear

$$:\ddot{O}:\ddot{S}:\ddot{Cl}:$$
$$:\ddot{Cl}:$$
trigonal pyramid

Use electronegativities to determine bond polarity H = 2.1, C = 2.5, N = 3.0, S = 2.5, Cl = 3.0, O = 3.5. Electronegativity differences give these bond polarities:

$$H \rightarrow C \rightarrow N \qquad O \rightarrow S \rightarrow Cl$$
$$\downarrow$$
$$Cl$$

Since both arrangements are unsymmetrical, polar molecules result.

PROBLEMS

2. Which of the following bonds is most polar? In each bond, indicate the atom that carries the partial negative charge.
   a. H—I   b. P—I   c. As—Br   d. N—S

3. Which of the following molecules are polar?
   a. CO   b. $AsCl_3$ c. H_2Se d. SO_3

SECTION REVIEW

1. How many electrons should be shown in Lewis structures of each of the following?
   a. HNO_3 b. CN^- c. O_2F_2 d. CS_2 e. $POBr_3$ f. $C_2O_4^{2-}$

2. Draw Lewis structures for each of the following.
   a. PH_3
   b. CS_2
   c. OH^-
   d. NO^+
   e. CO_3^{2-}
   f. HCN
   g. NH_3
   h. $SOCl_2$ (S is central atom)
   i. PCl_5

3. Why is the N—H bond angle in NH_3 less than a tetrahedral angle of 109.5°?

4. Predict the shape of the following using the electron pair repulsion model.
   a. BCl_3 b. MgI_2 c. H_2S d. Br_4 e. SiF_4 f. SCl_6

Chemistry: Concepts and Applications

5. Carbon atoms form how many single chemical bonds?

6. In carbon dioxide gas, the carbon atom forms two double bonds. What will the geometry of the bonds be?

7. In acetylene (ethyne) gas, used in welding, the carbon atom forms a triple bond. What geometry would you predict for this molecule?

8. Ethylene (ethene) gas is used to ripen fruit that is picked green. Each carbon atom in the gas has a double bond and two single bonds. Predict its bond geometry.

9. What do chemists call the process of separating a mixture into its parts?

10. What is a more formal name for "writing in color"?

11. What name is used to describe the phase that adsorbs the dissolved components in chromatography?

12. Why are polar solvents preferred for chromatography?

13. Which type of the chromatographies uses an electric current to aid in identifying the components of the mixture?

14. Use **Table B-8** to arrange the following bonds in order of increasing polarity: H—O, H—H, H—Cl, H—S, H—Br, H—Ga. Indicate the atom in each bond that carries the partial negative charge.

15. Which of the following molecules are polar?
    a. CO
    b. $SiCl_4$
    c. $COCl_2$ (C is central atom)
    d. $HCBr_3$ (C is central atom)

16. How does a polar covalent bond differ from a nonpolar covalent bond?

17. What type of molecules have polar bonds arranged in an asymmetrical pattern?

18. If two covalently bonded atoms have a large difference in electronegativities, will the bond be polar or nonpolar?

The Kinetic Theory of Matter

10.1 PHYSICAL BEHAVIOR OF MATTER

STATES OF MATTER

The **kinetic theory** is used to describe the motion of the particles of matter. Matter exists in four states—solid, liquid, gas, and plasma. The behavior of each state of matter can be explained by applying the kinetic theory.

Gas particles are independent of each other and are in constant, rapid, random motion. The particles move in straight lines between collisions, which are perfectly elastic. An elastic collision is one in which no energy is gained or lost. Gas particles have little or no attractive force between particles because they are usually at least ten diameters apart. Gases do not have a definite volume, but occupy the total volume of the container. As a consequence, gases take the shape of their container.

Liquids have a definite volume and take the shape of their container. Liquids have a definite volume because the particles are close together and have attractive forces between them. Still, the particles are free enough to slip past one another. Thus, a liquid flows and takes the shape of its container.

Solids have a definite volume and a definite shape. These properties result from the fact that the particles occupy a relatively fixed position in relation to surrounding particles.

When matter is heated to temperatures greater than 5000°C the collisions between particles are so violent that electrons are knocked away from atoms. This action produces a state of matter composed of electrons and positive ions which is called a **plasma.** Since a plasma consists of charged particles traveling at high speeds, it is affected by electric and magnetic fields. The study of plasma is called **magnetohydrodynamics.**

SECTION REVIEW

1. List the four states of matter.

10.2 KINETIC ENERGY AND CHANGES OF STATE

TEMPERATURE

Kinetic energy is the energy of motion. A measure of that kinetic energy is **temperature.** The average kinetic energy of molecules or atoms in a gas is the same for all samples at a particular temperature. The temperature and mass of gas particles determines their average speed. At a given temperature, a particle with large mass will move more slowly than a particle with small mass.

Particle speed is directly related to changes in temperature. Since molecular motion of a gas decreases as the temperature decreases, it should be possible theoretically to lower the temperature to a point where all molecular motion ceases. This temperature, known as **absolute zero,** is −273.15°C.

Scientists have made a temperature scale based on absolute zero. It is known as the absolute, or **kelvin scale.** The kelvin (K) is the SI unit of temperature. The zero point of the kelvin scale is absolute zero. The divisions, or degrees, are the same size as those of the Celsius scale. Thus,

$$K = °C + 273$$

PROBLEMS

1. Convert the following temperatures from Celsius to kelvin.
   a. 29°   **b.** −56°   **c.** 344°   **d.** −38°   **e.** 100°   **f.** 25°

2. Convert the following temperatures from kelvin to Celsius.
   a. 168   **b.** 255   **c.** 546   **d.** 300   **e.** 53   **f.** 273

KELVIN TEMPERATURE

All gases (in contrast to solids and liquids) expand and contract at approximately the same rate. When a gas is heated, it expands by 1/273 of its volume at 0° Celsius for each temperature increase of one Celsius degree. When a gas is cooled, it contracts 1/273 of its volume at 0° Celsius for each Celsius degree the temperature is lowered.

No gas has ever been cooled to −273°C. All gases liquefy or solidify at temperatures higher than −273°C. Remember, the temperature −273°C is called absolute zero. It is written zero kelvin or 0 K. Scientists have chosen 273 K (0°C) as a standard temperature for working with gases.

ENERGY AND CHANGE OF STATE

When a substance is heated, the energy of its particles is increased. If the kinetic energy is increased, the result is an increase in the temperature of the substance. If the increase is in potential energy, the physical state of the substance will change. The change, or combination of changes, that will take place depends upon the starting temperature of the substance. Similar considerations can be applied to removing energy from (cooling) a substance.

The changes of state from solid to liquid and liquid to solid take place at the same temperature, which is labeled the **melting point** or **freezing point.** The changes from liquid to gas and gas to liquid take place at the same temperature, which is labeled the **boiling point** or **condensing point.** The amount of energy

TABLE 10-1
Heats of Fusion and Vaporization for Some Substances (in J/kg)

Fusion (H_{fus})		Vaporization (H_{vap})	
aluminum	3.97×10^5	aluminum	1.08×10^7
arsenic	3.70×10^5	benzene	3.95×10^5
gold	6.30×10^4	gold	1.65×10^6
indium	2.83×10^4	helium	2.10×10^4
iron	2.47×10^5	iron	6.27×10^6
steel	2.47×10^5	selenium	3.33×10^5
titanium	2.95×10^5	sodium	4.24×10^6
water	3.34×10^5	water	2.26×10^6

required for a state change depends on the nature and amount of a substance. If we use q to represent the quantity of energy needed to melt a substance, then

$$q = m(H_{fus})$$

where m is the mass of the substance and H_{fus} is a property of a substance called **heat of fusion.** Similarly, to boil a substance, the relationship is

$$q = m(H_{vap})$$

where H_{vap} is a property of a substance called its **heat of vaporization.** **Table 10-1** lists the heat of fusion and vaporization for several substances.

EXAMPLE

How much energy is required to melt 8.63 kg of iron at its melting point?

Solving Process:
The energy required for this phase change depends upon the mass, 8.63 kg, and heat of fusion, 2.47×10^5 J/kg. Thus, the solution is

$$q = \text{mass} \times \text{heat of fusion}$$
$$= 8.63 \text{ kg Fe} \times 2.47 \times 10^5 \text{ J/kg}$$
$$= 2.13 \times 10^6 \text{ J}$$

PROBLEM

3. Compute the energy changes associated with the following transitions.
   a. melting 5.58 kg Ti at 1677°C
   b. condensing 1.42 kg H_2O at 100.0°C
   c. boiling 5.35 kg C_6H_6, benzene, at 80.1°C
   d. freezing 2.73 kg Al at 660°C
   e. melting 7.64 kg Au at 1064°C

SECTION REVIEW

1. Theoretically, all molecular motion ceases at what temperature?

2. At the same temperature, which molecule will move faster, the lighter or heavier one?

3. How does the amount of energy required to change the temperature 1 C° compare to that of one kelvin degree?

4. Convert the following temperatures from one temperature scale to another as indicated.
   a. 516 K to °C
   b. 155°C to K
   c. 26°C to K
   d. 14 K to °C
   e. 421°C to K
   f. 373 K to °C

5. In a closed, insulated system, ice is floating in water. The temperature is 0°C. Will all of the water freeze?

6. Water is boiling at 100°C. The hot plate's surface temperature is increased. Will the water now boil at a higher temperature?

Use **Table 10-1** to answer the following questions.

7. What is the energy change associated with melting 9.14 kg of indium at 156.6°C?

8. How much energy is required to boil 4.66 kg of selenium at 685°C?

9. How much energy is required to condense 1.75 kg of sodium at 883°C?

10. What is the energy change associated with freezing 1.15 kg of iron at 1538°C?

Behavior of Gases

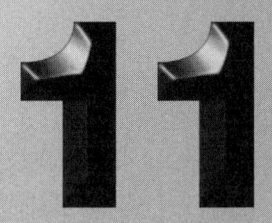

11.1 GAS PRESSURE

GAS PRESSURE

Recall, the effect on matter of temperature and pressure is described by the kinetic theory. The kinetic theory assumes that all matter is made up of very small particles that are in constant motion and undergo perfectly elastic collisions.

Gas molecules collide with each other billions of times per second. Gas molecules also strike the walls of their container. It is the number of collisions and the force of the collisions that cause gas pressure. **Pressure** is force per unit area. The scientific standard for pressure is defined in pascals. One pascal (Pa) is the pressure of 1 newton per square meter (N/m^2). Normal air pressure at sea level is 101 325 Pa or 101.325 kilopascals (kPa).

An instrument called a **manometer** (mah NAHM uh tuhr) is used to measure pressure. There are two types of manometers. In the "open" type, air exerts pressure on the column of liquid on one arm of a U-tube. The gas being studied exerts pressure on the other arm. The difference in liquid level between the two arms is a measure of the gas pressure relative to the air pressure. The "closed" type has a vacuum above the liquid in one arm.

A **barometer** is a closed-arm manometer used to measure atmospheric pressure. Most barometers are calibrated to read millimeters of mercury (mm Hg). For converting units,

$$101.325 \text{ kPa} = 760 \text{ mm or } 1 \text{ kPa} = 7.50 \text{ mm Hg}$$

FIGURE 11-1

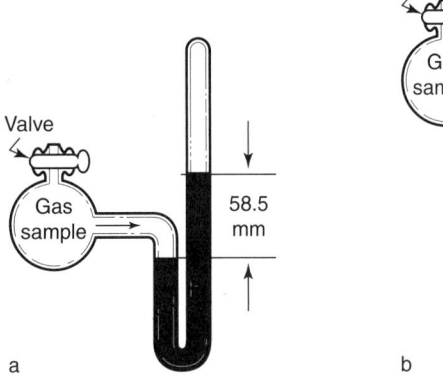

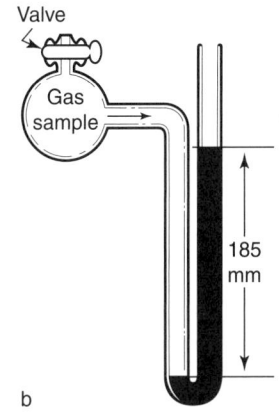

Chemistry: Concepts and Applications

EXAMPLE

In **Figure 11-1b,** the closed arm of the manometer is filled with oxygen. Compute the pressure of the oxygen in kilopascals. The difference in mercury levels is 185 mm and the atmospheric pressure is 98.95 kPa.

Solving Process:
The mercury is higher in the arm open to the atmosphere. Thus, the pressure exerted by the O_2 must be greater than that of the air. As a result, we must add the pressure of the mercury to the air pressure to get the O_2 pressure. Before adding, however, we must convert the 185 mm difference in height to kilopascals.

$$\text{number of kPa} = \frac{185 \text{ mm}}{} \cdot \frac{1 \text{ kPa}}{7.50 \text{ mm}} = 24.7 \text{ kPa}$$

Now we can add the two pressures.

$$\text{pressure of } O_2 = 98.95 + 24.7 = 124 \text{ kPa}$$

EXAMPLE

Suppose the difference in height of the two mercury levels in the closed manometer in **Figure 11-1a** is 58.5 mm. What is the pressure in kilopascals of the gas in the container?

Solving Process:
Since the column of mercury is 185 mm high and 7.50 mm of mercury equals 1 kPa, the pressure is

$$\text{pressure of gas} = \frac{58.5 \text{ mm}}{} \cdot \frac{1 \text{ kPa}}{7.50 \text{ mm}} = 7.80 \text{ kPa}$$

PROBLEMS

1. A closed manometer is filled with mercury and connected to a container of sulfur dioxide gas. The difference in the height of mercury in the two arms is 560 mm. What is the pressure of the SO_2 in kilopascals?

2. An open manometer is filled with mercury and connected to a container of hydrogen. The mercury level is 78.0 mm higher in the arm of the tube connected to the air. Air pressure is 100.7 kPa. What is the pressure of the hydrogen in kilopascals?

3. An open manometer is filled with mercury and connected to a container of nitrogen. The level of mercury is 26.0 mm higher in the arm of the tube connected to the container of nitrogen. Air pressure is 99.6 kPa. What is the pressure, in kilopascals, of the nitrogen?

4. A closed manometer is filled with mercury and connected to a container of argon gas. The difference in height of mercury in the two arms is 116.0 mm. What is the pressure, in kilopascals, of the argon?

SECTION REVIEW

1. What is an instrument called that is used to measure gas pressure?

2. Which theory explains the effect of temperature and pressure on matter?

3. What name is used to describe a closed manometer that directly measures the absolute pressure of the atmosphere?

4. What is the standard pressure in kPa of air at sea level under normal conditions?

5. What is caused by the force and number of collisions that gas molecules have with the container's walls?

6. An open manometer is filled with mercury and connected to a container of neon gas. The mercury level is 42.8 mm higher in the open arm. The barometric pressure is exactly 101.325 kPa. What is the pressure, in kilopascals, of the neon?

7. An open manometer is filled with mercury. The difference in the mercury level in the arms is 81.2 mm. The mercury level is higher in the gas sample arm. What is the pressure, in kilopascals, of the gas in the container if the air pressure is 95.6 kilopascals?

8. In a closed manometer assume that the height of the levels differs by 362 mm Hg. What is the pressure in kPa of the gas in the container?

11.2 THE GAS LAWS

Air in a tire exerts pressure. A partially filled balloon will expand if it is placed over a hot radiator. In marked contrast to solids and liquids, gas volumes change noticeably with small changes in pressure and temperature. These changes were studied by experimenting with real gases and the relations obtained were reduced to equations that defined the behavior of gases. These equations, known as the gas laws, are valid only for an ideal gas. An **ideal gas** is one composed of particles with no attractive forces and no volume. Although ideal gases do not actually exist, they give good approximations in most situations for real gases.

BOYLE'S LAW

If the pressure on an ideal gas in a confined container is increased, the volume decreases. When the pressure is doubled, the new gas volume is half the original gas volume. If the pressure is decreased to half the original pressure, the new volume is double the old volume. Robert Boyle found that gas volume and pressure vary inversely. **Boyle's law** *states that the pressure and volume of a gas at constant temperature are inversely proportional.*

When finding a new volume, we need to know the original volume and the change in pressure. The change in pressure can be represented by a pressure ratio.

The new volume of a gas after a change in pressure at a constant temperature is calculated by

$$V_2 = V_1 \times \frac{P_1}{P_2}$$

where V_1 is the initial volume and P_1 is the initial pressure. The given values can be substituted into the equation or the changes in the gas volume can be visualized using Boyle's law.

Mentally determine whether the new volume will be larger or smaller than the old volume and arrange the pressure ratio accordingly. If the new volume will be larger, multiply by a ratio that is greater than 1; if smaller, multiply by a ratio less than 1. The following points should be considered when solving Boyle's law problems.

1. A pressure increase decreases the volume, which means the pressure ratio should be less than 1.

2. A pressure decrease increases the volume, which means the pressure ratio should be greater than 1.

3. To calculate a new pressure when the old pressure and the volume change are known, use the relationship:

   new pressure = old pressure × volume ratio

   $$P_2 = P_1 \times \frac{V_1}{V_2}$$

4. The volume and pressure vary inversely.

EXAMPLE

If 425 mL of oxygen are collected at a pressure of 9.80 kPa what volume will the gas occupy if the pressure is changed to 9.40 kPa?

Solving Process:
The pressure decreases from 9.80 to 9.40 kPa. The volume should increase according to Boyle's law. To have a volume increase, the pressure ratio must be greater than 1. The pressure ratio is

$$\frac{9.80 \text{ kPa}}{9.40 \text{ kPa}}$$

In calculations, use the relationship:

new volume = old volume × pressure ratio

$$= \frac{425 \text{ mL} \mid 9.80 \text{ kPa}}{\mid 9.40 \text{ kPa}} = 443 \text{ mL}$$

EXAMPLE

Calculate the pressure of a gas that occupies a volume of 125 mL, if at a pressure of 95.0 kPa, it occupies a volume of 219 mL.

Solving Process:
The volume decreases from 219 mL to 125 mL. The pressure must increase, so the volume ratio must be greater than 1, or

$$\frac{219 \text{ mL}}{125 \text{ mL}}$$

new pressure = old pressure × volume ratio

$$= \frac{95.0 \text{ kPa}}{1} \cdot \frac{219 \text{ mL}}{125 \text{ mL}} = 166 \text{ kPa}$$

PROBLEMS

1. Correct the following gas volumes from the initial conditions to the new conditions (assume the temperature remains constant).
   a. 100.0 mL oxygen at 10.50 kPa to 9.91 kPa
   b. 50.0 mL hydrogen at 97.3 kPa to 101.000 Pa
   c. 500.0 mL sulfur dioxide at 95.6 kPa to 101.3 kPa
   d. 150.0 mL nitrogen at 101.30 kPa to 120.0 kPa
   e. 2000 L nitrogen at 158.0 kPa to 109.0 kPa
   f. 1.50 L neon at 98.2 kPa to 150 kPa

2. A flask containing 90.0 mL of hydrogen was collected under a pressure of 97.5 kilopascals. At what pressure would the volume be 70.0 mL, assuming the temperature is kept constant?

3. A gas has a volume of 275 mL when measured at a pressure of 9.80×10^4 Pa. If the temperature is not changed, what would the gas volume be at standard pressure?

4. A gas has a volume of 5.0×10^4 L at standard pressure. Assuming no temperature change, what volume will the gas occupy
   a. if the pressure is doubled?
   b. if the pressure is tripled?
   c. if the original pressure is cut in half?

5. What is the volume occupied by 10.0 L of gas at standard pressure after it has been compressed at constant temperature to 500.0 kPa?

6. A gas is confined in a cylinder with a movable piston at one end. When the volume of the cylinder is 760.0 mL the pressure of the gas is 125.0 kPa. When the cylinder volume is reduced to 450.0 mL, what is the pressure?

Chemistry: Concepts and Applications Supplemental Practice Problems, Chapter 11

CHARLES'S LAW

If the temperature of an ideal gas increases, the volume increases, when the pressure remains constant. If the temperature of a gas decreases, the volume decreases. **Charles's law** can be stated as *at constant pressure, the volume of a gas is directly proportional to its Kelvin temperature.* Note that temperature must be expressed in kelvin.

It is possible to predict the new volume of a gas when the old volume and the temperature change are known. The temperature change is expressed as an absolute temperature ratio. The equation used to calculate the new volume is

new volume = old volume × kelvin temperature ratio

$$V_2 = V_1 \times \frac{T_2}{T_1}$$

The subscripts represent the initial and final conditions, as in the Boyle's law relationship. The following points should be considered when solving Charles's law problems.

1. An absolute temperature increase gives a volume increase, which means an absolute temperature ratio greater than 1.

2. An absolute temperature decrease gives a volume decrease, which means an absolute temperature ratio less than 1.

3. The new temperature in kelvins can be calculated when the initial kelvin temperature and new and old volumes are known:

new temperature (K) = old temperature (K) × volume ratio

$$T_2 = T_1 \times \frac{V_2}{V_1}$$

4. The kelvin temperature varies directly as the volume.

EXAMPLE

What volume will a sample of nitrogen occupy at 28.0°C if the gas occupies a volume of 457 mL at a temperature of 0.0°C? Assume the pressure remains constant.

Solving Process:
Convert the temperatures from Celsius to kelvin.

$$K = 273 + °C$$

$$K = 273 + 28.0°C = 301 \text{ K} \quad \text{and} \quad K = 273 + 0.0°C = 273 \text{ K}$$

A kelvin temperature increase (from 273 K to 301 K) will cause a volume increase. The kelvin temperature ratio must be greater than 1.

$$\frac{301 \text{ K}}{273 \text{ K}}$$

new volume = old volume × kelvin temperature ratio

$$= \frac{457 \text{ mL} \mid 301 \text{ K}}{\mid 273 \text{ K}} = 504 \text{ mL}$$

EXAMPLE

If a gas occupies a volume of 733 mL at 10.0°C, at what temperature, in °C, will it occupy a volume of 1225 mL if the pressure remains constant?

Solving Process:
An increase in volume (from 733 mL to 1225 mL) indicates a temperature increase. The volume ratio must be greater than 1.

$$\frac{1225 \text{ mL}}{733 \text{ mL}}$$

$$T_2 = T_1 \times \frac{V_2}{V_1}$$

$$= \frac{283 \text{ K} \mid 1225 \text{ mL}}{\mid 733 \text{ mL}} = 473 \text{ K}$$

Convert 473 K to °C.

$$°C = 473 \text{ K} - 273 = 200°C$$

PROBLEMS

7. A gas has a volume of 1.00×10^4 L at standard temperature. Assuming no pressure change, what volume will the gas occupy
   a. if the kelvin temperature is doubled?
   b. if the original kelvin temperature is halved?

8. Correct the following gas volumes from the initial conditions to the new conditions (assume that the pressure remains constant).
   a. 250.0 mL chlorine at 10.0°C to 60.0°C
   b. 75.0 mL hydrogen at 20.0°C to −10.0°C
   c. 100.0 mL oxygen at 27.0°C to standard temperature
   d. 300.0 mL nitrogen at 15.0°C to 38.0°C
   e. 2.30 L nitrogen dioxide at standard temperature to 40.0°C
   f. 35.0 mL helium at 285 K to 92 K

9. A gas occupies a volume of 560 mL at a temperature of 120°C. To what temperature must the gas be lowered, if it is to occupy 400.0 mL? Assume a constant pressure.

COMBINED GAS LAW

Boyle's and Charles's laws can be used together to form a combined gas law. This law can be used in a situation where both a pressure and a temperature change occur. A pressure ratio and a kelvin temperature ratio are needed to calculate the new volume.

new volume = old volume × pressure ratio × kelvin temperature ratio

$$V_2 = V_1\left(\frac{P_1}{P_2}\right)\left(\frac{T_2}{T_1}\right)$$

Each ratio is considered independently in setting up the expression. You will want to construct a pressure-volume-temperature data table.

Value	Old Conditions	New Conditions	What happens to the gas volume?
Pressure			
Volume			
Temperature			

"What happens to the gas volume?" is answered with the word "decrease" or "increase," depending upon whether the pressure or temperature ratio is larger or smaller than 1.

The initials STP are often used in gas law problems. **STP** means standard temperature and pressure. The **standard pressure** for measuring gases is 101 325 Pa (101.325 kPa). For convenience in solving problems 101.3 kPa is used. **Standard temperature** is 0°C or 273 K. All temperature ratios must be expressed in kelvin.

EXAMPLE

Calculate the volume of a gas at STP if 502 mL of the gas are collected at 29.7°C and 96.0 kPa.

Solving Process:
Organize the data given as shown and convert the Celsius temperatures to kelvins.

Value	Old Conditions	New Conditions	What happens to the gas volume?
P	96.0 kPa	101.3 kPa	decreases
V	502 mL	?	?
T	302.7 K	273.2 K	decreases

new volume = old volume × pressure ratio × kelvin temperature ratio

$$= \frac{502.0 \text{ mL} \times 96.0 \text{ kPa} \times 273.2 \text{ K}}{101.3 \text{ kPa} \times 302.7 \text{ K}} = 429 \text{ mL}$$

EXAMPLE

If 400.0 mL of oxygen are collected over water at 20.0°C, and the atmospheric pressure is 97.0 kPa, what is the volume of the dry oxygen at STP?

Solving Process:
Organize the data. Convert C° to K and correct the total pressure for water vapor pressure.

Note that the gas is not actually wet when it is collected over water. When a gas is collected over water, some of the water molecules inevitably escape from the liquid surface and form water vapor. The collected gas, therefore, contains both gas and water molecules. To find the pressure due to gas molecules, you must account for and deduct the pressure due to water vapor molecules. You can find the pressure due to water vapor molecules in **Table B-9** in Appendix B.

Value	Old Conditions	New Conditions	What happens to the gas volume?
P	97.0 − 2.3 = 94.7 kPa	101.3 kPa	decreases
V	400.0 mL	?	?
T	293 K	273 K	decreases

new volume = old volume × pressure ratio × kelvin temperature ratio

$$= \frac{400.0 \text{ mL} \times 94.7 \text{ kPa} \times 273 \text{ K}}{101.3 \text{ kPa} \times 293 \text{ K}} = 348 \text{ mL}$$

PROBLEMS

10. Convert the following gas volumes to the new conditions using the combined gas law.
    a. 5.00×10^2 mL hydrogen at 20.0°C and 120 kPa to STP
    b. 2.50×10^2 mL oxygen at 27°C and 95.0 kPa to STP
    c. 1.00×10^2 mL chlorine at STP to 20.0°C and 98.0 kPa
    d. 140 mL hydrogen at 15°C and 110.0 kPa to 40.0°C and 94.5 kPa

11. The following gases are collected over water at the given conditions. Calculate the volume occupied by the dry gas at standard conditions.
    a. 2.00×10^2 mL oxygen at 15°C and 94 000 Pa
    b. 125 mL hydrogen at 20.0°C and 97 500 Pa
    c. 50.0 mL nitrogen at 28°C and 99 500 Pa
    d. 325 mL oxygen at 25°C and 98.6 kPa

12. A gas occupied 550.0 mL at a pressure of 9.95×10^4 Pa and a temperature of 21°C. Several days later it was measured at a pressure of 9.78×10^4 Pa and temperature of 15°C. What volume did the gas occupy under these new conditions?

13. A 47.0-mL volume of nitrogen gas is collected over water at a water temperature of 18°C and a pressure of 98.5 kPa. What volume will the gas occupy at standard conditions?

14. An automobile tire has a pressure of 210.0 kPa at 20.0°C. What will be the tire pressure after driving, if the tire temperature rises to 35.0°C?

Chemistry: Concepts and Applications

15. The respiratory rate for a person is about 15 breaths per minute. Assume that each average breath is about 510 mL of air at 20.0°C and 99.5 kPa. What volume of air in liters, corrected to standard conditions, does the individual breathe in one day?

GAS DENSITY

The volume of a gas changes with change in temperature or pressure. Specifically, if we increase the pressure on a gas we decrease the volume; thus, we would have a greater density. If we increase the temperature of a gas, the volume increases, and the density is lower. The density of a gas varies directly with the pressure and inversely with the temperature.

For convenience, gas density is usually expressed in grams per liter. Using g/mL would give very small numbers for gas densities. Remember that 1000 mL equal 1 L.

EXAMPLE

If the density of oxygen is 1.43 g/L at standard pressure and temperature, what is the density of oxygen at 99.0 kPa and 27.0°C?

Solving Process:
The original density must be adjusted by a pressure ratio and a kelvin temperature ratio to the new conditions.

Value	Old Conditions	New Conditions	What happens to the gas volume?
P	101.3 kPa	99.0 kPa	decreases
T	273 K	300.0 K	decreases
D	1.43 g/L	?	?

The pressure decreases and the temperature increases. A temperature increase gives a density decrease. The pressure and temperature ratios are

$$\frac{99.0 \text{ kPa}}{101.3 \text{ kPa}} \qquad \frac{273 \text{ K}}{300.0 \text{ K}}$$

new density = old density × pressure ratio × temperature ratio

$$= \frac{1.43 \text{ g}}{L} \times \frac{99.0 \text{ kPa}}{101.3 \text{ kPa}} \times \frac{273 \text{ K}}{300.0 \text{ K}} = 1.27 \text{ g/L}$$

PROBLEMS

16. Sulfur dioxide has a density of 2.927 g/L at STP. What is its density at a pressure of 120.0 kPa and a temperature of 50.0°C?

17. A gas has a density of 3.472 g/L at STP. Determine its density at a pressure of 95.0 kPa and a temperature of 27.0°C.

18. A gas has a density of 2.851 g/L at STP. The pressure is dropped by 20.0 kPa in order to attempt to change the density to 2.000 g/L. What must be the new temperature to achieve this lower density?

SECTION REVIEW

1. If the pressure on 100 mL of a gas is doubled, what volume will the gas occupy, assuming no other changes?

2. The volume of a gas at a pressure of 90.0 kPa is doubled and the temperature remains constant. What is the final pressure exerted by the gas?

3. If the temperature of a gas is 0°C and the temperature is changed so that the gas volume doubles, what is the new temperature of the gas?

4. Correct the following gas volumes from the initial conditions to the new conditions. Assume that the pressure or temperature is constant, if not given.
   a. 45.0 mL at 49°C to −29°C
   b. 270.0 mL at standard temperature to 25°C
   c. 75.0 mL at standard pressure to 90.8 kPa
   d. 165 mL at 75 000 Pa to 84 000 Pa
   e. 95.0 mL at STP to 24°C and 91.5 kPa
   f. 1.50 L at STP to −15°C and 110.0 kPa
   g. 325 mL at 30.0°C and 95.0 kPa to STP
   h. 240 mL at 5°C and 92.0 kPa to 40.0°C and 105.0 kPa

5. An unbreakable meteorological balloon is released from the ground. Ground level pressure is 98.5 kPa and the temperature is 18°C. The balloon contains 74.0 L of hydrogen gas. As the balloon ascends, the pressure drops to 7.0 kPa.
   a. What is the new volume of the balloon, assuming no temperature change?
   b. If a temperature drop of 79° occurs, what is the new volume of the balloon after the temperature change?
   c. Of the two factors, pressure and temperature, which had the greatest effect in changing the volume of the balloon?

6. A balloon will burst at a volume of 2.0 L. If the gas in a partially filled balloon occupies 0.75 L at a temperature of 21°C and a pressure of 9.90×10^4 Pa, what is the temperature at which it will burst if the pressure is 1.01×10^5 Pa at the time it breaks?

7. Oxygen has a density of 1.429 g/L at STP. Which change will result in a greater change in density? What is the new density?
   a. decreasing the temperature from 0.0°C to −40.0°C
   b. increasing the pressure from 100.0 kPa to 114.5 kPa

8. What is the density of a gas at STP if its density is 1.75 g/L at 110.0 kPa and 45°C?

9. At STP, the density of a gas is 3.24 mg/mL. What is its density in g/L at 30.0°C and 95.0 kPa?

Chemical Quantities

12.1 COUNTING PARTICLES OF MATTER

MOLECULAR MASS

Molecular mass of a covalent compound is the mass in atomic mass units of one molecule. Generally atomic masses will be rounded to tenths. For those elements with masses less than ten, masses will be rounded to hundredths unless more significant digits are suggested by the data of the problem.

EXAMPLE

Find the molecular mass of vitamin A, one of the fat-soluble vitamins. Its molecular formula is $C_{20}H_{30}O$.

Solving Process:

$$
\begin{array}{lrl}
\text{carbon} & 20 \times 12.0 \text{ u} = & 240 \text{ u} \\
\text{hydrogen} & 30 \times 1.01 \text{ u} = & 30.3 \text{ u} \\
\text{oxygen} & 1 \times 16.0 \text{ u} = & \underline{16.0 \text{ u}} \\
& \text{Molecular mass} = & 286 \text{ u}
\end{array}
$$

FORMULA MASS

Ionic compounds do not exist in the form of molecules. The **formula mass** of an ionic compound is the mass in atomic mass units of one formula unit. Both the molecular and formula masses are calculated in the same manner. It is possible to calculate masses without first determining whether the substance is ionic or molecular.

Formula mass is a more general term than molecular mass. Formula mass may be used in referring to all compounds. Molecular mass should be used only to refer to molecular compounds.

EXAMPLE

Determine the formula mass of calcium phosphate, $Ca_3(PO_4)_2$.

Solving Process:

$$
\begin{array}{lrl}
\text{calcium} & 3 \times 40.1 \text{ u} = & 120.3 \text{ u} \\
\text{phosphorus} & 2 \times 31.0 \text{ u} = & 62.0 \text{ u} \\
\text{oxygen} & 8 \times 16.0 \text{ u} = & \underline{128.0 \text{ u}} \\
& \text{Formula mass} = & 310.3 \text{ u}
\end{array}
$$

PROBLEMS

1. Calculate the formula or molecular mass of each of the following compounds.
   a. H_2SO_4
   b. NaOH
   c. NH_4NO_3
   d. $Fe(CH_3COO)_3$
   e. $C_3H_5N_3O_3$, nitroglycerin
   f. $Al(NO_3)_3$
   g. $C_{63}H_{84}N_{14}O_{14}PCo$, vitamin B_{12}
   h. SO_2

2. Aspirin can be used to decrease pain and fever. Calculate the molecular mass of 2-acetyloxybenzoic acid (aspirin) that has the following structural formula.

THE AVOGADRO CONSTANT

As stated earlier, the mass of a single atom or molecule is so small it cannot be measured easily. Laboratory quantities require many millions of atoms. If we express the international atomic masses of elements in grams, the masses can be readily measured in the laboratory.

Since atomic masses are relative quantities, the atomic mass in grams of one element contains the same number of atoms as the atomic mass in grams of any other element. It has been found that the atomic mass in grams of any element contains 6.02×10^{23} atoms. This number is called **Avogadro's constant,** and is abbreviated N_A. Another name for this quantity is the mole.

THE MOLE

The **mole** is the SI unit for amount of substance, and its symbol is mol. It represents both a formula mass and a number of formula units. Just as one million equals 1×10^6 things, one dozen equals 12 things, and one gross equals 144 things, one mole is 6.02×10^{23} things. Depending on the substance, the mass of the mole will be different. The mole is an important quantitative unit used in most chemical calculations. It is always understood to refer to one formula mass in grams, one atomic mass in grams, or one molecular mass in grams.

An element that is diatomic (such as nitrogen) can be measured as one mole of molecules or as one mole of atoms. Note the difference in **Table 12-1.**

These relationships are important in a number of different chemical calculations. They will be used in this chapter and in subsequent chapters.

Conversion ratios are used to convert from one unit (such as grams) to a different unit (such as moles). Since the atomic mass in grams of an element = 1 mole

TABLE 12-1
Mole Relationships

Substance	Mass	Number of Particles	Moles
C	12.0 g	6.02×10^{23} atoms	1 mol C
K^+	39.1 g	6.02×10^{23} ions	1 mol K^+
CO_2	44.0 g	6.02×10^{23} molecules	1 mol CO_2
NaCl	58.5 g	6.02×10^{23} ion pairs	1 mol NaCl
N_2	28.0 g	6.02×10^{23} molecules	1 mol N_2
N	14.0 g	6.02×10^{23} atoms	1 mol N

of the element = 6.02×10^{23} atoms of an element, four conversion factors can be written.

$$\frac{1 \text{ mol } K^+}{39.1 \text{ g } K^+} \quad \text{or} \quad \frac{39.1 \text{ g } K^+}{1 \text{ mol } K^+}$$

$$\frac{1 \text{ mol } K^+}{6.02 \times 10^{23} \text{ } K^+} \quad \text{or} \quad \frac{6.02 \times 10^{23} \text{ } K^+}{1 \text{ mol } K^+}$$

The actual form used depends upon the units desired in the answer.

EXAMPLE

Calculate the mass in grams of 2.23 mol of nitrogen molecules.

Solving Process:
To convert from moles to grams, use the conversion ratio 28.0 g N_2/mol N_2. This ratio gives the answer in grams by dividing out the unit mol.

$$\text{mass } N_2 = \frac{2.23 \text{ mol } N_2}{} \bigg| \frac{28.0 \text{ g } N_2}{1 \text{ mol } N_2}$$

$$= 62.4 \text{ g } N_2$$

EXAMPLE

Determine the number of atoms in 2.23 mol nitrogen molecules, N_2.

Solving Process:
The number of molecules in a mole is given by the Avogadro constant. To obtain atoms, this number must be multiplied by two, since N_2 is diatomic.

$$\text{atoms N} = \frac{2.23 \text{ mol } N_2}{} \bigg| \frac{6.02 \times 10^{23} \text{ molecules } N_2}{1 \text{ mol } N_2} \bigg| \frac{2 \text{ atoms N}}{1 \text{ molecule } N_2}$$

$$= 2.68 \times 10^{24} \text{ atoms N}$$

EXAMPLE

Find the number of atoms in 16.0 g sulfur.

Solving Process:
Convert from grams to moles of sulfur, then from moles of sulfur to atoms of sulfur. This conversion will involve two ratios.

$$\text{atoms S} = \frac{16.0 \text{ g S}}{} \times \frac{1 \text{ mol S}}{32.1 \text{ g S}} \times \frac{6.02 \times 10^{23} \text{ atoms S}}{1 \text{ mol S}}$$

$$= 3.00 \times 10^{23} \text{ atoms S}$$

PROBLEMS

3. Calculate the mass in grams of 0.354 mol of each of the following.
   a. ammonia gas, NH_3
   b. platinum metal, Pt
   c. cholesterol, $C_{27}H_{46}O$
   d. iron(II) ferricyanide, $Fe_3(Fe(CN)_6)_2$

4. Calculate the number of moles in 50.0 g of each of the following.
   a. borazon, BN
   b. thallium(I) sulfate, Tl_2SO_4
   c. calcium propanoate, $Ca(C_3H_5O_2)_2$
   d. penicillin G, $C_{16}H_{18}N_2O_4S$

5. Calculate the number of atoms, molecules, or ions for each of the following.
   a. 2.00 mol Na atoms
   b. 46.0 g Na atoms
   c. 3.00 mol K^+
   d. 68.0 g H_2S molecules

6. Calculate the mass in grams of each of the following.
   a. 6.02×10^{23} atoms of Na
   b. 3.01×10^{23} formula units of $Sr(OH)_2$
   c. 1.20×10^{24} molecules of CO_2
   d. 1.50×10^{23} ions of Na^+

SECTION REVIEW

1. Calculate the formula (or molecular) mass of the following compounds:
   a. K_3AsO_4
   b. $Na_2B_4O_7$
   c. $MnCl_2$
   d. $Al_2(SO_4)_3$
   e. N_2O_5
   f. $(NH_4)_3PO_4$
   g. Na_2CO_3
   h. $CHCl_2COOH$
   i. NaCl

2. Hydrocarbons and various oxides of nitrogen react photochemically (a chemical process that requires light) to form a variety of pollutants. The formula of one of the pollutants, peroxyacetylnitrate, is

$$CH_3C\begin{matrix}\nearrow O \\ \searrow OONO_2\end{matrix}$$

What is the molecular mass of this compound?

3. An amino acid that cannot be made (synthesized) by the body and must be obtained in the diet is lysine. Determine the molecular mass of lysine, which has the following formula.

$$H_2N-(CH_2)_3-\underset{\underset{NH_2}{|}}{CHCOOH}$$

4. Calculate the mass in grams of each of the following.
   a. 6.38 mol O_2
   b. 4.00 mol Al
   c. 2.25 mol H_2SO_4
   d. 5.49 mol KI
   e. 1.500 mol $Ba(IO_4)_2$
   f. 0.602 mol $Ca(NO_3)_2$

5. Calculate the number of moles in each of the following.
   a. 188.0 g Zn
   b. 160.0 g Br_2
   c. 293.0 g Fe
   d. 32.0 g SO_2
   e. 10.0 g Na_2S
   f. 84.2 g K_2SO_4

6. Calculate the number of atoms, molecules, or ions in each of the following quantities.
   a. 20.0 g Ca atoms
   b. 3.34 mol CO_2 molecules
   c. 68.0 g H_2S molecules
   d. 0.125 mol Mg^{2+} ions

7. Calculate the mass in grams of each of the following.
   a. 3.01×10^{23} atoms of S
   b. 2.41×10^{24} molecules of H_2O

12.2 USING MOLES

MASS-MASS RELATIONSHIPS

Stoichiometry is the study of quantitative relationships in chemical reactions. A basic idea used in solving stoichiometric problems is the mole concept. If you are given the mass of one substance and know the balanced equation, you can calculate the reactants needed or the products produced because the equation shows relative number of moles of reactants and products. A general procedure for mass-mass problems uses the following steps.

1. Write a balanced equation.

2. Convert from mass of given material to moles.

3. Determine the mole ratio from the coefficients of the balanced equation and convert from moles of given material to moles of required material.

4. Express the moles of required material in grams.

The setup for a mass-mass calculation follows the format given below.

$$\begin{pmatrix}\text{start with}\\\text{grams given}\end{pmatrix} \rightarrow \begin{pmatrix}\text{grams}\\\text{to moles}\end{pmatrix} \rightarrow \begin{pmatrix}\text{use}\\\text{mole ratio}\end{pmatrix} \rightarrow \begin{pmatrix}\text{moles}\\\text{to grams}\end{pmatrix} \rightarrow \begin{pmatrix}\text{end with}\\\text{grams required}\end{pmatrix}$$

EXAMPLE

Calculate the mass of HCl needed to react with 10.0 g Zn.

Solving Process:
Step 1. Begin with the balanced equation.

$$Zn(s) + 2HCl(aq) \rightarrow ZnCl_2(aq) + H_2(g)$$

Step 2. Convert grams of zinc to moles.

$$\frac{10.0 \text{ g Zn}}{} \left| \frac{1 \text{ mole Zn}}{65.4 \text{ g Zn}} \right.$$

Step 3. Determine the mole ratio that exists between Zn and HCl and convert from moles Zn to moles HCl.

1 mole Zn reacts with 2 moles HCl

$$\frac{10.0 \text{ g Zn}}{} \left| \frac{1 \text{ mol Zn}}{65.4 \text{ g Zn}} \right| \frac{2 \text{ mol HCl}}{1 \text{ mol Zn}}$$

Step 4. Convert moles of HCl to grams of HCl.

$$\text{grams HCl} = \frac{10.0 \text{ g Zn}}{} \left| \frac{1 \text{ mol Zn}}{65.4 \text{ g Zn}} \right| \frac{2 \text{ mol HCl}}{1 \text{ mol Zn}} \left| \frac{36.5 \text{ g HCl}}{1 \text{ mol HCl}} \right.$$

$$= 11.2 \text{ g HCl}$$

Note that the conversion ratios are chosen and arranged so all the units divide out except the desired unit, in this case, grams of HCl. Since all the ratios are equal to 1, multiplying by one of them, or by all of them, changes only the units of the answer.

EXAMPLE

Calculate the mass of O_2 produced if 2.50 g $KClO_3$ are completely decomposed by heating.

Solving Process:
Step 1. Write the balanced equation.

$$2KClO_3(s) \rightarrow 2KCl(s) + 3O_2(g)$$

Step 2. Convert mass of $KClO_3$ to moles.

$$\frac{2.50 \text{ g KClO}_3}{} \left| \frac{1 \text{ mol KClO}_3}{123 \text{ g KClO}_3} \right.$$

Step 3. Determine the mole ratio that exists between $KClO_3$ and O_2.

2 moles $KClO_3$ yields 3 moles O_2

$$\frac{2.50 \text{ g KClO}_3}{} \left| \frac{1 \text{ mol KClO}_3}{123 \text{ g KClO}_3} \right| \frac{3 \text{ mol O}_2}{2 \text{ mol KClO}_3}$$

Step 4. Convert moles of O$_2$ to grams.

$$\text{grams O}_2 = \frac{2.50 \text{ g KClO}_3}{} \cdot \frac{1 \text{ mol KClO}_3}{123 \text{ g KClO}_3} \cdot \frac{3 \text{ mol O}_2}{2 \text{ mol KClO}_3} \cdot \frac{32.0 \text{ g O}_2}{1 \text{ mol O}_2}$$

$$= 0.976 \text{ g O}_2$$

PROBLEMS

Solve the following problems. The reactions may not be balanced.

1. If 20.0 g of magnesium react with excess hydrochloric acid, how many grams of magnesium chloride are produced?

   Mg(s) + HCl(aq) → MgCl$_2$(aq) + H$_2$(g)

2. How many grams of chlorine gas must be reacted with excess sodium iodide if 10.0 g of sodium chloride are needed?

   NaI(aq) + Cl$_2$(g) → NaCl(aq) + I$_2$(s)

3. How many grams of oxygen are produced in the decomposition of 5.00 g of potassium chlorate?

   KClO$_3$(s) → KCl(s) + O$_2$(g)

4. What mass of copper is required to replace silver from 4.00 g of silver nitrate dissolved in water?

   Cu(s) + AgNO$_3$(aq) → Cu(NO$_3$)$_2$(aq) + Ag(s)

5. If excess ammonium sulfate reacts with 20.0 g of calcium hydroxide, how many grams of ammonia are produced?

   (NH$_4$)$_2$SO$_4$(aq) + Ca(OH)$_2$(s) → CaSO$_4$(s) + NH$_3$(s) + H$_2$O(l)

6. If excess sulfuric acid reacts with 30.0 g of sodium chloride, how many grams of hydrogen chloride are produced?

   NaCl(aq) + H$_2$SO$_4$(aq) → HCl(g) + Na$_2$SO$_4$(aq)

7. How much silver phosphate is produced if 10.0 g of silver acetate react with excess sodium phosphate?

   AgCH$_3$COO(aq) + Na$_3$PO$_4$(aq) → Ag$_3$PO$_4$(s) + NaCH$_3$COO(aq)

8. How many grams of sodium hydroxide are needed to completely neutralize 25.0 g of sulfuric acid?

   NaOH(aq) + H$_2$SO$_4$(aq) → Na$_2$SO$_4$(s) + H$_2$O(g)

AVOGADRO'S PRINCIPLE AND MOLAR VOLUME

What is the relationship between the mass of a gas and its volume? **Avogadro's principle** states that *equal volumes of all gases, measured under the same conditions of pressure and temperature, contain the same number of particles or moles.* One mole of any gas has a mass equal to its molecular mass. For example:

$$1 \text{ mole } N_2 = 28.0 \text{ g } N_2 = 6.02 \times 10^{23} \text{ molecules of } N_2$$

$$1 \text{ mole } CO_2 = 44.0 \text{ g } CO_2 = 6.02 \times 10^{23} \text{ molecules of } CO_2$$

The volume of one mole of a gas at STP is the molar volume of the gas. One mole of a gas at STP occupies 22.4 liters (L). This volume is the same for all gases at STP. The mass and volume of any gas are related as follows.

$$1 \text{ mole of any gas} = \text{molecular mass} = 22.4 \text{ L}$$

EXAMPLE

How many grams of carbon dioxide, CO_2, will occupy a volume of 500.0 mL at STP?

Solving Process:
The conversion equalities are

$$1 \text{ mol } CO_2 = 22.4 \text{ L } CO_2 \text{ (STP)}$$
$$1 \text{ mol } CO_2 = 44.0 \text{ g } CO_2$$

$$\text{grams } CO_2 = \frac{500.0 \text{ mL } CO_2}{} \times \frac{1 \text{ L}}{1000 \text{ mL}} \times \frac{1 \text{ mol}}{22.4 \text{ L}} \times \frac{44.0 \text{ g } CO_2}{1 \text{ mol } CO_2}$$

$$= 0.982 \text{ g}$$

PROBLEMS

Assume the volumes given are at STP unless other conditions are specified.

9. Calculate the number of moles contained in each of the following gas volumes.
   a. 5.00×10^4 mL H_2
   b. 1.000×10^3 mL N_2
   c. 6500 mL SO_2
   d. 15 000 mL NH_3
   e. 2500 mL O_2
   f. 2.000×10^3 mL CO_2

10. Calculate the mass of each of the following volumes of gas.
    a. 2.00×10^4 L CH_4
    b. 1500.0 mL Cl_2
    c. 70.0 mL SO_3
    d. 3.000×10^2 L N_2O
    e. 3.0×10^3 L N_2
    f. 3500.0 mL H_2S

11. Calculate the volume in L of each of the following.
    a. 4.0 mol Br_2
    b. 200.0 g H_2S
    c. 25.5 g SO_2
    d. 600.0 g Cl_2
    e. 2.50 mol NH_3
    f. 50.0 g NO_2
    g. 7.00 mol O_2
    h. 10.0 g HCl

MASS-GAS VOLUME PROBLEMS

Many chemical reactions involve gases. It is often necessary to know the volume of gas involved with a known mass of material in a reaction. Problems of this type are similar to mass-mass problems, however one additional piece of information is needed. In mass-volume problems, mass is changed to moles of the desired substance and then converted to volume using the relationship:

$$1 \text{ mole of any gas} = 22.4 \text{ L of that gas at STP}$$

The reverse calculation may also be done. Volume is changed to moles and moles are changed to mass.

EXAMPLE

Calculate the volume of oxygen produced at STP by the decomposition of 10.0 g of potassium chlorate, $KClO_3$.

Solving Process:
Write the balanced equation.

$$2KClO_3(s) \rightarrow 2KCl(s) + 3O_2(g)$$

Start with the known mass of $KClO_3$ given in the problem and convert to volume of oxygen at STP.

$$\text{volume } O_2 = \frac{10.0 \text{ g } KClO_3}{} \cdot \frac{1 \text{ mol } KClO_3}{123 \text{ g } KClO_3} \cdot \frac{3 \text{ mol } O_2}{2 \text{ mol } KClO_3} \cdot \frac{22.4 \text{ L}}{1 \text{ mol } O_2} = 2.73 \text{ L}$$

EXAMPLE

A student performs an experiment involving the reaction of magnesium metal with hydrochloric acid to form hydrogen gas. From the given data, calculate the mass of magnesium.

1. volume of hydrogen gas formed   42.0 mL
2. temperature of hydrogen   20.0°C
3. pressure   99.3 kPa
4. vapor pressure of water   2.3 kPa
5. pressure of dry hydrogen   (99.3 − 2.3) 97.0 kPa

Solving Process:
Determine the volume of dry hydrogen at STP. Use the combined gas law.

$$\text{volume dry } H_2 = \frac{42.0 \text{ mL } H_2 \mid 97.0 \text{ kPa} \mid 273.2 \text{ K}}{101.3 \text{ kPa} \mid 293.2 \text{ K}}$$

$$= 37.5 \text{ mL}$$

Use the volume of dry H_2 (37.5 mL) and the molar volume to find the moles of hydrogen gas formed at STP.

$$\text{mol } H_2 = \frac{37.5 \text{ mL } H_2 \mid 1 \text{ mol } H_2 \mid 1 \text{ L}}{22.4 \text{ L } H_2 \mid 1000 \text{ mL}}$$

$$= 1.67 \times 10^{-3} \text{ mol}$$

Write a balanced equation and use it to find the mass of magnesium.

$$Mg(s) + 2HCl(aq) \rightarrow MgCl_2(aq) + H_2(g)$$

$$\text{mass Mg} = \frac{1.67 \times 10^{-3} \text{ mol } H_2 \mid 1 \text{ mol Mg} \mid 24.3 \text{ g Mg}}{1 \text{ mol } H_2 \mid 1 \text{ mol Mg}} = 0.0406 \text{ g}$$

PROBLEMS

Assume that all volumes are at STP.

12. How many mL of hydrogen are produced if 4.00 g zinc react with excess hydrochloric acid?

$$Zn(s) + 2HCl(aq) \rightarrow ZnCl_2(aq) + H_2(g)$$

13. If excess chlorine gas reacts with a solution containing 20.0 g of potassium bromide, how many milliliters of bromine gas can be produced?

$$2KBr(aq) + Cl_2(g) \rightarrow 2KCl(aq) + Br_2(g)$$

14. How many grams of copper(II) oxide can be reduced to copper metal with 10.0 L of H_2?

$$CuO(s) + H_2(g) \rightarrow Cu(s) + H_2O(g)$$

15. Calculate the mL of oxygen that can be produced by the electrolysis of 5.00 g of water.

$$2H_2O(l) \rightarrow 2H_2(g) + O_2(g)$$

16. In the reaction between aluminum and oxygen, how many grams of aluminum are required to react with 5.00 L of oxygen?

$$4Al(s) + 3O_2(g) \rightarrow 2Al_2O_3(s)$$

VOLUME-VOLUME PROBLEMS

It is possible to calculate the volume of a gas in a reaction when the volume of another gas in the reaction is known. Two methods can be used in solving these volume-volume problems. The first method is the same as the mass-mass or mass-volume method.

Use the following steps.

Step 1. Convert the given volume to moles.

Step 2. From the balanced equation, convert the moles of given substance to moles of required substance.

Step 3. Convert the moles of required substance back to its volume.

In each case, the temperature and pressure must be taken into consideration. Two methods of solving for gas volume are given. The second method usually involves only an inspection and simple mental calculation. It can be used easily when the temperature and pressure remain constant.

EXAMPLE

If 6.00 L of oxygen are available to burn carbon disulfide, CS_2, how many L of carbon dioxide are produced? The products of the combustion of carbon disulfide are carbon dioxide and sulfur dioxide.

Solving Process:
Balance the equation for this reaction.

$$CS_2(l) + 3O_2(g) \rightarrow CO_2(g) + 2SO_2(g)$$

Convert 6.00 L O_2 to L of CO_2.

$$\text{volume } CO_2 = \frac{6.00 \text{ L } O_2}{} \bigg| \frac{1 \text{ mol } O_2}{22.4 \text{ L } O_2} \bigg| \frac{1 \text{ mol } CO_2}{3 \text{ mol } O_2} \bigg| \frac{22.4 \text{ L } CO_2}{1 \text{ mol } CO_2} = 2.00 \text{ L}$$

Therefore, 6.00 L O_2 will produce 2.00 L CO_2. Note that the changes to and from moles divide out.

Alternate Method: *Temperature and Pressure Constant*
The balanced equation indicates the relative number of moles of reactant and product. The coefficients also indicate the relative volumes of the gases at constant temperature and pressure. The relationship is a result of the principle stated in Avogadro's hypothesis: *equal volumes of gases at the same temperature and pressure contain the same number of particles*. If the gases are measured at the same temperature and pressure then 3 volumes O_2:1 volume CO_2 or 3 L O_2:1 L CO_2. The volume of CO_2 will be one-third the volume of O_2. Since the O_2 volume is 6.00 L, the CO_2 volume is 2.00 L. Conversion ratios could be used as follows.

$$\text{volume } CO_2 = \frac{6.00 \text{ L } O_2}{} \bigg| \frac{1 \text{ L } CO_2}{3 \text{ L } O_2}$$
$$= 2.00 \text{ L}$$

PROBLEMS

17. In the electrolysis of water, 75.0 mL of oxygen gas are produced. How many mL of hydrogen are produced?

$$2H_2O(l) \rightarrow 2H_2(g) + O_2(g)$$

18. If an electric discharge produces 20.0 mL of ozone, O_3, how many milliliters of oxygen are required?

$$3O_2(g) \rightarrow 2O_3(g)$$

19. Ammonia can be produced by the Haber process. If 60.0 L of NH_3 are produced, how many L of hydrogen and nitrogen are necessary?

$$3H_2(g) + N_2(g) \rightarrow 2NH_3(g)$$

20. How many mL of chlorine gas are required to produce 50.0 mL of hydrogen chloride gas?

$$H_2(g) + Cl_2(g) \rightarrow 2HCl(g)$$

21. The residue from the complete decomposition of potassium chlorate is found to contain 1.80 g of potassium chloride. Determine the following:
    a. grams of $KClO_3$ originally present
    b. grams of oxygen produced
    c. milliliters of oxygen at STP

LIMITING REACTANTS

Many reactions continue until one of the reactants is consumed. The reactant that is used up first is called the **limiting reactant.** The other reactant is said to be in excess. When discussing limiting reactants, we will deal only with nonreversible reactions. It is possible to determine whether a material is in excess or is deficient in a reaction by experiment or by calculation.

Limiting reactant problems are most easily solved by comparing the moles of the reactants present using the following steps.

Step 1. Write a balanced equation.

Step 2. Change both given quantities to moles.

Step 3. From the balanced equation, determine the moles of required substance that each given quantity will produce.

Step 4. Complete the problem using the quantity that yields the lesser amount of product. This reactant is the limiting reactant.

EXAMPLE

If 40.0 g of H_3PO_4 react with 60.0 g of $MgCO_3$, calculate the volume of CO_2 produced at STP.

Solving Process:

Step 1. Write the balanced equation.

$$2H_3PO_4(aq) + 3MgCO_3(s) \rightarrow Mg_3(PO_4)_2(s) + 3CO_2(g) + 3H_2O(l)$$

Step 2. Change grams of reactant to moles of reactant.

$$\text{mol } H_3PO_4 = \frac{40.0 \text{ g } H_3PO_4}{} \cdot \frac{1 \text{ mol } H_3PO_4}{98.0 \text{ g } H_3PO_4} = 0.408 \text{ mol}$$

$$\text{mol } MgCO_3 = \frac{60.0 \text{ g } MgCO_3}{} \cdot \frac{1 \text{ mol } MgCO_3}{84.3 \text{ g } MgCO_3} = 0.712 \text{ mol}$$

Step 3. From the balanced equation determine the moles of CO_2 that will be produced by each reactant.

$$\text{mol } CO_2 = \frac{0.408 \text{ mol } H_3PO_4}{} \cdot \frac{3 \text{ mol } CO_2}{2 \text{ mol } H_3PO_4} = 0.612 \text{ mol}$$

$$\text{mol } CO_2 = \frac{0.712 \text{ mol } MgCO_3}{} \cdot \frac{3 \text{ mol } CO_2}{3 \text{ mol } MgCO_3} = 0.712 \text{ mol}$$

The limiting reactant produces the lesser amount of product, so in this case, H_3PO_4 is the limiting reactant.

Step 4. Use the limiting reactant to complete the problem.

$$\text{volume } CO_2 = \frac{0.612 \text{ mol } CO_2}{} \cdot \frac{22.4 \text{ L}}{1 \text{ mol } CO_2} = 13.7 \text{ L at STP.}$$

Therefore, 40.0 g of H_3PO_4 will produce 13.7 L of CO_2 measured at standard temperature and pressure.

The same approach for finding limiting reactants can also be used in mass-mass or volume-volume problems.

PROBLEMS

22. If 20.0 g of NaOH react with 30.0 g of H_2SO_4 to produce Na_2SO_4, which reactant is limiting?

$$2NaOH(aq) + H_2SO_4(aq) \rightarrow Na_2SO_4(aq) + 2H_2O(l)$$

23. If 5.00 g of copper metal react with a solution containing 20.0 g of AgNO$_3$ to produce silver metal, which reactant is limiting?

$$Cu(s) + 2AgNO_3(aq) \rightarrow Cu(NO_3)_2(aq) + 2Ag(s)$$

24. What reactant is limiting if 3.00 L of Cl$_2$ at STP react with a solution containing 25.0 g of NaBr to produce Br$_2$?

25. If 20.0 g of KOH react with 15.0 g of (NH$_4$)$_2$SO$_4$, calculate the L of NH$_3$ produced at STP.

26. Magnesium acetate can be prepared by a reaction involving 15.0 g of iron(III) acetate with either 10.0 g of MgCrO$_4$ or 15.0 g of MgSO$_4$. Which reaction will give the greatest yield of Mg(CH$_3$COO)$_2$? How many grams of Mg(CH$_3$COO)$_2$ will be produced?

$$2Fe(CH_3COO)_3(aq) + 3MgCrO_4(s) \rightarrow 3Mg(CH_3COO)_2(aq) + Fe_2(CrO_4)_3(s)$$

$$2Fe(CH_3COO)_3(aq) + 3MgSO_4(s) \rightarrow 3Mg(CH_3COO)_2(aq) + Fe_2(SO_4)_3(s)$$

NONSTANDARD CONDITIONS

Gas volume changes dramatically when pressure or temperature change. The molar volume is 22.4 L only at STP. If the experimental conditions are different from STP in a problem, it is still necessary to calculate the gas volume at STP.

The secret to success in these problems is to remember that the central step (moles of given to moles of unknown) must take place at STP. Thus, if you are given a volume of gas at other than STP, you must convert to STP before performing the moles to moles step in the solving process. On the other hand, if you are requested to find the volume of a gas at conditions other than STP, you must convert the volume after the moles to moles step.

EXAMPLE

How many grams of ammonium sulfate must react with excess sodium hydroxide to produce 408 mL of ammonia measured at 27°C and 98.0 kPa?

Solving Process:
Write the balanced equation.

$$(NH_4)_2SO_4(s) + 2NaOH(aq) \rightarrow Na_2SO_4(aq) + 2NH_3(g) + 2H_2O(l)$$

Convert 408 mL NH$_3$ at 27°C and 98.0 kPa to STP and then convert to g of (NH$_4$)$_2$SO$_4$. Since the temperature decreases, the volume decreases and the absolute temperature ratio is

$$\frac{273 \text{ K}}{300 \text{ K}}$$

Since pressure increases, volume decreases and the pressure ratio is

$$\frac{98.0 \text{ kPa}}{101.3 \text{ kPa}}$$

$$\text{mass (NH}_4)_2\text{SO}_4 = \frac{408 \text{ mL NH}_3}{} \left| \frac{1 \text{ L}}{1000 \text{ mL}} \right| \frac{273 \text{ K}}{300 \text{ K}} \left| \frac{98.0 \text{ kPa}}{101.3 \text{ kPa}} \right. \cdots$$

$$\frac{1 \text{ mol NH}_3}{22.4 \text{ L}} \left| \frac{1 \text{ mol (NH}_4)_2\text{SO}_4}{2 \text{ mol NH}_3} \right| \frac{132 \text{ g (NH}_4)_2\text{SO}_4}{1 \text{ mol (NH}_4)_2\text{SO}_4} = 1.06 \text{ g}$$

To produce 408 mL NH$_3$ at 27°C and 98.0 kPa, it is necessary to react 1.06 g (NH$_4$)$_2$SO$_4$ with excess sodium hydroxide.

EXAMPLE

What volume of hydrogen collected over water at 27°C and 97.5 kPa is produced by the reaction of 3.00 g of Zn with an excess of sulfuric acid? The vapor pressure of water at 27°C is 3.6 kPa.

Solving Process:

Step 1. Write the balanced equation.

$$\text{Zn(s)} + \text{H}_2\text{SO}_4(\text{aq}) \rightarrow \text{ZnSO}_4(\text{aq}) + \text{H}_2(\text{g})$$

Step 2. Convert from grams of Zn to liters of dry H$_2$ at 27°C and 97.5 kPa. Then convert to liters of H$_2$ at STP by using the absolute temperature and pressure ratios.

$$\frac{3.00 \text{ g Zn}}{} \left| \frac{1 \text{ mol Zn}}{65.4 \text{ g Zn}} \right| \frac{1 \text{ mol H}_2}{1 \text{ mol Zn}} \left| \frac{22.4 \text{ L H}_2}{1 \text{ mol H}_2} \right.$$

Step 3. The liters of H$_2$ at STP must be converted to the conditions given in the problem. As the temperature is increased, the volume will increase, so the absolute temperature ratio is

$$\frac{300 \text{ K}}{273 \text{ K}}$$

Step 4. As pressure is decreased volume will increase, so the pressure ratio is

$$\frac{101.3 \text{ kPa}}{97.5 \text{ kPa}}$$

This ratio must be corrected for the vapor pressure of water, which is 3.6 kPa at this temperature. The corrected ratio is

$$\frac{101.3 \text{ kPa}}{97.5 - 3.6 \text{ kPa}} \quad \text{or} \quad \frac{101.3 \text{ kPa}}{93.9 \text{ kPa}}$$

Chemistry: Concepts and Applications *Supplemental Practice Problems, Chapter 12*

Step 5. Then, combine Steps 2 through 4 and multiply it out.

$$\text{volume H}_2 = \frac{3.00 \text{ g Zn}}{} \left| \frac{1 \text{ mol Zn}}{65.4 \text{ g Zn}} \right| \frac{1 \text{ mol H}_2}{1 \text{ mol Zn}} \cdots$$

$$\frac{22.4 \text{ L H}_2}{1 \text{ mol H}_2} \left| \frac{300 \text{ K}}{273 \text{ K}} \right| \frac{101.3 \text{ kPa}}{93.9 \text{ kPa}} = 1.22 \text{ L H}_2$$

Hence, 3.00 g Zn will react with excess H_2SO_4 to give 1.22 L of H_2 measured at 27°C and 97.5 kPa over water.

PROBLEMS

27. If 14.7 g of sodium peroxide (Na_2O_2) react with water to produce sodium hydroxide and oxygen gas, how many L of oxygen are produced at 22°C and 1.12×10^5 Pa?

28. How many L of chlorine gas measured at 18.5°C and 98.0 kPa can be produced by the electrolysis of 62.3 g NaCl to give sodium metal and chlorine gas?

29. How many L of nitrogen measured at 21.5°C and 9.55×10^4 Pa are required to react with excess calcium carbide, CaC_2, to produce 100.0 g of calcium cyanamid, $CaCN_2$, and carbon?

30. How many grams of iron metal must react with excess steam to produce 10.0 L of hydrogen collected over water at 20.0°C and 9.90×10^4 Pa? The other product is iron(II,III) oxide, Fe_3O_4 (Fe_3O_4 is actually $FeO \cdot Fe_2O_3$).

IDEAL GAS EQUATION

The **ideal gas equation** combines the four physical variables (pressure, volume, temperature, and number of particles) for gases into one equation. Remember that an ideal gas is composed of point masses that do not take up space, and these masses are not attracted to each other at all. All real gases deviate somewhat from the gas laws since the molecules of real gases are not point masses (they take up space) and they attract one another.

The ideal gas equation is $PV = nRT$, where P is the pressure in kilopascals. V is the volume in cubic decimeters and T is the temperature in kelvin. The n represents the number of moles of a gas. With these units, the value of the constant R is 8.31 L · kPa/mol · K. There are other values of R depending upon the units used to derive R.

We can use the ideal gas equation to determine the molecular mass (M) of a gas. The number of moles (n) of any species is equal to its mass (m) divided by the molecular mass (M). Thus, the ideal gas equation can also be written as follows.

$$PV = nRT \quad \text{or} \quad PV = \frac{m}{M}RT \quad \text{or} \quad M = \frac{mRT}{PV}$$

EXAMPLE

How many moles of gas will a 1250-mL flask hold at 35.0°C and a pressure of 95.4 kPa?

Solving Process:
The ideal gas equation can be solved for the number of moles, n, of a substance.

$$PV = nRT \quad or \quad n = \frac{PV}{RT}$$

Before we can substitute the known values into the ideal gas equation, 35.0°C must be converted to 308.2 K. We get the following expression.

$$n = \frac{\overset{P}{95.4 \text{ kPa}} \quad \Big| \quad \overset{V}{1250 \text{ mL}} \quad \Big| \quad 1 \text{ L}}{\underset{R}{8.31 \frac{\text{L} \cdot \text{kPa}}{\text{mol} \cdot \text{K}}} \quad \Big| \quad \underset{T}{308.2 \text{ K}} \quad \Big| \quad 1000 \text{ mL}} = 0.0466 \text{ mol}$$

The solution is 0.0466 mol. Note that all other units in the problem divide out.

EXAMPLE

A flask has a volume of 258 mL. A gas with mass 1.475 g is introduced into the flask at a temperature of 302.0 K and a pressure of 9.86×10^4 Pa. Calculate the molecular mass of the gas using the ideal gas equation.

Solving Process:
The number of moles, n, of a substance is equal to mass, m, divided by the molecular mass, M. Therefore, the ideal gas equation may be written

$$PV = \frac{mRT}{M} \quad or \quad M = \frac{mRT}{PV}$$

$$M = \frac{1.475 \text{ g}}{9.86 \times 10^4 \text{ Pa}} \quad \Big| \quad \frac{8.31 \text{ L} \cdot \text{kPa}}{\text{mol} \cdot \text{K}} \quad \Big| \quad \frac{302.0 \text{ K}}{258 \text{ mL}} \quad \Big| \quad \frac{1000 \text{ mL}}{1 \text{ L}} = 146 \text{ g/mol}$$

Remember that the units of volume, pressure, temperature, and quantity of gas must be consistent with the value of R.

PROBLEMS

31. What is the molecular mass of sulfur dioxide, SO_2, if 300.0 mL of the gas has a mass of 0.855 g at STP?

32. A sample of hydrogen iodide, HI, has a mass of 2.28 g and occupies 400.0 mL at STP. What is the molecular mass of this compound?

33. If 0.179 g of methane, CH_4, occupy 0.250 L, what is the molecular mass of methane if the volume is given at standard conditions?

34. From the volume, temperature, and pressure, calculate the number of moles for each gas listed using the ideal gas equation.
   a. 750.0 mL O_2 at 27°C and 99.0 kPa
   b. 3.00 L CO_2 at −15°C and 103.0 kPa

35. Calculate the volume each gas will occupy under the conditions listed using the ideal gas equation.
   a. 3.00 mol H_2 at 24°C and 100.5 kPa
   b. 150.0 g Cl_2 at −12.5°C and 98.5 kPa

36. The density of a sample of phosphorus trifluoride, PF_3, is 3.90 g/L. What is the molecular mass of this gas at STP?

$$\left(\text{Hint: } D = \frac{m}{V} = \frac{MP}{RT}\right)$$

MASS PERCENTS

The **mass percent** of elements in a compound gives the relative amount of each element present. The percent of an element in a compound is determined by the following equation.

$$\% = \text{number of atoms of element} \times \frac{\text{atomic mass of element}}{\text{formula mass of compound}} \times 100\%$$

To calculate mass percent:

(a) calculate the total mass for each element,

(b) calculate the formula mass for the entire compound,

(c) divide the total mass of each element by the formula mass of the compound, and

(d) multiply by 100%.

EXAMPLE

Find the mass percent of nitrogen in ammonium nitrate, NH_4NO_3, an important source of nitrogen in fertilizers.

Solving Process:
Calculate the formula mass; then find the percentage.

$$\begin{aligned}
\text{nitrogen} & \quad 2 \times 14.0 = 28.0 \\
\text{hydrogen} & \quad 4 \times 1.01 = 4.04 \\
\text{oxygen} & \quad 3 \times 16.0 = 48.0 \\
& \quad \text{Formula mass} = 80.0 \text{ g}
\end{aligned}$$

$$\% N = \frac{\text{total mass N}}{\text{formula mass } NH_4NO_3} \times 100\%$$

$$= \frac{28.0 \text{ g}}{80.0 \text{ g}} \times 100\% = 35.0\% \text{ N}$$

PROBLEMS

37. Calculate the mass percent of each element of the following compounds.
   a. Fe_2O_3 **b.** Ag_2O **c.** HgO **d.** Na_2S

38. Determine the mass percent of sodium in sodium sulfate, Na_2SO_4.

39. Urea, $CO(NH_2)_2$, and ammonia, NH_3, are two compounds used as a source of nitrogen in fertilizers. Calculate the mass percent of nitrogen in each.

40. Calculate the percentage of each of the following in the compound sodium sulfate decahydrate, $Na_2SO_4 \cdot 10\ H_2O$.
   a. Na   **b.** S   **c.** O   **d.** H_2O

MOLECULAR AND EMPIRICAL FORMULAS

The **empirical formula** of a compound is the smallest whole number ratio of the number of atoms of each element in the substance. The **molecular formula** gives the actual number of atoms in the molecule. For instance, CH_2 is the empirical formula for the series of molecular compounds C_2H_4, C_3H_6, C_4H_8, and so on.

There is a definite relationship between the empirical and the molecular formula. Note that the molecular formula is always a whole number multiple of the empirical formula. As can be seen in **Table 12-2** the empirical formula and the molecular formula are not always the same.

TABLE 12-2
Empirical and Molecular Formulas

Compound	Empirical Formula	Molecular Formula
water	H_2O	H_2O
hydrogen peroxide	HO	H_2O_2
mercury(I) bromide	HgBr	Hg_2Br_2
methane	CH_4	CH_4
butane	C_2H_5	C_4H_{10}
ethene	CH_2	C_2H_4
butene	CH_2	C_4H_8

PROBLEM

41. Write the empirical formula for each of the following.
   a. C_6H_6 (benzene)   **f.** SO_3
   b. C_2H_2 (ethyne)   **g.** N_2O_4
   c. $C_6H_{12}O_6$ (glucose)   **h.** NO_2
   d. C_4H_{10} (butane)   **i.** $Ag_2C_4H_4O_6$
   e. P_4O_{10} **j.** K_2S_4

EMPIRICAL FORMULAS

Earlier, we used the formula of a compound to determine its mass percents. Now we reverse the procedure and determine the empirical formula from the mass percents. The elements in compounds combine in simple whole number ratios of atoms. To determine an empirical formula, masses of elements are converted to moles and then a ratio of moles is determined.

EXAMPLE

Determine the empirical formula for sodium sulfite. Sodium sulfite contains 36.5% sodium, 25.4% sulfur, and 38.1% oxygen.

Solving Process:
A percentage indicates a part of one hundred. Therefore, the percentage composition data indicates that there are 36.5 g Na, 25.4 g S, and 38.1 g O in 100 g of compound.

Step 1. Find the number of moles.

$$\text{Na} \quad \frac{36.5 \text{ g Na}}{} \cdot \frac{1 \text{ mol Na}}{23.0 \text{ g Na}} = 1.59 \text{ mol Na}$$

$$\text{S} \quad \frac{25.4 \text{ g S}}{} \cdot \frac{1 \text{ mol S}}{32.1 \text{ g S}} = 0.791 \text{ mol S}$$

$$\text{O} \quad \frac{38.1 \text{ g O}}{} \cdot \frac{1 \text{ mol O}}{16.0 \text{ g O}} = 2.38 \text{ mol O}$$

Step 2. Determine the ratio of moles.

$$\text{Na} \quad \frac{1.59 \text{ mol}}{0.791 \text{ mol}} = 2.01 \qquad \text{S} \quad \frac{0.791 \text{ mol}}{0.791 \text{ mol}} = 1.00 \qquad \text{O} \quad \frac{2.38 \text{ mol}}{0.791 \text{ mol}} = 3.01$$

The ratio is 2.01:1.00:3.01, Na:S:O.
The empirical formula is Na_2SO_3.

EXAMPLE

What is the empirical formula of a compound that contains 53.73% Fe and 46.27% S?

Solving Process:
There are 53.73 g Fe and 46.27 g S in 100 g of compound.

Step 1. Find the number of moles.

$$\text{mol Fe} = \frac{53.73 \text{ g Fe}}{} \cdot \frac{1 \text{ mol Fe}}{55.85 \text{ g Fe}} = 0.9620 \text{ mol Fe}$$

$$\text{mol S} = \frac{46.27 \text{ g S}}{} \cdot \frac{1 \text{ mol S}}{32.07 \text{ g S}} = 1.443 \text{ mol S}$$

Step 2. Determine the ratio of moles.

$$\frac{\text{Fe}}{0.9620 \text{ mol}} / 0.9620 \text{ mol} = 1.000 \qquad \frac{\text{S}}{1.443 \text{ mol}} / 0.9620 \text{ mol} = 1.500$$

The ratio is 1.000:1.500, giving $FeS_{1.500}$

In the previous example problem, the relative numbers of atoms were small whole numbers and we could write the formula directly from them. The ratio 1 to 1.5 must be expressed in terms of whole numbers, since a fractional part of an atom does not exist. By multiplying both numbers in the ratio by two, we obtain two atoms Fe and three atoms S. The empirical formula is Fe_2S_3.

PROBLEMS

42. Calculate the empirical formula for compounds with the following compositions.
    a. Fe 63.5%, S 36.5%
    b. Mn 63.1%, S 36.9%
    c. K 26.6%, Cr 35.4%, O 38.0%

43. Calculate empirical formulas for the following two compounds containing sodium, sulfur, and oxygen.
    a. Na 32.4%, S 22.6%, O 45.0%
    b. Na 29.1%, S 40.5%, O 30.4%

44. Calculate the empirical formulas for the following three iron ores.
    a. Fe 77.7%, O 22.3%
    b. Fe 72.4%, O 27.6%
    c. Fe 70.0%, O 30.0%

MOLECULAR FORMULAS

The molecular formula indicates not only the ratio of the atoms of the elements in a compound but also the actual number of atoms of each element in one molecule of the compound.

The molecular formula calculation is the same as the empirical formula calculation, except that the molecular mass is used in an additional step. Remember, the molecular formula is always a whole number multiple of the empirical formula.

EXAMPLE

An organic compound is found to contain 92.25% carbon and 7.75% hydrogen. If the molecular mass is 78 u, what is the molecular formula?

Solving Process:
Determine the empirical formula.

Step 1. Find the number of moles.

$$\frac{92.25 \text{ g C}}{} \cdot \frac{1 \text{ mol C}}{12.01 \text{ g C}} = 7.681 \text{ mol C}$$

$$\frac{7.75 \text{ g H}}{} \cdot \frac{1 \text{ mol H}}{1.01 \text{ g H}} = 7.67 \text{ mol H}$$

Step 2. Divide by the smaller number of moles to determine ratio of moles.

$$\text{H} \quad \frac{7.67 \text{ mol}}{7.67 \text{ mol}} = 1.00 \qquad \text{C} \quad \frac{7.681 \text{ mol}}{7.67 \text{ mol}} = 1.00$$

Step 3. Use the empirical formula to find the molecular formula.

The empirical formula is CH. Since the CH unit has a formula mass of 13 u and a molecular mass of 78 u there will be six units in each molecule.

$$(13 \text{ u})x = 78 \text{ u}$$
$$x = 78 \text{ u}/13 \text{ u} = 6.0$$

Six times the molecular formula is C_6H_6.

PROBLEMS

45. There are two oxides of phosphorus. Both oxides can exist in different forms depending on the temperature and the pressure. Calculate the empirical and molecular formulas from the following data.
   a. P 56.4%, O 43.6%, molecular mass 220 u
   b. P 43.7%, O 56.3%, molecular mass 284 u

46. The formula mass of a compound is 92 u. Analysis of the compound shows that there are 0.608 g of nitrogen and 1.388 g of oxygen. What is the molecular formula of this compound?

SECTION REVIEW

1. Molten iron and carbon monoxide are produced in a blast furnace by the reaction of iron(III) oxide and coke (carbon). If 25.0 kg of pure Fe_2O_3 are used, how many moles of iron can be produced?

2. Ammonia gas produced as a by-product in an industrial reaction can be reacted with sulfuric acid in order that the gas does not escape into the atmosphere. The product, ammonium sulfate, can be used as a fertilizer. Determine how many kilograms of acid are required to produce 1000.0 kg of $(NH_4)_2SO_4$.

3. Coal gasification is a process that is carried out industrially in a series of steps. The net reaction involves coal (carbon) reacting with water to form methane, CH_4, and carbon dioxide. How many kilograms of methane can be produced from 1.00×10^3 kg of coal?

4. A source of acid rain is automobile exhaust. Nitric oxide, formed in an internal combustion engine, reacts with oxygen in the air to produce nitrogen dioxide. The NO₂ reacts with water to form nitric acid. It is determined that the average car produces 1.00×10^4 L of exhaust gas per mile driven. Assume that the average concentration of NO₂ in auto exhaust is 0.10 µg/L and that traffic surveys have shown an average of 2.00×10^6 vehicle miles driven per day. From this data, determine the kilograms of nitric acid that could be produced annually.

$$2NO_2 + H_2O \rightarrow HNO_2 + HNO_3$$

5. Photosynthesis is a complex process composed of many steps. The initial reactants are carbon dioxide and water and the final products are glucose and oxygen gas. If a plant needs to make 30.0 g of glucose, $C_6H_{12}O_6$, through the process of photosynthesis, how many grams of water are required?

6. One mole of He has a mass of 4.0026 g and 1.000 L of He (at STP) has a mass of 0.1787 g. Calculate the molar volume of helium.

7. What is the molecular mass of a gas if 5.75 g of the gas occupy a volume of 3.50 L? The pressure was recorded as 9.525×10^4 Pa and the temperature is 52°C.

8. How many milliliters of hydrogen at STP are produced by the reaction of 0.750 g of sodium metal with excess water?

$$2Na(s) + 2H_2O(l) \rightarrow 2NaOH(aq) + H_2(g)$$

9. What mass of magnesium will react with excess hydrochloric acid to produce 5.00×10^2 mL of H₂ at STP?

$$Mg(s) + 2HCl(aq) \rightarrow MgCl_2(aq) + H_2(g)$$

10. When lead(II) sulfide is burned in air, lead(II) oxide and sulfur dioxide are produced. If 20.0 L of sulfur dioxide were produced, how many liters of oxygen gas were required to react with the lead(II) sulfide?

$$2PbS(s) + 3O_2(g) \rightarrow 2PbO(s) + 2SO_2(g)$$

11. In a reaction involving carbon monoxide and iron(III) oxide, the products are iron metal and carbon dioxide. If 84.75 L of carbon dioxide are produced, how many L of carbon monoxide are required?

12. Hydrogen burns to give water. If 200.0 mL of H₂ reacts with 150.0 mL of O₂, what volume of water vapor is produced? How many milliliters of gas remain unreacted and what gas remains? Assume that all volumes are measured at any given temperature above the normal boiling point of water.

13. How many grams of sodium hydrogen carbonate, NaHCO₃, must be heated to produce 2.50 L of carbon dioxide measured at 22.5°C and 97.5 kPa? The other products are sodium carbonate and water.

14. If 3.20 g of aluminum react with excess hydrochloric acid, how many mL of hydrogen collected over water at 20.0°C and 99.5 kPa are produced?

15. A sample of gas has a mass of 1.248 g and occupies 300.0 mL at STP. What is the molecular mass of this gas?

16. From the volume, temperature, and pressure data given, calculate the number of moles and the mass in grams for each gas listed using the ideal gas equation.
    a. 2000.0 mL NH_3 at 10.0°C and 105.0 kPa
    b. 5.00 L SO_2 at 21.0°C and 100.0 kPa

17. Calculate the volume each gas will occupy under the conditions listed using the ideal gas equation.
    a. 5.00 mol CH_4 at 27.0°C and 97.2 kPa
    b. 200.0 g NH_3 at 12.0°C and 104.5 kPa

18. The sugar substitute sodium benzosulfimide (sodium saccharin) has a sweetness of about 500 times that of sucrose. Calculate the percentage of sodium and carbon in the sweetener. Its formula is

19. Copper phthalocyanine is a complex organic molecule possessing a brilliant greenish blue color. Millions of pounds are produced yearly to color products such as plastics, automobile finishes, rubber goods, and printing inks. Determine the percent carbon in copper phthalocyanine that has the formula $Cu(C_8H_4N_2)_4$.

20. Write the empirical formula for each of the following.
    a. C_6H_{14}
    b. CO_2
    c. N_2F_4
    d. $C_3H_6Cl_2$
    e. $C_5H_{10}O_2$
    f. $P_3N_3Cl_6$

21. Two compounds are analyzed and found to contain:
    a. 0.89 g K, 1.18 g Cr, 1.27 g O
    b. 1.03 g K, 0.69 g Cr, 0.84 g O
    Determine the empirical formulas for these two compounds.

22. A fat is composed, in part, of long chains of carbon and hydrogen atoms. In a reaction with a strong base, a fat forms a soap and glycerol. What is the empirical formula of a fat containing 76.5% C, 11.3% O and 12.2% H, if it has a molecular mass of 847 u?

23. Citric acid, an organic acid found in lemons and other citrus fruits, contains 37.5% carbon, 58.3% oxygen, and 4.20% hydrogen. What is the empirical formula of citric acid if it has a molecular mass of 192 u?

Water and Its Solutions 13

13.1 UNIQUELY WATER

HYDROGEN BONDING

Water, H_2O, has a molecular mass of 18 u. Hydrogen sulfide, H_2S, has a molecular mass of 34 u. At 25°C, hydrogen sulfide is a gas. If you did not already know that water is a liquid at 25°C, you might predict it to be gas on the basis of its smaller molecular mass compared to H_2S. How can you explain the fact that water is, instead, a liquid? The explanation lies in the existence of an attractive force between water molecules called **hydrogen bonding.**

The hydrogen bond is not a chemical bond. It is an intermolecular attractive force. When hydrogen is covalently bonded to a highly electronegative element, such as fluorine, nitrogen, or oxygen, a strongly polar molecule results. The positive side of the polar molecule (oxygen) is attracted to the negative side (hydrogen) of other polar molecules. Hydrogen is the only element to exhibit this property.

The effects of hydrogen bonding can be observed when water freezes and melts. When water freezes, hydrogen bonding between water causes the molecules to become arranged in an open crystal structure. This arrangement results in a decrease in density. When ice melts, many of the hydrogen bonds are broken and the lattice collapses. The water molecules move closer together. Water is most dense at 3.98°C. Because ice is less dense than the liquid, it floats.

SECTION REVIEW

1. When hydrogen is bonded to a highly electronegative element, what intermolecular attractive force results?

2. List three elements that bond with hydrogen to produce hydrogen bonds between the molecules.

3. Why does ice float in liquid water when most solids sink in their liquids?

4. A hydrogen bond is not a true chemical bond. True or false?

13.2 SOLUTIONS AND THEIR PROPERTIES

SOLUTE—SOLVENT

A solution consists of a dissolved substance, the **solute,** and a dissolving medium, the **solvent.** A solution is a homogeneous mixture (has a constant composition throughout). A solute need not be a solid. It can be a gas, such as HCl in hydrochloric acid, or a liquid, such as the ethylene glycol in a car's cooling system. If the solution contains two liquids, the liquid that is in the greater amount is called the solvent. The most common solvent is water.

Knowing the actual strength of a solution is more useful than knowing in general terms that it is dilute or concentrated. The concentration of solutions can be described quantitatively in many ways. Molarity and mole fraction are discussed in this chapter.

MOLARITY

The mole is also used to express the concentration of a solution. A 1 molar solution contains 1 mole of solute dissolved in enough solvent (usually water) to make 1 liter of solution.

$$\text{molarity } (M) = \frac{\text{moles of solute}}{\text{liter of solution}}$$

Chemists express concentration in terms of **molarity** because they measure most solutions by volume and because they are interested in obtaining a certain number of particles. One mole of sodium chloride, NaCl, is 58.5 grams. If 2 moles of NaCl (117.0 grams) are dissolved in enough water to make 1 liter of solution, the solution is a 2M solution. Fifty milliliters of a solution will have the same concentration, 2M. The total number of particles changes when the volume is changed but the concentration of particles (the number of particles per unit volume) does not change.

EXAMPLE

Calculate the molarity of 1.50 L of solution that contains 200.0 g of $MgCl_2$.

Solving Process:
The problem requires the calculation of molarity. Molarity is moles of solute per (divided by) L of solution. Therefore, the data concerning solute is placed in the numerator, and the data concerning the solution in the denominator. The solute data in the numerator is then converted to moles, and the solution data in the denominator to L.

$$\text{molarity} = \frac{200.0 \text{ g MgCl}_2}{1.50 \text{ L}} \times \frac{1 \text{ mol MgCl}_2}{95.3 \text{ g MgCl}_2}$$

$$= 1.40 \text{ mol/L} = 1.40M$$

EXAMPLE

Calculate the molarity of a solution that contains 10.0 g of sodium hydroxide in 5.00×10^2 mL of solution.

Solving Process:
Convert 10.0 g of NaOH per 5.00×10^2 mL to moles of NaOH per L of solution.

$$\text{molarity} = \frac{10.0 \text{ g NaOH}}{5.00 \times 10^2 \text{ mL}} \times \frac{1 \text{ mol NaOH}}{40.0 \text{ g NaOH}} \times \frac{1000 \text{ mL}}{1 \text{ L}}$$

$$= 0.500 \text{ mol/L} = 0.500M$$

PROBLEMS

1. Calculate the molarity of each of the following solutions.
   a. 0.500 L containing 30.0 g of acetic acid, CH_3COOH
   b. 2.000 L containing 49.0 g of phosphoric acid, H_3PO_4
   c. 1.50 L containing 102 g of potassium hydroxide, KOH

2. Calculate the mass of solute in the following solutions:
   a. 750.0 mL of $CaCl_2$ solution that is 0.500M
   b. 3000.0 mL of a KOH solution that is 2.50M
   c. 250.0 mL of a Na_2SO_4 solution that is 2.00M

3. How many liters of each solution can be made according to the following specifications?
   a. a 2.00M solution using 80.0 g sodium hydroxide
   b. a 0.500M solution using 80.0 g sodium hydroxide
   c. a 1.50M solution using 188 g silver nitrate, $AgNO_3$

MOLE FRACTION

Another way to express solution concentration is mole fraction. The mole fraction (X) of a substance in a solution is defined as the moles of substance divided by the moles of solution (sum of moles of solute + moles of solvent).

$$X = \frac{moles\ solute}{(moles\ of\ solute\ +\ moles\ of\ solvent)}$$

The sum of the mole fractions of all the components of a solution equals one.

EXAMPLE

What are the mole fractions of glucose and water in a solution made of 7.59 g of glucose, $C_6H_{12}O_6$, dissolved in 125 g of water?

Solving Process:
The molecular mass of glucose is 180.0 g. Find the moles of glucose.

$$\text{mol glucose} = \frac{7.59\ g\ C_6H_{12}O_6}{} \left| \frac{1\ mol\ C_6H_{12}O_6}{180.0\ g\ C_6H_{12}O_6} \right. = 0.0422\ mol$$

The molecular mass of H_2O is 18.0 u. Find the moles of water.

$$\text{mol } H_2O = \frac{125\ g\ H_2O}{} \left| \frac{1\ mol\ H_2O}{18.0\ g\ H_2O} \right. = 6.94\ mol$$

Chemistry: Concepts and Applications

Determine the mole fraction of $C_6H_{12}O_6$.

$$\text{mol fraction} = \frac{\text{mol solute}}{(\text{mol solute} + \text{mol solvent})}$$

$$= \frac{0.0422 \text{ mol}}{(0.0422 + 6.94) \text{ mol}} = \frac{0.0422}{6.98} = 0.006\ 05$$

Determine the mole fraction of H_2O.

$$\text{mol fraction} = \frac{6.94}{6.98} = 0.994$$

If one multiplies the mole fraction by 100, you have the mole percent. In the above problem 99.4% of the molecules in the solution are H_2O.

PROBLEMS

Calculate the mole fraction for each component in the following solutions.

4. 22.5 g CH_3CH_2OH in 1.00×10^2 g H_2O

5. 39.5 g $C_6H_5CH_3$, toluene, in 1.5×10^2 g C_6H_6, benzene

COLLOIDS

Colloids contain particles that are evenly distributed through a dispersing medium, and remain distributed over time rather than settling out. Colloids are classified as a heterogeneous mixture, but they represent a transition between heterogeneous mixtures and solutions. Colloid particles (dispersed phase) are larger than the single atoms, ions, or molecules found in solutions. They are smaller than the particles of heterogeneous mixtures. The particles of a suspension can be seen with a light microscope and settle out of suspension on standing.

TABLE 13-1
Classifications of Some Colloids

Phase of Colloid Particles	Phase of material colloid particles are in	Name	Example
liquid	gas	aerosol	fog
solid	gas	aerosol	smoke
gases	liquid	liquid foam	whipped cream
gases	solid	solid foam	marshmallows
liquid	liquid	emulsion	mayonnaise
liquid	solid	emulsion	cheese
solids	liquids	sols	jellies and paint
solids	solids	sols	pearls and opals

Particles from 1 nm to 100 nm in size usually remain dispersed throughout the medium. Such a mixture is called a colloid. Substances show unusual properties even when only one of the three dimensions of the particle's size is in the colloidal range.

TABLE 13-2
Comparison of Solutions, Suspensions (heterogeneous mixtures), and Colloids

Type	Particle size	Permanence
Solution	<1 nm	permanent
Colloid	>1 nm but <100 nm	permanent
Suspension	>100 nm	settle out

You may have seen the beam of a searchlight in the night air. The suspended water droplets in air are large enough to scatter the light, and the beam becomes visible from the side. This scattering of light by suspended particles is called the **Tyndall effect.**

Colloidal particles are visible under an ultramicroscope. They are in continuous random motion because of the constant bombardment by the smaller molecules of the medium they are in. This motion is called **Brownian motion.**

TABLE 13-3
Properties of Solutions, Colloids, and Suspensions

Solution	Colloids	Suspensions
Do not settle out	Do not settle out	Settle out on standing
Pass unchanged through ordinary filter paper	Pass unchanged through ordinary filter paper	Separated by ordinary filter paper
Pass unchanged through membrane	Separated by a membrane	Separated by a membrane
Do not scatter light	Scatter light	Scatter light

SECTION REVIEW

1. Calculate the molarity of the following solutions.
    a. 500.0 mL that contains 82.0 g calcium nitrate
    b. 250.0 mL that contains 50.0 g copper(II) sulfate pentahydrate
    c. 1000.0 mL that contains 116 g sodium carbonate heptahydrate

2. Calculate the mass of solute in the following solutions.
    a. 250.0 mL of $Na_2SO_4 \cdot 7H_2O$ solution that is 2.00M
    b. 1.500 L of KH_2PO_4 solution that is 0.240M
    c. 2500.0 mL of a HNO_3 solution that is 4.00M

3. How many liters of solution can be made from each of the following?
    a. a 0.100M solution using 117 g sodium chloride
    b. a 1.00M solution using 50.0 g copper(II) sulfate pentahydrate
    c. a 0.200M solution using 200.0 g sodium sulfide

4. How many grams of lead(II) acetate, Pb(CH$_3$COO)$_2$, must be used to make 500.0 mL of a solution that is to contain 10.0 mg/mL of lead ion? What is the molarity of this solution?

5. A laboratory experiment requires 0.100M Pb(NO$_3$)$_2$. How many grams of Pb(NO$_3$)$_2$ are needed to make 175 mL of the solution?

6. A teacher needs to prepare 15 sets of solutions for a chemistry lab. Each set must have 70.0 mL of 0.200M FeSO$_4$ · 7H$_2$O. What mass of FeSO$_4$ · 7H$_2$O is required to prepare enough solution for the class?

7. Calculate the molarity of each of the following solutions.
   a. 500.0 mL that contains 82.0 g Ca(NO$_3$)$_2$
   b. 250.0 mL that contains 50.0 g NiSO$_4$ · 6H$_2$O

8. Calculate the mass of solute in each of the following solutions.
   a. 250.0 mL of a Na$_2$SO$_4$ · 7H$_2$O solution that is 2.00M
   b. 1.500 L of KH$_2$PO$_4$ solution that is 0.240M

9. How many liters of solution can be made from each of the following?
   a. a 0.100M solution using 117 g NaCl
   b. a 1.25M solution using 55.0 g Na$_2$S$_2$O$_3$ · 5H$_2$O

10. Calculate the mole fraction of methanol, CH$_3$OH, when 3.20 of methanol are dissolved in 4.61 g of ethanol, CH$_3$CH$_2$OH.

11. How is a colloid different from a solution?

12. What term refers to the scattering of light by particles in a colloid?

13. Arrange the words suspension, solution, and colloid in order of increasing particle size.

14. What size particles exhibit colloidal behavior?

15. The random jiggling of bacteria in a drop of water is described with what name?

Acids, Bases, and pH   14

14.1 ACIDS AND BASES

NAMING ACIDS AND SALTS

Water solutions of binary hydrides form acids. The stem derived from the hydride is given a prefix *hydro-* and a suffix *-ic* and is followed by the word *acid*. The binary hydride HCl is called hydrogen chloride as a gas, but as an aqueous solution it is called hydrochloric acid.

TABLE 14-1
Binary Acids

Formula	Name	Anion
HF(aq)	hydrofluoric acid	F^-, fluoride ion
HCl(aq)	hydrochloric acid	Cl^-, chloride ion
HBr(aq)	hydrobromic acid	Br^-, bromide ion
H_2S(aq)	hydrosulfuric acid	S^{2-}, sulfide ion

Many common acids contain only oxygen, hydrogen, and a nonmetallic ion or a polyatomic ion. Such acids are called **oxyacids.** The suffixes *-ous* and *-ic* indicate the oxidation state of the atom bound to the oxygen and hydrogen. The *-ous* suffix indicates a lower oxidation state. **Table 14-2** lists common acids and anions.

TABLE 14-2
Common Oxyacids

Formula	Name		Anion
$HClO_4$	perchloric acid	ClO_4^-	perchlorate
$HClO_3$	chloric acid	ClO_3^-	chlorate
$HClO_2$	chlorous acid	ClO_2^-	chlorite
HClO	hypochlorous acid	ClO^-	hypochlorite
HNO_3	nitric acid	NO_3^-	nitrate
HNO_2	nitrous acid	NO_2^-	nitrite
H_2SO_4	sulfuric acid	SO_4^{2-}	sulfate
H_2SO_3	sulfurous acid	SO_3^{2-}	sulfite
CH_3COOH	acetic acid	CH_3COO^-	acetate
H_2CO_3	carbonic acid	CO_3^{2-}	carbonate
H_3PO_4	phosphoric acid	PO_4^{3-}	phosphate
$H_2C_2O_4$	oxalic acid	$C_2O_4^{2-}$	oxalate

In a **neutralization reaction** an acid reacts with a base to form a salt and H_2O. (Many bases can easily be recognized because they are composed of a metallic ion combined with the hydroxide ion. Others, like ammonia, are more difficult to recognize.) The reaction goes to completion since a molecular compound (water) is formed. The water is only slightly ionized. For practical purposes, the water does not react again.

$$H_2SO_4 + 2NaOH \rightarrow Na_2SO_4 + 2H_2O$$
Acid   Base   Salt   Water

The other compound formed is called a salt. **Salts** are crystalline solids. A salt contains the positive ion of a base and the negative ion of an acid. In addition to common salts such as NaCl and Na_2SO_4, another group of salts, termed acid salts, contain hydrogen, $NaHSO_4$, sodium hydrogen sulfate; K_2HPO_4, potassium monohydrogen phosphate; KH_2PO_4, potassium dihydrogen phosphate.

Salts may be soluble or insoluble in water. The common solubility rules are indicated in **Table B-10** in Appendix B.

PROBLEMS

1. Name the following acids.
   a. HCl
   b. HNO_3
   c. H_2SO_4
   d. H_3PO_4
   e. $HClO_3$
   f. CH_3COOH
   g. HNO_2
   h. HClO
   i. H_2SO_3
   j. H_2CO_3
   k. $HClO_2$
   l. $HClO_4$

2. Name the following salts. Include the name of the acid from which the salt is obtained.
   a. $NaClO_3$
   b. $Fe(ClO_4)_2$
   c. NH_4BrO_3
   d. $Mg(IO_3)_2$
   e. MnI_2
   f. $Ba(NO_3)_2$
   g. $PbCl_2$
   h. $Hg(BrO_3)_2$
   i. $ZnSO_4$
   j. $Ca(ClO)_2$

3. Write formulas for each salt and write the formula of the acid from which the salt can be obtained.
   a. ammonium sulfate
   b. barium hypochlorite
   c. lithium chlorate
   d. cobalt(II) sulfite
   e. mercury(I) bromate
   f. chromium(III) nitrate
   g. magnesium chloride
   h. potassium perchlorate

SECTION REVIEW

1. Name the following acids.
   a. HBr
   b. HNO_2
   c. H_2SO_4
   d. H_2S
   e. H_3PO_3
   f. $HClO_3$
   g. HI
   h. CH_3COOH
   i. H_3AsO_4
   j. HIO_3
   k. H_2SiO_3
   l. H_2CO_3

2. Write formulas for the following. Identify each as acid, base, or salt.

   a. magnesium hydroxide
   b. hydrochloric acid
   c. zinc nitrate
   d. sulfurous acid
   e. sodium hypochlorite
   f. potassium hydroxide

14.2 STRENGTHS OF ACIDS AND BASES

STRENGTHS OF ACIDS AND BASES

A strong acid such as hydrochloric acid exists in solution as ions.

$$H_2O(l) + HCl(g) \rightarrow H_3O^+(aq) + Cl^-(aq)$$

The concentration of H_3O^+ ions determines the strength of an acid. When a weak acid dissolves in water, an equilibrium is established between the molecular form and the ionic form of the substance.

$$H_2O(l) + CH_3COOH(l) \rightleftharpoons H_3O^+(aq) + CH_3COO^-(aq)$$

The reverse reaction is favored. As a result, there is a small concentration of ions. The amount of ionization is directly related to acid strength.

Strong bases, such as sodium hydroxide, also dissolve in water to form ions.

$$NaOH(s) \rightarrow Na^+(aq) + OH^-(aq)$$

When $NH_3(g)$, a weak base, dissolves in water, few ions are produced.

$$H_2O(l) + NH_3(g) \rightleftharpoons NH_4^+(aq) + OH^-(aq)$$

About 99% of the $NH_3(g)$ remains in the molecular form. As with acids, the amount of ionization is directly related to base strength.

Acids and Bases React 15

15.1 ACID AND BASE REACTIONS

ACID–BASE THEORIES

Several definitions have been proposed for acids and bases. Depending upon the situation, each definition has its advantages and disadvantages. Three acid-base theories are Arrhenius, Brønsted-Lowry, and Lewis.

The **Arrhenius theory** is the oldest approach to acid-base theory. It is adequate for most introductory chemistry concepts. The theory explains acids and bases by the concept of ion formation. An acid ionizes in solution to produce hydrogen ions, H^+. For example, hydrochloric acid ionizes in one step.

$$HCl \rightarrow H^+ + Cl^-$$

Sulfuric acid, a polyprotic compound, ionizes in two steps.

$$H_2SO_4 \rightarrow H^+ + HSO_4^-$$
$$HSO_4^- \rightarrow H^+ + SO_4^{2-}$$

A base ionizes or dissociates in solution to produce hydroxide ions, OH^-.

$$NaOH \rightarrow Na^+ + OH^-$$

The Arrhenius theory accounts for the characteristic properties of acids and bases.

Brønsted and Lowry expanded the definition of a base to include any substance that would accept a proton. Remember that a hydrogen ion is just a proton since there are no neutrons in the nucleus. An acid is defined as a proton donor. The products that result from an acid-base reaction are called the conjugate acid and the conjugate base.

$$HF(aq) + HCO_3^-(aq) \rightleftharpoons H_2CO_3(aq) + F^-(aq)$$
$$\text{acid} \qquad \text{base} \qquad \text{conjugate} \quad \text{conjugate}$$
$$\qquad\qquad\qquad\qquad\qquad \text{acid} \qquad \text{acid}$$

The conjugate base is the particle that remains after a proton is donated by an acid. The conjugate acid is formed when a base accepts a proton from an acid. The hydrogen carbonate ion, HCO_3^-, behaves as a base but does not contain ionizable hydroxide.

The **Lewis** definition of acids and bases is the broadest of the three theories. Lewis defined an acid as an electron-pair acceptor and a base as an electron-pair donor. This definition includes reactions that contain neither hydrogen nor hydroxide ions. Molecules as well as ions can be treated as acids or bases. Consider the reaction

$$Na_2O + SO_3 \rightarrow Na_2SO_4$$

Sodium is a spectator ion. Using the Lewis electron dot symbols

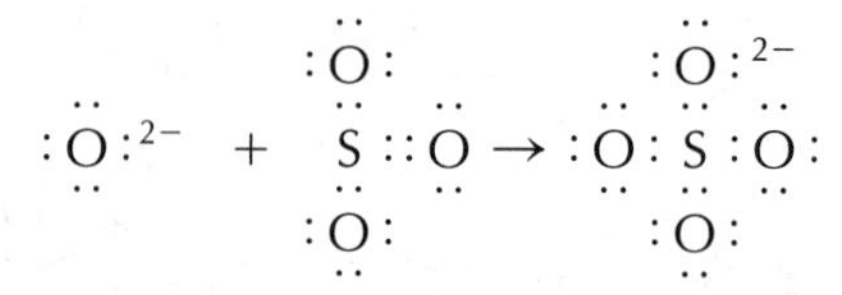

base electron-pair donor   acid electron-pair acceptor

The oxide ion can donate the electron pair to the SO_3 molecule.

PROBLEMS

1. Identify the acid, base, conjugate acid, and conjugate base in the following reactions.
   a. $HCN(aq) + SO_4^{2-}(aq) \rightarrow HSO_4^-(aq) + CN^-(aq)$
   b. $CH_3COO^-(aq) + H_2S(aq) \rightarrow CH_3COOH(aq) + HS^-(aq)$

2. Identify the Lewis acid and Lewis base in the following reactions.
   a. $Al^{3+} + 6H_2O \rightarrow Al(H_2O)_6^{3+}$
   b. $2NH_3 + Ag^+ \rightarrow Ag(NH_3)_2^+$

NET IONIC EQUATIONS

When an aqueous solution of silver nitrate is added to an aqueous solution of zinc chloride, a white precipitate, silver chloride, forms.

$$2AgNO_3(aq) + ZnCl_2(aq) \rightarrow 2\ AgCl(s) + Zn(NO_3)_2(aq)$$

The equation above shows all the substances as molecules even though three of them are actually existing as ions in solution. The equation would be more accurate if it were written in ionic form.

$$2Ag^+(aq) + 2NO_3^-(aq) + Zn^{2+}(aq) + 2Cl^-(aq)$$
$$\rightarrow 2AgCl(s) + Zn^{2+}(aq) + 2NO_3^-(aq)$$

You will notice that some ions appear in the same form on both the reactant and product sides. These ions, called **spectator ions,** do not take part in the reaction. Spectator ions can be subtracted from both sides of the equation to leave the **net ionic equation.**

$$2Ag^+(aq) + 2Cl^-(aq) \rightarrow 2AgCl(s)$$

We divide each coefficient by two to reduce the net ionic equation to its final form.

$$Ag^+(aq) + Cl^-(aq) \rightarrow AgCl(s)$$

The net ionic equation shows that mixing any solution of silver ions with any solution of chloride ions will produce the precipitate AgCl.

The following rules are used to write net ionic equations.

Rule 1. The binary acids HCl, HBr, and HI are strong and are written in ionic form. All others are weak, and are written in molecular form.

Rule 2. The number of oxygen atoms in a strong acid containing three elements exceeds the number of hydrogen atoms by two or more. Strong acids are written in ionic form.

Rule 3. The second and subsequent ionizations of polyprotic acids are always weak, even if the original acid is strong. Weak acids are written in molecular form.

Rule 4. Group 1 and 2 metal hydroxides are strong bases and are written in ionic form. All other hydroxides are written in molecular form.

Rule 5. Soluble salts are written in ionic form. Insoluble salts are written in molecular form. Use **Table B-10** in Appendix B to determine the solubility of a salt.

Rule 6. Oxides are written in molecular form.

Rule 7. Gases are written in molecular form.

EXAMPLE

Write the net ionic equation for the following reaction.

zinc metal + hydrochloric acid → zinc chloride + hydrogen gas

Solving Process:

Rule 1: HCl is a strong acid (ionic).

Rule 5: $ZnCl_2$ is soluble (ionic).

Rule 7: H_2 gas is molecular.

(a) Write the balanced molecular equation.

$$Zn(s) + 2HCl(aq) \rightarrow ZnCl_2(aq) + H_2(g)$$

(b) Write the ionic equation.

$$Zn(s) + 2H^+(aq) + 2Cl^-(aq) \rightarrow Zn^{2+}(aq) + 2Cl^-(aq) + H_2(g)$$

(c) Determine the net ionic equation by subtracting out any spectator ions.

$$Zn(s) + 2H^+(aq) \rightarrow Zn^{2+}(aq) + H_2(g)$$

PROBLEM

3. Write the net ionic equation for each word equation.
   a. sodium + water → sodium hydroxide + hydrogen
   b. phosphoric acid + magnesium hydroxide → magnesium phosphate + water
   c. barium chloride + sodium sulfate → sodium chloride + barium sulfate
   d. magnesium hydroxide + ammonium phosphate → magnesium phosphate + ammonia + water
   e. iron(III) bromide + ammonium sulfide → iron(III) sulfide + ammonium bromide

SECTION REVIEW

1. Define an acid according to the following theories.
   a. Arrhenius theory
   b. Brønsted-Lowry theory
   c. Lewis theory

2. Label the acid, base, conjugate acid, and conjugate base in the following reactions.
   a. $HSO_4^-(aq) + Cl^-(aq) \rightarrow SO_4^{2-}(aq) + HCl(aq)$
   b. $OH^-(aq) + CH_3COOH(aq) \rightarrow CH_3COO^-(aq) + H_2O(l)$

3. Identify the Lewis acid and Lewis base in the reaction of Ni^{2+} with four water molecules.

   $$Ni^{2+}(aq) + 4H_2O(l) \rightarrow Ni(H_2O)_4^{2+}(aq)$$

4. Apply the rules for writing the net ionic equations to these reactions.
   a. sodium hydroxide + hydrochloric acid → sodium chloride + water
   b. potassium metal + water → potassium hydroxide + hydrogen gas
   c. silver nitrate + sodium chloride → sodium nitrate + silver chloride

15.2 APPLICATIONS OF ACID-BASE REACTIONS

TITRATIONS

Titration is the general process of determining the molarity of an acid or a base through the use of an acid-base reaction. It is an experimental procedure in which a standard solution is used to determine the molarity of an unknown medium. A **standard solution** is one of known molarity. The titration involves the gradual addition of one solution to another until the solute in the first solution has completely reacted with the solute in the second solution. This point is called the equivalence point. The equivalence point is detected using an indicator. The point at which the indicator changes color is called the endpoint of the titration.

The most common titrations involve the reaction of an acid solution with a basic solution. The reaction of the acid and base is termed a neutralization. The products of this reaction are a salt and water.

$$\text{acid + base} \rightarrow \text{salt + water}$$

The reaction between a strong acid (e.g., HCl or HNO$_3$) and a strong base (e.g., NaOH) gives salts (e.g., NaCl or NaNO$_3$). Since these salts are products of strong acids and strong bases, the resulting solution is neutral.

For a strong acid/strong base titration, the pH at the equivalence point is 7; but only a small amount of reagent causes a major pH change. The titration curve for the neutralization reaction is shown in **Figure 15-1a.** Curves can be produced using a pH meter connected to a chart recorder. The indicator selected should change color in the pH range from about 4 to 10. Phenolphthalein is usually used since it is easy to detect visually a slight pink color from a colorless liquid.

Reaction between a strong acid (HCl, HNO$_3$, or H$_2$SO$_4$) and a weak base (NH$_3$) also produces salts (NH$_4$Cl, NH$_4$NO$_3$, or (NH$_4$)$_2$SO$_4$). These salts hydrolyze to form slightly acidic solutions. The titration curve for this reaction is shown in **Figure 15-1b.** Methyl orange can be used as an indicator because of the low pH region in which it changes color.

The reaction between a weak acid (CH$_3$COOH) and a strong base (NaOH) gives a salt (NaCH$_3$COO). Such salts hydrolyze to give a slightly basic solution. The titration curve for this reaction is shown in **Figure 15-1c.** Any indicator changing color in the higher pH ranges could be used, but phenolphthalein is most frequently used.

The concentration of the acid and basic solutions will change the position of the curves only slightly (especially at the start and completion of the titration) in relation to the pH.

FIGURE 15-1a

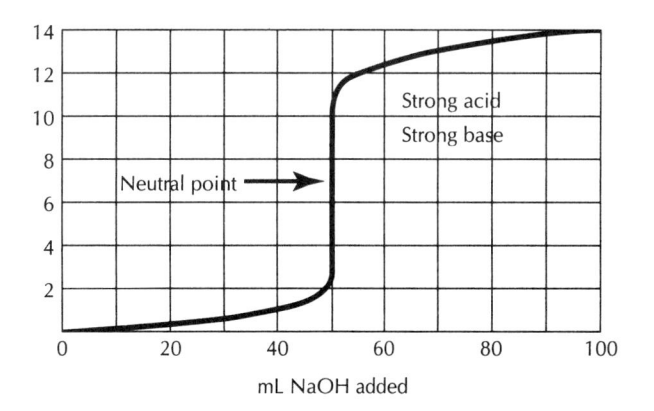

FIGURE 15-1b

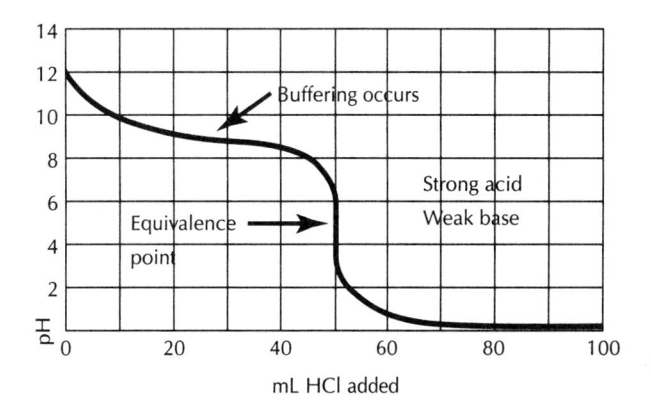

Chemistry: Concepts and Applications

FIGURE 15-1c

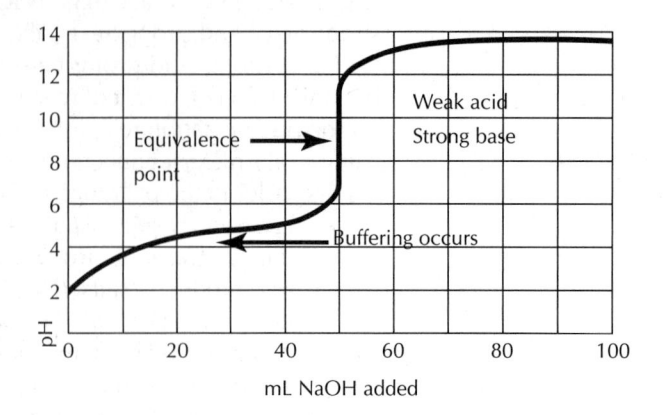

[Titration curve: pH vs mL NaOH added, showing Weak acid / Strong base titration with Equivalence point near 50 mL, and Buffering region labeled.]

EXAMPLE

If 20.0 mL of a 0.300M solution of NaOH is required to neutralize completely 30.0 mL of a sulfuric acid solution, what is the molarity of the H_2SO_4 solution?

Solving Process:
(a) First write the balanced equation.

$$2NaOH(aq) + H_2SO_4(aq) \rightarrow Na_2SO_4(aq) + 2H_2O(l)$$

(b) Since the concentration of the base is given, determine the moles of NaOH.

$$\text{number of moles} = \frac{20.0 \text{ mL soln}}{} \Big| \frac{0.300 \text{ mol NaOH}}{1.00 \text{ L soln}} \Big| \frac{1 \text{ L}}{1000 \text{ mL}}$$

$$= 0.006\ 00 \text{ mol NaOH}$$

(c) From the coefficients of the balanced equation, 2 moles of base are required for reaction with 1 mole of acid.

$$\text{number of moles} = \frac{0.006\ 00 \text{ mol NaOH}}{} \Big| \frac{1 \text{ mol } H_2SO_4}{2 \text{ mol NaOH}}$$

$$= 0.003\ 00 \text{ mol } H_2SO_4$$

(d) Determine the molarity of the acid.

$$\text{molarity} = \frac{0.003\ 00 \text{ mol } H_2SO_4}{30.0 \text{ mL soln}} \Big| \frac{1000 \text{ mL}}{1 \text{ L}}$$

$$= 0.100 \text{ mol } H_2SO_4/L = 0.100M \text{ } H_2SO_4$$

EXAMPLE

What volume of 0.500M HNO_3 is required to neutralize 25.0 mL of a 0.200M NaOH solution?

Solving Process:
(a) The balanced equation is

$$HNO_3(aq) + NaOH(aq) \rightarrow NaNO_3(aq) + H_2O(l)$$

(b) Since the concentration of the base is given, determine the moles of NaOH.

$$\text{mol NaOH} = \frac{25.0 \text{ mL soln}}{} \bigg| \frac{0.200 \text{ mol NaOH}}{1.00 \text{ L soln}} \bigg| \frac{1 \text{ L}}{1000 \text{ mL}}$$

$$= 0.005\ 00 \text{ mol NaOH}$$

(c) From the coefficients of the balanced equation, 1 mole of acid will react completely with 1 mole of base.

$$0.005\ 00 \text{ mol NaOH} = 0.005\ 00 \text{ mol } HNO_3$$

(d) Therefore

$$\text{volume} = \frac{0.005\ 00 \text{ mol } HNO_3}{} \bigg| \frac{1.00 \text{ L soln}}{0.500 \text{ mol } HNO_3} \bigg| \frac{1000 \text{ mL}}{1 \text{ L}}$$

$$= 10.0 \text{ mL soln}$$

PROBLEMS

1. Calculate the unknown quantity for the complete neutralization of the following.

	Acid		Base	
	concentration	volume	concentration	volume
a.	0.250M HCl	30.00 mL	? NaOH	25.00 mL
b.	0.500M H_2SO_4	?	0.750M KOH	20.00 mL
c.	? HNO_3	15.00 mL	1.50M NH_3	25.00 mL
d.	0.400M HNO_3	35.00 mL	0.800M NaOH	?

2. What is the molarity of a NaOH solution if 25.00 mL is required to completely neutralize 40.00 mL of a 1.50M solution of H_2SO_4?

3. Calculate the mL of a 0.600M solution of HNO_3 necessary to neutralize 28.55 mL of a 0.450M solution of KOH.

4. A titration of 15.00 mL of household ammonia, NH_3(aq), required 38.57 mL of 0.780M HCl. Calculate the molarity of the ammonia.

SECTION REVIEW

1. How many mL of 0.500M NaOH are necessary to neutralize completely 20.0 mL of each of the following acids?
   a. 0.150M HNO_3
   b. 0.250M H_2SO_4
   c. 0.220M HCl
   d. 0.450M H_3PO_4

2. In a laboratory experiment, 20.00 mL of NH_3(aq) solution is titrated to the methyl orange endpoint using 15.65 mL of a 0.200M HCl solution. What is the concentration of the aqueous ammonia solution?

3. How many mL of 0.750M sulfuric acid are needed to neutralize completely 20.00 mL of 0.427M NaOH solution?

Oxidation-Reduction Reactions

16.1 THE NATURE OF OXIDATION-REDUCTION REACTIONS

OXIDATION NUMBERS

In most of the equations considered in previous chapters one species displaces another species that is similarly charged. Double displacement reactions such as the neutralizations are common examples. The species are ionic and retain the same charge as reactants and products.

$$2NaOH(aq) + H_2SO_4(aq) \rightarrow Na_2SO_4(aq) + 2HOH(l)$$

$$2Na^+(aq) + 2OH^-(aq) + 2H^+(aq) + SO_4^{2-}(aq)$$
$$\rightarrow 2Na^+(aq) + SO_4^{2-}(aq) + 2H_2O(l)$$

An oxidation-reduction reaction or **redox reaction** involves a change in the charges of the ions. Reactions such as synthesis and single displacement are oxidation-reduction reactions since there have been changes in the charges.

Recall, the **oxidation number** is the charge on an ion or element. The oxidation states of an atom may be assigned from the following rules.

1. All free elements are assigned an oxidation number of zero. Thus, hydrogen in H_2, oxygen in O_2, and phosphorus in P_4, all have an oxidation number of zero.

2. The oxidation number of a monatomic ion is equal to the charge on the ion.
   a. Group 1 elements form only 1+ ions.
   b. Group 2 elements form only 2+ ions.
   c. Halogen elements have a 1− oxidation number except in inter-halogen compounds.

3. In practically all hydrogen-containing compounds, the oxidation number of hydrogen is 1+. The exception occurs with the metal hydrides, in which the oxidation number of hydrogen is 1−.

4. The oxidation number of oxygen in compounds is generally 2−. The exceptions are the peroxides, in which the oxidation number is 1−, and in oxygen difluoride, OF_2, where oxygen has an oxidation number of 2+.

5. All oxidation numbers that are assigned must be consistent with the conservation of charge. For neutral particles, the oxidation numbers of all atoms

must add up to zero. For a polyatomic ion, the oxidation numbers of the atoms must add up to the charge on the polyatomic ion. Review the following examples.

	hydrogen	oxygen	sulfur	Total Charge
sulfuric acid H_2SO_4	2(1+)	4(2−)	? oxidation number of S = 6+	= 0
sulfite ion SO_3^{2-}		3(2−)	? oxidation number of S = 4+	= 2−

PROBLEM

1. In the following, give the oxidation number for the indicated atoms.
   a. Al in Al_2O_3
   b. S in $Na_2S_2O_3$
   c. Mn in MnO_4^-
   d. Cl in ClO_3^-
   e. Fe in $FeCl_3$
   f. Cr in $Cr_2O_7^{2-}$
   g. C in K_2CO_3
   h. N in NO_3^-

HALF-REACTIONS

Oxidation is the process by which electrons are removed from atoms or ions. **Reduction** is the process by which electrons are added to atoms or ions. Oxidation and reduction must occur at the same time in a reaction, and the number of electrons lost must equal the number gained.

A redox equation can be separated into an oxidation half-reaction and a reduction half-reaction. The method of balancing oxidation-reduction equations is to balance separately the oxidation half-reaction and the reduction half-reaction. The two half-reactions are added to obtain the balanced equation for the total reaction.

Use the following general approach to balance redox reactions.

1. Write the separate half-reactions.

2. Balance the electrons using oxidation numbers.

3. Balance the atoms in each half-reaction as follows:
   a. Balance all atoms with the use of coefficients, except hydrogen and oxygen atoms.
   b. Add enough water (H_2O) to the side deficient in oxygen to balance the oxygen.
   c. Add sufficient hydrogen ion (H^+) to the side deficient in hydrogen to balance the hydrogen.

4. Multiply the half-reactions by small whole numbers to balance the electrons.

5. Add the two half-reactions and subtract any duplications on either side of the equation.

EXAMPLE

Write a balanced oxidation-reduction equation for the following reaction.

$$MnO_4^- + H_2SO_3 \rightarrow Mn^{2+} + HSO_4^- + H_2O$$

Solving Process:

Separate the reaction into two half-reactions. Balance the half-reactions separately. The reduction half-reaction is

$$MnO_4^- \rightarrow Mn^{2+}$$

The first step in balancing the half-reaction is to indicate the number of electrons gained or lost. In the reduction half-reaction being considered here, the manganese has an oxidation number 7+ before the reaction and 2+ after the reaction. Thus manganese must gain 5 electrons.

$$MnO_4^- + 5e^- \rightarrow Mn^{2+}$$

The next step is to balance all elements other than oxygen and hydrogen. In the reaction above, one manganese atom appears on each side of the equation. The equation is balanced with respect to manganese atoms, the only element present in addition to oxygen. No change is needed to balance the manganese.

Next, oxygen should be balanced. You may assume that all the oxidation-reduction reactions in this book take place in water solution. Thus, oxygen atoms are always available in the form of water molecules.

$$MnO_4^- + 5e^- \rightarrow Mn^{2+} + 4H_2O$$

Finally, the hydrogen atoms must be balanced. Hydrogen is available in water molecules but using water to balance hydrogen atoms would throw the oxygen atoms out of balance. If you note that the solution is acidic (H_2SO_3 is one of the reactants) then you will realize that H^+ ions will be abundant in the solution and can be used to balance the hydrogen atoms.

$$MnO_4^- + 8H^+ + 5e^- \rightarrow Mn^{2+} + 4H_2O$$

The reduction half-reaction is now balanced.

The oxidation half-reaction must now be balanced. The sulfur atoms change oxidation number from 4+ to 6+, and they lose two electrons each.

$$H_2SO_3 \rightarrow HSO_4^- + 2e^-$$

Again, use the available H_2O and H^+ to balance the half-reaction with respect to oxygen and hydrogen.

$$H_2SO_3 + H_2O \rightarrow HSO_4^- + 2e^- + 3H^+$$

Before the two half-reactions can be combined to give the overall equation, the coefficients of the electrons must be adjusted so that the same number of electrons are lost as are gained. The manganese half-reaction requires five electrons

Chemistry: Concepts and Applications

while the sulfur half-reaction produces two. The least common multiple of five and two is ten, so the reduction half-reaction is multiplied by two and the oxidation half-reaction by five.

Reduction half-reaction × 2

$$2MnO_4^- + 16H^+ + 10e^- \rightarrow 2Mn^{2+} + 8H_2O$$

Oxidation half-reaction × 5

$$5H_2SO_3 + 5H_2O \rightarrow 5HSO_4^- + 10e^- + 15H^+$$

Adding the two half-reactions and eliminating the electrons that appear in equal numbers on both sides gives

$$2MnO_4^- + H^+ + 5H_2SO_3 \rightarrow 2Mn^{2+} + 5HSO_4^- + 3H_2O$$

Reactions of the oxidation-reduction type can also take place in basic solution. Balance these just as you would an acidic reaction and then add sufficient hydroxide ions (OH^-) to each side to change all H^+ ions to H_2O molecules. Remember that the same number of hydroxide ions must be added to each side of the reaction.

EXAMPLE

Write a balanced oxidation-reduction equation for the following reaction.

$$NO_2 + OH^- \rightarrow NO_2^- + NO_3^-$$

Solving Process:
Note that nitrogen is both oxidized and reduced in this reaction.

		Reduction	Oxidation
1.	Write skeleton.	$NO_2 \rightarrow NO_2^-$	$NO_2 \rightarrow NO_3^-$
2.	Balance electrons.	$NO_2 + e^- \rightarrow NO_2^-$	$NO_2 \rightarrow NO_3^- + e^-$
3.	Balance nitrogen.	*Nitrogen atoms are balanced.*	
4.	Balance oxygen.	$NO_2 + e^- \rightarrow NO_2^-$	$H_2O + NO_2 \rightarrow NO_3^- + e^-$
5.	Balance hydrogen.	(same)	$H_2O + NO_2 \rightarrow NO_3^- + 2H^+ + e^-$
6.	Convert to basic solution.	(same)	$H_2O + NO_2 + 2OH^- \rightarrow NO_3^- + 2H_2O + e^-$
7.	Eliminate the excess water molecules on both sides.		$NO_2 + 2OH^- \rightarrow NO_3^- + H_2O + e^-$

The number of electrons in each half-reaction is the same, so they may be added directly. The nitrogen dioxide molecules appearing in each half-reaction are combined in the final equation just as the electrons appearing on each side are eliminated.

$$2NO_2 + 2OH^- \rightarrow NO_2^- + NO_3^- + H_2O$$

PROBLEMS

Balance the following oxidation-reduction equations. All reactions take place in an acidic solution unless otherwise indicated.

2. $Cr(s) + Sn^{4+}(aq) \rightarrow Cr^{3+}(aq) + Sn^{2+}(aq)$

3. $Al(s) + H^+(aq) \rightarrow Al^{3+}(aq) + H_2(g)$

4. $Zn(s) + Ag^+(aq) \rightarrow Zn^{2+}(aq) + Ag(s)$

5. $NO_3^-(aq) + S(s) \rightarrow NO_2(g) + H_2SO_4(aq)$

6. $Br_2(l) + SO_3^{2-}(aq) \rightarrow Br^-(aq) + SO_4^{2-}(aq)$ (*basic*)

7. $Fe^{2+}(aq) + MnO_4^-(aq) \rightarrow Mn^{2+}(aq) + Fe^{3+}(aq)$

8. $Cu(s) + SO_4^{2-}(aq) \rightarrow Cu^{2+}(aq) + SO_2(g)$

9. $Cu(s) + NO_3^-(aq) \rightarrow Cu^{2+}(aq) + NO(g)$

10. $MnO_4^-(aq) + S^{2-}(aq) \rightarrow Mn^{2+}(aq) + S(s)$

11. $CuS(s) + NO_3^-(aq) \rightarrow Cu^{2+}(aq) + NO_2(g) + S(s)$

12. $NO_2(g) + ClO^-(aq) \rightarrow NO_3^-(aq) + Cl^-(aq)$ (*basic*)

13. $Fe^{2+}(aq) + Cr_2O_7^{2-}(aq) \rightarrow Fe^{3+}(aq) + Cr^{3+}(aq)$

14. $MnO_4^-(aq) + Cl^-(aq) \rightarrow Mn^{2+}(aq) + Cl_2(g)$

15. $IO_3^-(aq) + H_2S(g) \rightarrow I_2(g) + SO_3^{2-}(aq)$ (*basic*)

16. $H_2SeO_3(aq) + Br^-(aq) \rightarrow Se(s) + Br_2(g)$

17. $BrO_3^-(aq) + MnO_2(s) \rightarrow Br^-(aq) + MnO_4^-(aq)$ (*basic*)

18. $H_2S(g) + NO_3^-(aq) \rightarrow S(s) + NO(g)$

SECTION REVIEW

1. Give the oxidation number for the following.
   a. Te in TeO_2
   b. Cl in $HClO_2$
   c. N in N_2O
   d. P in PO_4^{3-}
   e. Sb in Sb_2O_5
   f. I in IO_3^-

Balance the following oxidation-reduction equations. All reactions take place in an acidic solution unless otherwise indicated.

2. $AsH_3(g) + ClO_3^-(aq) \rightarrow H_3AsO_4(aq) + Cl^-(aq)$

3. $HNO_2(aq) + I^-(aq) \rightarrow NO(g) + I_2(g)$

4. $MnO_4^-(aq) + H_2O_2(aq) \rightarrow Mn^{2+}(aq) + O_2(g)$

5. $MnO_2(s) + ClO_3^-(aq) \rightarrow MnO_4^-(aq) + Cl^-(aq)$ (basic)

6. $Br_2(l) \rightarrow Br^-(aq) + BrO_3^-(aq)$ (basic)

7. $N_2O_4(aq) + Br^-(aq) \rightarrow NO_2^-(aq) + BrO_3^-(aq)$ (basic)

8. $H_2PO_2^-(aq) + SbO_2^-(aq) \rightarrow HPO_3^{2-}(aq) + Sb(s)$ (basic)

9. $CrO_2^-(aq) + ClO^-(aq) \rightarrow CrO_4^{2-}(aq) + Cl^-(aq)$ (basic)

10. $Cu(OH)_2(s) + HPO_3^{2-}(aq) \rightarrow Cu_2O(s) + PO_4^{3-}(aq)$

11. $HS^-(aq) + IO_3^-(aq) \rightarrow I^-(aq) + S(s)$

12. $N_2O(g) + ClO^-(aq) \rightarrow Cl^-(aq) + NO_2^-(aq)$ (basic)

13. $H_2SO_3(aq) + MnO_2(s) \rightarrow SO_4^{2-}(aq) + Mn^{2+}(aq)$

14. $IO_4^-(aq) + I^-(aq) \rightarrow I_2(g)$

15. $CrO_4^{2-}(aq) + I^-(aq) \rightarrow Cr^{3+}(aq) + I_2(g)$

Electrochemistry

17.1 ELECTROLYSIS: CHEMISTRY FROM ELECTRICITY

REDUCTION POTENTIAL AND REACTION POTENTIAL

Redox reactions can be used to generate electricity or can be produced by electricity. The study of these electrochemical changes is called **electrochemistry**.

Oxidation is the loss of electrons. A substance that acquires electrons from other substances easily is called an oxidizing agent. It is an oxidizing agent because it causes other substances to be oxidized. By convention, a series of half-reactions, termed the standard reduction potential table, is set up with the best oxidizing agent at the bottom left position. (See **Table B-11** in Appendix B.) Each half-reaction has a characteristic reduction potential ($E°$) that is compared to a standard reference half-reaction.

$$2H^+(aq) + 2e^- \rightarrow H_2(g)$$

This reaction is assumed to have a reduction potential of 0.000 volt (V) at 25°C, 101.325 kPa pressure and 1 molar H^+. Fluorine, F_2, is at the bottom of the list because it shows the greatest tendency to acquire electrons and become the fluoride ion. The fluoride ion is a very weak reducing agent since F^- does not readily give up its electrons.

The lithium ion, Li^+, is a weak oxidizing agent, as it does not readily gain electrons. However, the lithium atom easily gives up electrons, so it is a strong reducing agent.

A large positive potential indicates a great tendency for the reaction to occur. Fluorine gas will proceed readily to fluoride ion, since the potential is +2.87 volts. For all practical purposes, fluoride ion will not go to fluorine gas. Lithium ion will not proceed spontaneously to lithium metal since the potential is negative, −3.04 volts.

The potentials given in **Table B-11** apply when the half-reaction takes place in the forward direction. In the reverse direction, the sign of the voltage is reversed. The E° values do not depend upon the number of electrons transferred.

Use the table to see if two half-reactions will react by adding the half-reaction potentials. It is necessary to balance the chemical quantities and the number of electrons, but no adjustment need be made in potential values. The potential is the ease with which certain electrons per atom or ion are lost. Potentials are dependent on temperature, pressure, and concentration. Keep in mind that the given potential applies to the forward reaction. For the reverse direction, the sign of the potential is reversed.

EXAMPLE

The following equation represents copper metal placed in a colorless silver ion solution.

$$Cu(s) + 2Ag^+(aq) \rightarrow Cu^{2+}(aq) + 2Ag(s)$$

Solving Process:
Write the half-reactions and obtain each voltage from the reduction potential table. Remember that the sign of the voltage may be reversed. Balance the electrons and add.

$$\begin{array}{ll} Cu \rightarrow Cu^{2+} + 2e^- & -0.340 \text{ V} \\ 2Ag^+ + 2e^- \rightarrow 2Ag & +0.7991 \text{ V} \\ \hline Cu + 2Ag^+ \rightarrow Cu^{2+} + 2Ag & +0.459 \text{ V} \end{array}$$

Since the voltage is positive, this reaction should occur spontaneously. Spontaneous does not mean instantaneous. A reaction occurs spontaneously when it occurs without additional energy such as heat or light. Note that the reverse reaction does not take place.

$$\begin{array}{ll} Cu^{2+} + 2e^- \rightarrow Cu & +0.340 \text{ V} \\ 2Ag \rightarrow 2Ag^+ + 2e^- & -0.7991 \text{ V} \\ \hline \text{No reaction} & -0.459 \text{ V} \end{array}$$

This reaction does not occur spontaneously since the voltage is negative.

PROBLEM

1. Calculate the potential in volts for each of the following reactions.
    a. $Cr(s) + Ni^{2+}(aq) \rightarrow Cr^{2+}(aq) + Ni(s)$
    b. $Al(s) + H^+(aq) \rightarrow Al^{3+}(aq) + H_2(g)$
    c. $Br_2(l) + I^-(aq) \rightarrow Br^-(aq) + I_2(s)$
    d. $Fe^{2+}(aq) + MnO_4^-(aq) \rightarrow Fe^{3+}(aq) + Mn^{2+}(aq)$
    e. $Cl_2(g) + Sn^{2+}(aq) \rightarrow Cl^-(aq) + Sn^{4+}(aq)$
    f. $Hg(l) + Hg^{2+}(aq) \rightarrow Hg_2^{2+}(aq)$

SECTION REVIEW

1. Calculate the positive or negative potential for each equation. Determine if the reactions will occur.
    a. $Ni(s) + Cu^{2+}(aq) \rightarrow Ni^{2+}(aq) + Cu(s)$
    b. $Cl^-(aq) + Br_2(l) \rightarrow Cl_2(g) + Br^-(aq)$
    c. $Cu(s) + H^+(aq) \rightarrow Cu^{2+}(aq) + H_2(g)$
    d. $Mn(s) + Co^{2+}(aq) \rightarrow Mn^{2+}(aq) + Co(s)$
    e. $Zn^{2+}(aq) + Pb(s) \rightarrow Zn(s) + Pb^{2+}(aq)$

17.2 GALVANIC CELLS: ELECTRICITY FROM CHEMISTRY

GALVANIC CELLS

Chemists refer to a battery as an electrochemical cell. It consists of electrodes in contact with an electrolyte. An electric current is produced when the two half-cells are physically separated but electrically connected and electrons move through an external circuit. This process occurs spontaneously in a **galvanic cell.** The galvanic cell is usually made of two half-cells connected by a salt bridge. The salt bridge completes the internal circuit by allowing ions to migrate between the cells. A porous ceramic cup can serve the same purpose as the salt bridge.

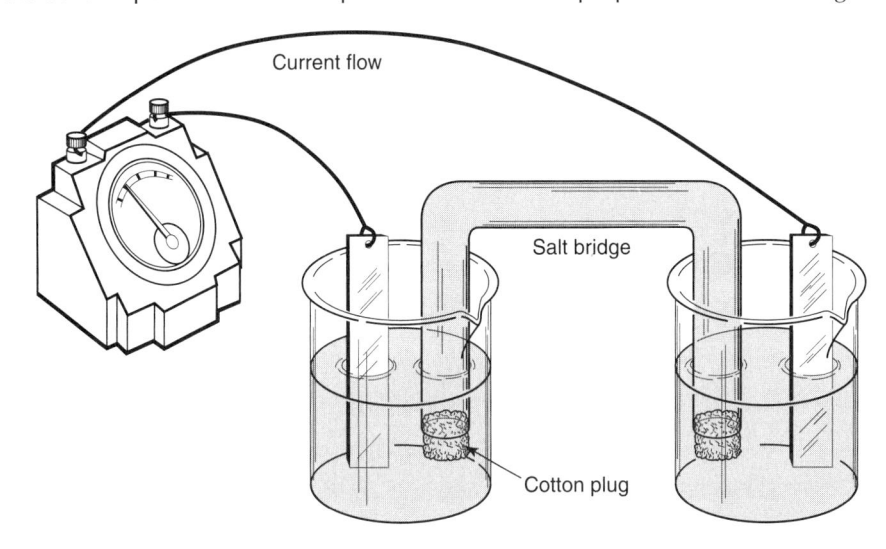

A convenient notation is used to represent a particular voltaic cell. The nickel-cadmium cell pictured above is represented by $Cd|Cd^{2+}||Ni^{2+}|Ni$. In this form the anode (oxidation half-cell) is written on the left. The cathode (reduction half-cell) is written on the right. The salt bridge connecting the two half-cells is represented by the two parallel vertical lines. The single line between Cd and Cd^{2+} represents the phase boundary between the solid Cd electrode and the solution (electrolyte).

EXAMPLE

Consider the following electrochemical cell.

$$Li|Li^+||Ag^+|Ag$$

Use **Table B-11** in Appendix B to help you analyze the cell.

Solving Process:
From **Table B-11** find the two reduction half-reactions, and their E° value.

$$Li^+ + e^- \rightarrow Li, \;-3.040 \text{ V}$$

$$Ag^+ + e^- \rightarrow Ag, \;+0.7991 \text{ V}$$

The lower positive voltage indicates which half-reaction is written in reverse order. The sign on the voltage is also changed. The oxidation half-reaction is

$$Li \rightarrow Li^+ + e^-, \quad +3.040 \text{ V}$$

This reaction occurs at the anode. Here the Li electrode loses both electrons and mass as it dissolves to form the Li^+ cation. Lithium metal is the reducing agent. The electrons leave the Li electrode and travel through the external circuit to the Ag electrode.

The reduction half-reaction is

$$Ag^+ + e^- \rightarrow Ag, \quad +0.7991 \text{ V}$$

This reaction occurs at the cathode. The cathode gains both electrons and mass. The silver cations migrate to the cathode, gain an electron, and plate out as silver metal. The Ag^+ is the oxidizing agent. The theoretical voltage on the meter would be

$$3.040 \text{ V} + 0.7991 \text{ V} = +3.839 \text{ V}$$

PROBLEMS

Use **Table B-11** to help you answer the following questions.

1. Refer to the electrochemical cell below to answer each of the following questions.

    $$Zn|Zn^{2+}||Pb^{2+}|Pb$$

    a. At which electrode does oxidation occur?
    b. Which electrode is the cathode?
    c. Electrons will flow from which electrode?
    d. Which electrode will gain in mass?
    e. What is the oxidizing agent?
    f. Write the half-reaction for the zinc half-cell.
    g. What is the theoretical voltage on the meter?

2. Refer to the electrochemical cell below to answer each of the following questions.

    $$Al|Al^{3+}||Au^{3+}|Au$$

    a. At which electrode does reduction occur?
    b. Which electrode is the anode?
    c. Which electrode will lose in mass?
    d. To which electrode will the cations migrate?
    e. What is the reducing agent?
    f. Write the half-reaction for the gold half-cell.
    g. What is the theoretical voltage on the meter?

FARADAY'S LAWS

Electrochemistry is the study of the relationship between chemical change and electric energy. Michael Faraday experimented extensively to determine the relationship between electric charge and chemical energy. The following statements are known as Faraday's laws.

1. The mass of an element released at the electrode during electrolysis varies directly as the quantity of electricity that is passed through a solution.

2. The quantity of different elements that can be deposited by the same amount of electricity depends on the equivalent masses of these elements. Chemists measure the quantity of electrons in moles. Electricity is measured in coulombs (C). One coulomb is the quantity of electricity in one ampere (A) flowing for one second. The relationship of all these quantities is

$$1 \text{ mole } e^- = 96\,500 \text{ coulomb} = 1 \text{ ampere} \cdot \text{second}$$

Thus 96 500 coulombs passing through molten Al_2O_3 will liberate 1/3 of an equivalent mass of aluminum (27.0 g) and 1/2 of an equivalent mass of oxygen (16.0 g).

$$96\,500 \text{ C} = 9.0 \text{ g Al} = 1/3 \text{ mol Al} = 6.02 \times 10^{23} \, e^-$$
$$96\,500 \text{ C} = 8.0 \text{ g O} = 1/2 \text{ mol O} = 6.02 \times 10^{23} \, e^-$$

EXAMPLE

How many grams of aluminum will be deposited if 31 500 coulombs of electricity pass through an aluminum nitrate solution?

Solving Process:
Begin with the balanced equation for the reaction.

$$Al^{3+} + 3e^- \rightarrow Al$$

Convert coulombs to moles of electrons, to moles, to grams.

$$\text{grams Al} = \frac{31\,500 \text{ C}}{} \cdot \frac{1 \text{ mol } e^-}{96\,500 \text{ C}} \cdot \frac{1 \text{ mol Al}}{3 \text{ mol } e^-} \cdot \frac{27.0 \text{ g Al}}{1 \text{ mol Al}} = 2.94 \text{ g}$$

EXAMPLE

If 10.0 amperes of current flow for 20.0 minutes through a solution of copper(II) nitrate, how many moles of copper are deposited?

Solving Process:

$$Cu^{2+} + 2e^- \rightarrow Cu$$

$$\text{mol Cu} = \frac{10.0 \text{ A}}{} \cdot \frac{20.0 \text{ min}}{} \cdot \frac{60 \text{ s}}{1 \text{ min}} \cdot \frac{1 \text{ C}}{A \cdot s} \cdot \frac{1 \text{ mol } e^-}{96\,500 \text{ C}} \cdot \frac{1 \text{ mol Cu}}{2 \text{ mol } e^-}$$

$$= 0.0622 \text{ mol Cu}$$

EXAMPLE

Calculate the mass of silver metal that can be deposited if a 5.12 A current is passed through a silver nitrate solution for 2.00 hours. The equation for the reaction is $Ag^+ + e^- \rightarrow Ag$.

Solving Process:
Obtain ampere · seconds by converting hours to seconds and multiplying by the number of amperes given. Convert ampere · seconds to coulombs. Finally change to moles of electrons, to moles, to grams.

$$\text{grams Ag} = \frac{5.12 \text{ A}}{} \left| \frac{2.00 \text{ h}}{1 \text{ h}} \right| \frac{60 \text{ min}}{1 \text{ min}} \left| \frac{60 \text{ s}}{} \right| \frac{1 \text{ C}}{A \cdot s} \cdots$$

$$\frac{1 \text{ mol } e^-}{96\,500 \text{ C}} \left| \frac{1 \text{ mol Ag}}{1 \text{ mol } e^-} \right| \frac{108 \text{ g Ag}}{1 \text{ mol Ag}} = 41.3 \text{ g}$$

EXAMPLE

How many liters of chlorine gas measured at STP are released by the passage of 8.12 amperes for 2.00 hours through molten magnesium chloride?

Solving Process:
The equation would be $2Cl^- \rightarrow Cl_2 + 2e^-$.

$$\text{volume Cl}_2 = \frac{8.12 \text{ A}}{} \left| \frac{2.00 \text{ h}}{1 \text{ h}} \right| \frac{60 \text{ min}}{1 \text{ min}} \left| \frac{60 \text{ s}}{} \right| \frac{1 \text{ C}}{A \cdot s} \cdots$$

$$\frac{1 \text{ mol } e^-}{96\,500 \text{ C}} \left| \frac{1 \text{ mol Cl}_2}{2 \text{ mol } e^-} \right| \frac{22.4 \text{ L Cl}_2}{1 \text{ mol Cl}_2} = 6.79 \text{ L Cl}_2$$

PROBLEMS

3. How many seconds are required to deposit 2.51 g Fe on an object using 15.4 A of current passing through an iron(III) nitrate solution? The equation for the reaction is $Fe^{3+} + 3e^- \rightarrow Fe$.

4. How many amperes are required to deposit 0.504 g Fe in 40.0 minutes by passing a current through a solution of iron(II) acetate?

5. Calculate the current required to liberate 5.60 L Cl_2 at STP in 2.00 hours in the electrolysis of molten NaCl.

6. During the operation of a lead storage battery, the reaction at the two electrodes is as follows.

$$\text{cathode} \quad PbO_2 + 4H^+ + SO_4^{2-} + 2e^- \rightarrow PbSO_4 + 2H_2O$$
$$\text{anode} \quad Pb + SO_4^{2-} \rightarrow PbSO_4 + 2e^-$$

How much PbO_2 (in grams) is used when a current of 50.0 A in 1 hour is withdrawn from the battery?

SECTION REVIEW

1. Determine the theoretical voltage for the following electrochemical cell.

   $Mn|Mn^{2+}||Fe^{2+}|Fe$

2. Write the half-reaction that occurs at the anode in the following electrochemical cell.

   $Cr|Cr^{2+}||Sn^{2+}|Sn$

3. How many moles of electrons are required to produce a 5.00 A current for 2.00 hours?

4. If 3.00 moles of electrons are required in producing 10.0 A of current, how many seconds are required?

5. What mass of copper is produced if 10 000.0 A · s pass through a copper(II) nitrate solution?

6. Calculate the grams of zinc deposited if 5.00 moles of electrons pass through a zinc acetate solution.

7. Using 2.50 moles of electrons how many grams of cadmium metal will be deposited from a cadmium sulfate solution?

8. If 193 000 coulombs of electricity pass through a silver nitrate solution, how many grams of silver metal are produced?

9. In the electrolysis of molten NaCl, how many moles of sodium metal are produced if 20.0 A of current flowing for 8.00 hours are used?

10. If it is necessary to deposit 1.50 g Ag on an object, how many seconds must 5.00 A of electricity flow through a solution of silver nitrate?

11. How many amperes of electricity flowing for 30.0 minutes are required to deposit 0.250 g Fe from an iron(III) nitrate solution?

Chemistry: Concepts and Applications   Supplemental Practice Problems, Chapter 17

Organic Chemistry 18

18.1 HYDROCARBONS

HYDROCARBONS

Organic compounds are compounds that contain carbon atoms linked together in chains or rings. **Hydrocarbons** are compounds that contain carbon and hydrogen. They are the simplest organic compounds. Hydrocarbons may be grouped into families. In some of these families, all the carbon-carbon bonds are single bonds. These compounds are said to be **saturated.** In other families, the compounds contain double or triple bonds and are **unsaturated.**

ALKANES

Alkanes are saturated hydrocarbons conforming to the general formula C_nH_{2n+2}, where n is a whole number equal to the number of carbon atoms. The alkane series is also termed the methane or paraffin series. The simplest alkanes are as follows.

CH_4 methane

CH_3CH_3 ethane

$CH_3CH_2CH_3$ propane

The first formula is a condensed structural formula. The second formula is an expanded structural formula.

Table 18-1 lists the stem name for each number of carbon atoms in a continuous chain or ring. It also gives some information about the alkanes of low molecular mass.

TABLE 18-1
Alkanes

Stem Name	Alkane Name	Condensed Structural Formula (unbranched)	Chemical Formula	Number of Isomers
meth-	methane	CH_4	CH_4	1
eth-	ethane	CH_3CH_3	C_2H_6	1
prop-	propane	$CH_3CH_2CH_3$	C_3H_8	1
but-	butane	$CH_3(CH_2)_2CH_3$	C_4H_{10}	2
pent-	pentane	$CH_3(CH_2)_3CH_3$	C_5H_{12}	3
hex-	hexane	$CH_3(CH_2)_4CH_3$	C_6H_{14}	5
hept-	heptane	$CH_3(CH_2)_5CH_3$	C_7H_{16}	9
oct-	octane	$CH_3(CH_2)_6CH_3$	C_8H_{18}	18
non-	nonane	$CH_3(CH_2)_7CH_3$	C_9H_{20}	35
dec-	decane	$CH_3(CH_2)_8CH_3$	$C_{10}H_{22}$	75

With C_4H_{10}, the carbon atoms may be connected to give two different structural formulas. These two arrangements are **isomers.** Isomers have the same chemical formula but different structural formulas.

RULES FOR NAMING HYDROCARBONS

The following rules are used to name hydrocarbons.

1. Pick the longest continuous chain of carbon atoms and determine its name.

2. Number the carbon atoms in the chain beginning at the end closest to a branch. In straight-chain hydrocarbons, the numbering can begin at either end.

3. Name the hydrocarbon groups attached to the longest chain by adding -yl to the stem name. Indicate the point of attachment by the number of the carbon atoms to which the group is attached. Common group names are meth*yl*, —CH_3, and eth*yl*, —CH_2CH_3.

For example, consider the following compound.

$$CH_3-CH-CH_2-CH_2-CH_3$$
$$|$$
$$CH_2$$
$$|$$
$$CH_3$$

The longest chain, which consists of six carbon atoms, is enclosed in a box. A chain of six carbon atoms is termed *hexane*. The carbon atoms in the longest chain are numbered in such a way as to give the lowest number possible to the attached group. At position 3 the attached group is termed *methyl*. The name of the compound is 3-methylhexane. Note that position numbers are separated from the name by hyphens.

The C_4H_{10} isomers we discussed previously are named butane and 2-methylpropane. The following are the isomers of pentane.

$CH_3CH_2CH_2CH_2CH_3$ $CH_3CHCH_2CH_3$ with CH_3 branch CH_3CCH_3 with two CH_3 branches

pentane   2-methylbutane   2,2-dimethylpropane

Note that the position numbers are separated from each other by commas. The following are the isomers of hexane.

$CH_3CH_2CH_2CH_2CH_2CH_3$ $CH_3CHCH_2CH_2CH_3$ with CH_3 branch $CH_3CH_2CHCH_2CH_3$ with CH_3 branch

hexane   2-methylpentane   3-methylpentane

$CH_3CH-CHCH_3$ with two CH_3 branches $CH_3CCH_2CH_3$ with two CH_3 branches

2,3-dimethylbutane   2,2-dimethylbutane

4. When two or more groups are attached to a compound, the groups are named in alphabetical order. Consider the following example.

$$CH_3-CH-CH-CH_2-CH-CH_2-CH_3$$
with CH_3 branches at positions 2 and 5, and a CH_2CH_3 (ethyl) branch at position 3

3-ethyl-2,5-dimethylheptane

The longest continuous chain of carbon atoms is named heptane. The branched groups are ethyl and methyl. Since there are two methyl groups the prefix *di-* is used to indicate this number.

Chemistry: Concepts and Applications   Supplemental Practice Problems, Chapter 18   **141**

PROBLEMS

1. Name the following hydrocarbons.

a.
$$CH_3-CH_2-\underset{\underset{\underset{CH_3}{|}}{\underset{CH_2}{|}}}{CH}-\underset{\underset{CH_3}{|}}{CH}-CH_3$$

b.
$$CH_3-\underset{\underset{CH_3}{|}}{\overset{\overset{CH_3}{|}}{C}}-\underset{\overset{CH_3}{|}}{CH}-CH_3$$ with CH_2 on top right carbon

c.
$$CH_3-\underset{\underset{CH_2}{|}}{\overset{\overset{CH_3}{|}}{C}}-CH_3$$
with CH_3 below CH_2

d.
$$CH_3-CH_2-\underset{\underset{CH_2-CH_3}{|}}{\overset{\overset{CH_2-CH_2-CH_3}{|}}{C}}-CH_2-CH_3$$

e.
$$CH_3-\underset{\underset{}{}}{\overset{\overset{CH_3}{|}}{CH}}-\underset{\underset{CH_3}{|}}{CH}-\underset{\overset{CH_2}{|} \overset{|}{CH_3}}{CH}-CH_3$$

f.
$$CH_3-CH_2-\underset{\overset{CH_3}{|}}{CH}-\underset{}{CH}-\underset{\overset{CH_2}{|} \overset{|}{CH_3}}{CH}-CH_3$$
with CH_3 below middle CH

g.
$$CH_3-\underset{}{CH}-\underset{\underset{CH-CH_2-CH_3}{|}}{CH}-CH_3$$ with CH_2 / CH_3 chain on top and CH_3 branch

h.
$$CH_3-\underset{\underset{CH_3-CH-CH_3}{|}}{CH}-\underset{\overset{CH_2-CH_3}{|}}{CH}-CH_3$$

2. Name the following hydrocarbons.

a.
$$CH_3CH_2CH_2\underset{\overset{CH_3}{|}}{CH}CH_3$$

b.
$$CH_3\underset{\overset{CH_3}{|}}{CH}CH_2CH_3$$

c.
$$CH_3\underset{\underset{CH_2CH_3}{|}}{\overset{\overset{CH_3}{|}}{CH}}CHCH_3$$

d.
$$CH_3CH_2\underset{\underset{CH_3}{|}\underset{}{}}{\overset{\overset{}{}}{CH}}CH_2CH_3$$ with CH_2–CH_3 branch

e.
$$CH_3\underset{\overset{CH_3}{|}}{CH}CH_2\underset{\overset{CH_3}{|}}{CH}CH_3$$

f.
$$\text{CH}_3\text{CHCHCH}_2\text{CH}_3$$
with CH₃ above middle C and CH₃ below the adjacent C

f.
```
        CH₃
         |
CH₃CHCHCH₂CH₃
       |
       CH₃
```

g. CH₃CHCH₂CH₃
         |
         CH₂
         |
         CH₃

h.
```
        CH₃
         |
         CH₂
         |
CH₃CHCHCH₃
       |
       CH₃
```

3. Listed below are the condensed structural formulas or names of the nine isomers of heptane, C₇H₁₆. Write either the formula or name for each.

   a. CH₃CH₂CH₂CH₂CH₂CH₂CH₃

   b.
   ```
      CH₃   CH₃
       |     |
   CH₃CHCH₂CHCH₃
   ```

   c.
   ```
      CH₃  CH₃
       |    |
   CH₃C────CHCH₃
       |
      CH₃
   ```

   d. 2,3-dimethylpentane

   e. 3,3-dimethylpentane

   f.
   ```
              CH₃
               |
   CH₃CH₂CHCH₂CH₂CH₃
   ```

   g.
   ```
         CH₃
          |
   CH₃CCH₂CH₂CH₃
          |
         CH₃
   ```

   h. 2-methylhexane

   i. 3-ethylpentane

CYCLOALKANES

The cycloalkanes are saturated ring compounds having the general formula C_nH_{2n}. The following are some examples of cycloalkanes.

C₃H₆
cyclopropane

CH₂—CH₂
    \ /
    CH₂

C₅H₁₀
methylclobutane

```
CH₂—CH—CH₃
 |      |
CH₂—CH₂
```

C₄H₈
cyclobutane

```
CH₂—CH₂
 |    |
CH₂—CH₂
```

C₄H₈
methylcyclopropane

```
      CH₃
       |
       CH
      / \
   CH₂—CH₂
```

C₅H₁₀
cyclopentane

```
      CH₂
     /   \
   CH₂   CH₂
    |     |
   CH₂—CH₂
```

C₅H₁₀
1,1-dimethylcyclopropane

```
CH₂—CH₂
   \ /
    C
   / \
 CH₃  CH₃
```

ISOMERS

Recall, when two or more substances have the same molecular formula, but different molecular structures, they are called **isomers.** There are different classifications of isomers.

Structural isomers have a different molecular skeleton because the carbon chain is different. For example, pentane and 2,2-dimethylpropane are structural isomers.

$$CH_3-CH_2-CH_2-CH_2-CH_3$$
pentane

$$CH_3-\underset{\underset{CH_3}{|}}{\overset{\overset{CH_3}{|}}{C}}-CH_2$$
$$CH_3$$
2,2-dimethylpropane

Geometric isomers are composed of the same atoms bonded in the same order, but with a different arrangement of atoms around a double bond. As when two nails hold a piece of wood, there can be no free rotation about a double bond. Because of this lack of rotation, the positions above and below the plane of the double bond are different. When like groups are on the same side of a double bond, *cis* precedes the name. When the like groups are on opposite sides of the double bond, *trans* is used in the name.

cis-2-butene   trans-2-butene

Positional isomers form when another element, such as oxygen, may occupy two or more positions in the molecule. The —OH group when attached to a hydrocarbon chain forms an alcohol. It can be found in different positions.

$$CH_3-CH_2-CH_2-OH \qquad CH_3-\underset{}{\overset{\overset{OH}{|}}{CH}}-CH_3$$
1-propanol   2-propanol

Functional isomers form when another element, such as oxygen, may bond in two or more different ways. Ethanol is a liquid alcohol. Methoxymethane is an ether and is a gas at room temperature. Both have the molecular formula C_2H_6O.

$$CH_3-CH_2-OH \qquad CH_3-O-CH_3$$
ethanol   methoxymethane

ALKENES

Alkenes are unsaturated compounds containing one double bond and having the general formula C_nH_{2n}. The -ene ending indicates a double bond. The position of the double bond is indicated by using the lower number of the two carbon atoms that the double bond joins. In compounds containing branched groups, the numbering of the double bond takes precedence. Note the following examples.

$$CH_2=CH_2 \qquad CH_3CH=CH_2 \qquad CH_3CH=CHCH_3$$
$$\text{ethene} \qquad\qquad \text{propene} \qquad\qquad \text{2-butene}$$

$$\underset{\text{2-methyl-1-butene}}{CH_3CH_2\overset{\overset{\displaystyle CH_3}{|}}{C}=CH_2} \qquad \underset{\text{3-methyl-1-butene}}{CH_3\overset{\overset{\displaystyle CH_3CHCH=CH_2}{|}}{} \; }$$

If a compound contains more than one double bond, the numbers of double bonds are noted with a Greek prefix preceding the -ene ending. For example,

$$CH_2=CHCH_2CH=CH_2 \qquad CH_2=CHCH=CH_2 \qquad CH_2=C=CHCH_2CH_3$$
$$\text{1,4-pentadiene} \qquad\qquad \text{1,3-butadiene} \qquad\qquad \text{1,2-pentadiene}$$

ALKYNES

Alkynes contain a triple bond and have the general formula C_nH_{2n-2}. They are named by replacing the -ane of the corresponding saturated hydrocarbon with -yne, except for the first compound in the series, for which the common name is used.

$$HC\equiv CH \qquad CH_3-C\equiv C-CH_3$$
$$\text{acetylene} \qquad\qquad \text{2-butyne}$$
$$\text{(ethyne)}$$

TABLE 18-2
Hydrocarbon Summary

Family	Formula	Prefix or Suffix	Type of Compound
alkanes	C_nH_{2n+2}	-ane	single bonds, saturated
cycloalkanes	C_nH_{2n}	cyclo-	ring structure, saturated
alkenes	C_nH_{2n}	-ene	double bond, unsaturated
alkynes	C_nH_{2n-2}	-yne	triple bond, unsaturated

AROMATIC HYDROCARBONS

All aromatic hydrocarbons contain one or more flat rings of carbon atoms. The compounds are named as derivatives of basic ring systems. Consider the ring structure of benzene.

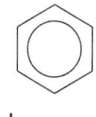

benzene

Chemistry: Concepts and Applications

All positions on the benzene ring are equivalent. Thus, only one monosubstituted compound is possible. The following are examples of monosubstituted aromatic hydrocarbons.

methylbenzene (toluene)   ethylbenzene   propylbenzene

For two substituents on the benzene ring three positions are possible. These positions may be designated by numbers or names, although the use of numbers is more correct.

position number	name
1,2	ortho- (o-)
1,3	meta- (m-)
1,4	para- (p-)

Disubstituted aromatic hydrocarbons include the following.

1,2-dimethylbenzene
(*ortho*-dimethylbenzene)

1,3-dimethylbenzene
(*meta*-dimethylbenzene)

1,4-dimethylbenzene
(*para*-dimethylbenzene)

Thousands of compounds are derived from benzene or other ring systems. These other rings may be considered to be fused benzene rings. Two examples of fused rings are naphthalene, $C_{10}H_8$, and anthracene, $C_{14}H_{10}$.

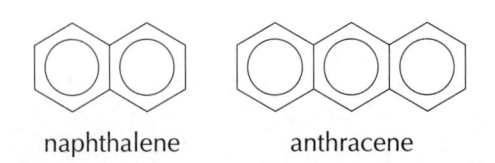

naphthalene   anthracene

The radical —C₆H₅, which is the benzene ring with one less hydrogen, is termed the **phenyl radical.** Note the following examples.

phenyl radical   ethylbenzene (phenylethane)   2-phenylbutane

2-acetyloxybenzoic acid (acetylsalicyclic acid or aspirin)   styrene

2,4,6-trinitrotoluene (TNT)   dichlorodiphenyltrichloroethane (DDT)

PROBLEMS

4. Name the compounds represented by the following formulas.
   a. CH₃CH=CHCH₂CH₃
   b. [benzene ring with two CH₃ groups]
   c. [cyclohexane]
   d. [benzene ring with —C≡CH]
   e. [cyclobutene]
   f. CH≡CCH₃

5. Draw the structural formulas for the following:
   a. 3-heptyne
   b. cyclopentene
   c. 3-phenyl-2,2-dimethylhexane
   d. 1,3-butadiene
   e. 1-ethyl-2-methylbenzene
   f. 2,4-dimethyl-2-pentene

SECTION REVIEW

1. Write structural formulas for the following compounds.
   a. 2-butene
   b. 1,8-nonadiyne
   c. 3-methyl-2-pentene
   d. 2-phenylbutane
   e. propene
   f. 2-pentyne

2. Define isomerism.

3. Draw three structural isomers of C_6H_{14} that have only single bonds.

4. Identify which molecule is the *cis* and which is the *trans* geometric isomer.

   a. 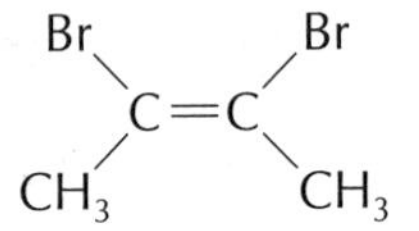
   $$\begin{array}{c} Br \\ \\ CH_3 \end{array} C=C \begin{array}{c} Br \\ \\ CH_3 \end{array}$$

   b. 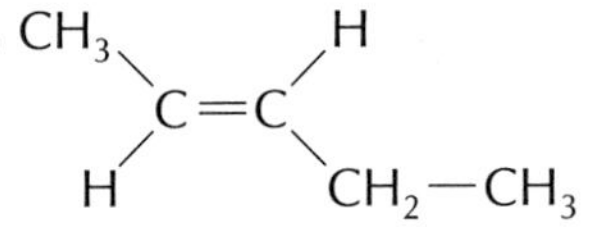
   $$\begin{array}{c} CH_3 \\ \\ H \end{array} C=C \begin{array}{c} H \\ \\ CH_2-CH_3 \end{array}$$

5. Identify the following pair of molecules as positional isomers or functional isomers.
   a. $CH_3-CH_2-CH_2-OH \quad CH_3-CH_2-O-CH_3$
   b. $CH_3-CH_2-CH_2-CH_2-NH_2 \quad CH_3-CH_2-CH(NH_2)-CH_3$

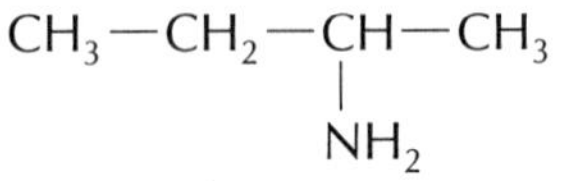

18.2 SUBSTITUTED HYDROCARBONS

HALOGENATED COMPOUNDS

By replacing a hydrogen atom with a halogen atom (—F, *fluoro;* —Cl, *chloro;* —Br, *bromo;* and —I, *iodo*) on a hydrocarbon, additional isomers are possible. When naming these alkyl halides, the longest chain must contain the halogen-bearing carbon that is given the lowest possible number. For example,

$CH_3CH_2CH_2Cl$
1-chloropropane

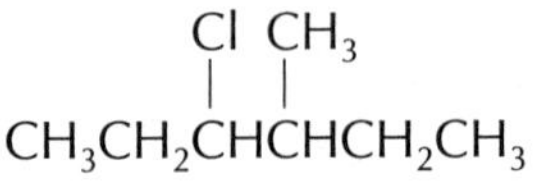

$CH_3CH_2CHClCH(CH_3)CH_2CH_3$
3-chloro-4-methylhexane

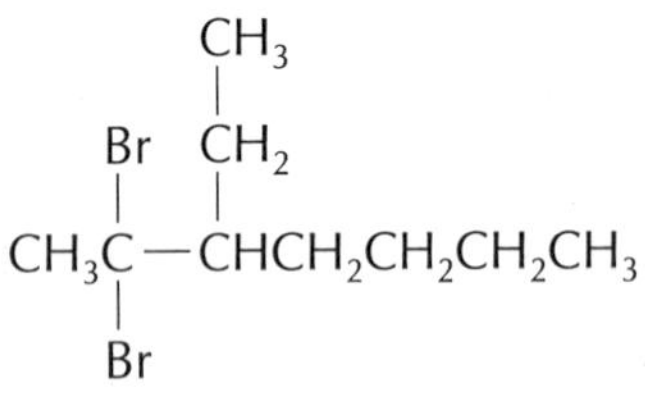

2,2-dibromo-3-ethylheptane

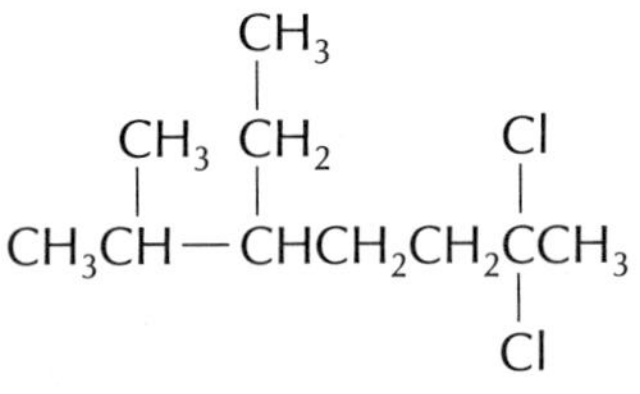

2,2-dichloro-5-ethyl-6-methylheptane

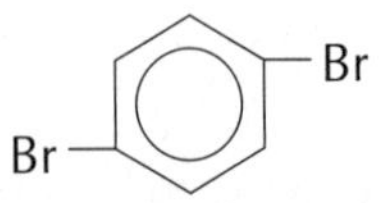

1,4-dibromobenzene

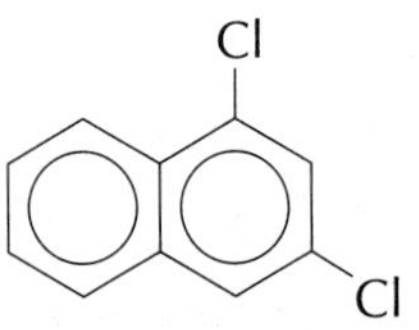

1,3-dichloronaphthalene

PROBLEMS

1. Listed below are the condensed structural formulas or the names of the eight isomers of C$_5$H$_{11}$Cl. Write either the formula or the name for each.

   a. CH$_3$CH$_2$CH$_2$CH$_2$CH$_2$Cl

   b. $\quad\;\;$ CH$_3$
      $\quad\;\;$ |
      CH$_3$CHCH$_2$CH$_2$Cl

   c. 2-chloropentane

   d. 2-chloro-2-methylbutane

   e. $\quad\quad\;\;$ Cl
      $\quad\quad\;\;$ |
      CH$_3$CH$_2$CHCH$_2$CH$_3$

   f. $\quad\;$ CH$_3$ $\;$ Cl
      $\quad\;$ | $\quad\;\;$ |
      CH$_3$CH—CHCH$_3$

   g. 1-chloro-2-methylbutane

   h. 1-chloro-2,2-dimethylpropane

2. Name the following compounds.

   a. $\quad\quad\;\;$ CH$_3$
      $\quad\quad\;\;$ |
      CH$_3$CH$_2$CCH$_2$CH$_2$Br
      $\quad\quad\;\;$ |
      $\quad\quad\;\;$ CH$_2$
      $\quad\quad\;\;$ |
      $\quad\quad\;\;$ CH$_3$

   b. $\quad\quad\;\;$ CH$_3$
      $\quad\quad\;\;$ |
      CH$_2$=CHCHCH=CH$_2$

   c. $\quad\quad\;\;$ CH$_3$
      $\quad\quad\;\;$ |
      CH$_2$=CHCCH$_3$
      $\quad\quad\;\;$ |
      $\quad\quad\;\;$ CH$_3$

   d. C$_6$H$_5$Cl

   e. CH$_3$CH=CHCH$_2$CH$_3$

   f. $\quad\;\;$ CH$_3$
      $\quad\;\;$ |
      CH$_3$C=CHCH$_3$

   g. CH$_3$CH$_2$CH=CH$_2$

   h. $\quad\quad\;\;$ CH$_3$
      $\quad\quad\;\;$ |
      CH$_3$CHCH=CHCH$_3$

   i. $\quad\;\;$ CH$_3$ $\;\;$ CH$_3$
      $\quad\;\;$ | $\quad\quad$ |
      CH$_3$C=CCH$_2$CH$_3$

   j. $\quad\quad\;\;$ CH$_3$ $\;\;$ CH$_3$
      $\quad\quad\;\;$ | $\quad\quad$ |
      CH$_2$=CCH$_2$C=CH$_2$

   k. $\quad\quad\;\;$ CH$_3$ $\;\;$ CH$_3$
      $\quad\quad\;\;$ | $\quad\quad$ |
      CH$_2$=C—C—CH=CHCH$_3$
      $\quad\quad\quad\quad\;\;$ |
      $\quad\quad\quad\quad\;\;$ CH$_3$

   l. (naphthalene with Br at positions 1 and 4)

3. Draw structural formulas for the following.

   a. 3-heptene
   b. 2-methylnaphthalene
   c. trichloromethane
   d. 2-chloro-3-phenylhexane
   e. 1,3-cyclopentadiene
   f. toluene (methylbenzene)
   g. 1,4-dibromobenzene
   h. 2-bromo-3-methyl-2-butene

ALCOHOLS

The alcohols, or hydroxy compounds, have a **hydroxyl group,** —OH, attached to the alkyl group. They are named by dropping the -e of the alkane series and adding -ol. If the hydroxyl group is attached to an aromatic group, the compound is called a **phenol.** Consider the following examples.

$$\text{CH}_3\text{OH} \quad \text{CH}_3\text{CH}_2\text{OH} \quad \text{CH}_3\text{CH}_2\text{CH}_2\text{OH}$$
methanol ethanol 1-propanol

$$\underset{\text{2-propanol}}{\text{CH}_3\underset{\underset{\text{OH}}{|}}{\text{CH}}\text{CH}_3} \quad \underset{\text{1-butanol}}{\text{CH}_3\text{CH}_2\text{CH}_2\text{CH}_2\text{OH}} \quad \underset{\text{2-butanol}}{\text{CH}_3\underset{\underset{\text{OH}}{|}}{\text{CH}}\text{CH}_2\text{CH}_3}$$

$$\underset{\text{2-methyl-1-propanol}}{\text{CH}_3\underset{\underset{\text{CH}_3}{|}}{\text{CH}}\text{CH}_2\text{OH}} \quad \underset{\text{2-methyl-2-propanol}}{\text{CH}_3\underset{\underset{\text{OH}}{|}}{\overset{\overset{\text{CH}_3}{|}}{\text{C}}}\text{CH}_3}$$

CARBOXYLIC ACIDS

All organic acids have the functional group

$$-\text{C}\underset{\text{OH}}{\overset{\text{O}}{\diagup\hspace{-0.5em}\diagdown}}$$

which is called the **carboxyl group.** The carboxylic acid group is usually written as —COOH. The carbon of this group is considered the first carbon of the chain in naming compounds. The -e in the chain name is dropped and -oic plus the word *acid* is added. The common names are given in parenthesis.

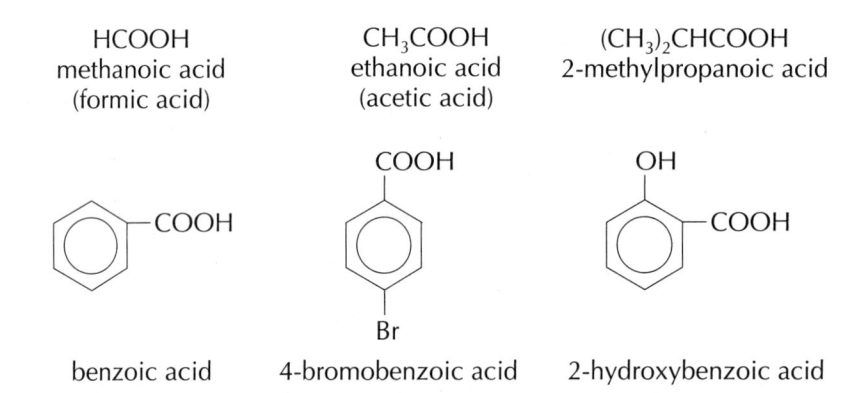

HCOOH   CH₃COOH   (CH₃)₂CHCOOH
methanoic acid   ethanoic acid   2-methylpropanoic acid
(formic acid)   (acetic acid)

benzoic acid   4-bromobenzoic acid   2-hydroxybenzoic acid

ESTERS

Esters contain the group

$$-\overset{\overset{\text{O}}{\|}}{\text{C}}-\text{O}-$$

and are formed from organic acids. The *-ic* of the acid name is dropped and the ending *-ate* is added. The alkyl group replacing the hydrogen atom in the carboxyl group is named first as a separate word.

$$\underset{\text{ethyl propanoate}}{CH_3CH_2\overset{\overset{O}{\|}}{C}-OCH_2CH_3} \qquad \underset{\text{ethyl 2-methylpropanoate}}{CH_3\overset{\overset{CH_3}{|}}{CH}-\overset{\overset{O}{\|}}{C}-OCH_2CH_3}$$

$$\underset{\text{2-methylethyl propanoate}}{CH_3CH_2\overset{\overset{O}{\|}}{C}-O\overset{\overset{CH_3}{|}}{C}HCH_3} \qquad \underset{\text{methyl benzoate}}{C_6H_5-\overset{\overset{O}{\|}}{C}-OCH_3}$$

ETHERS

Ethers have the general formula R—O—R′ in which an oxygen atom is joined to two separate hydrocarbon groups. Ethers are named as *oxy-* derivatives of hydrocarbons.

$$\underset{\text{methoxyethane}}{CH_3-O-CH_2CH_3} \qquad \underset{\text{1-ethoxypropane}}{CH_3CH_2CH_2-O-CH_2CH_3} \qquad \underset{\text{methoxybenzene}}{CH_3-O-C_6H_5}$$

KETONES

Ketones contain the functional group

$$\overset{\diagdown}{\underset{\diagup}{C}}=O$$

These compounds have the ending *-one*. The functional group is given the lowest possible number.

$$\underset{\substack{\text{propanone}\\\text{(acetone)}}}{CH_3\overset{\overset{O}{\|}}{C}CH_3} \qquad \underset{\text{2-butanone}}{CH_3CH_2\overset{\overset{O}{\|}}{C}CH_3} \qquad \underset{\text{3-pentanone}}{CH_3CH_2\overset{\overset{O}{\|}}{C}CH_2CH_3}$$

$$\underset{\text{2-pentanone}}{CH_3\overset{\overset{O}{\|}}{C}CH_2CH_2CH_3} \qquad \underset{\text{3-methyl-2-butanone}}{CH_3\overset{\overset{O}{\|}}{C}\overset{\overset{}{|}}{\underset{\underset{CH_3}{|}}{C}}HCH_3} \qquad \underset{\text{1-phenylethanone}}{C_6H_5-\overset{\overset{O}{\|}}{C}-CH_3}$$

$$\underset{\text{diphenylmethanone}}{C_6H_5-\overset{\overset{O}{\|}}{C}-C_6H_5}$$

ALDEHYDES

The functional group characteristic of aldehydes is

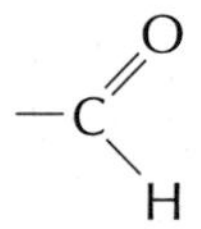

$$-C\overset{\displaystyle O}{\underset{\displaystyle H}{}}$$

These compounds are named by dropping the -e and adding -al to the chain name. The aldehyde carbon is given the number 1 in naming.

HCHO
methanal
(formaldehyde)

CH₃CHO
ethanal

CH₃CH₂CHO
propanal

CH₃CH₂CH₂CHO
butanal

(CH₃)₂CHCHO
2-methylpropanal

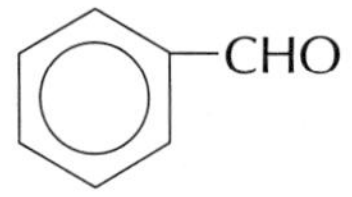

C₆H₅—CHO
benzaldehyde

TABLE 18-3

Organic Compounds Containing Oxygen

Compound	General Formula*	Characteristic Group	Ending
Alcohol	R—OH	—OH	-ol
Carboxylic Acid	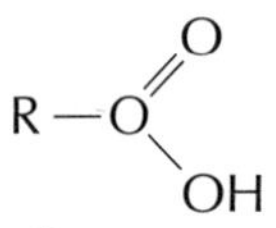 R—C(=O)OH	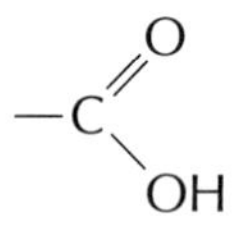 —C(=O)OH	-oic acid
Aldehyde	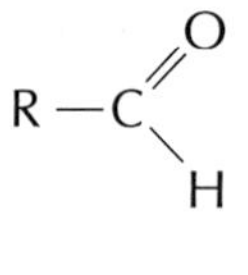 R—C(=O)H	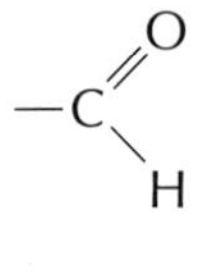 —C(=O)H	-al
Ketone	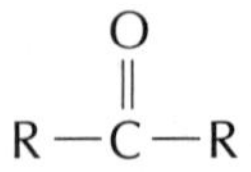 R—C(=O)—R	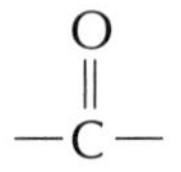 —C(=O)—	-one
Ester	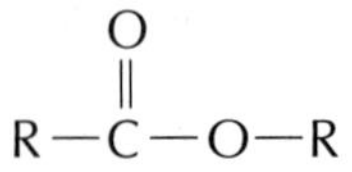 R—C(=O)—O—R	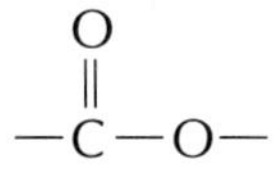 —C(=O)—O—	-yl -oate
Ether	R—O—R	—O—	-oxy-

*R represents any alkyl group such as -CH₃, methyl; -CH₃CH₂, ethyl; etc.

NITROGEN CONTAINING COMPOUNDS

Amines are organic compounds containing nitrogen. Amines are derivatives of ammonia. One, two, or three of the hydrogens in ammonia can be replaced with an alkyl group. General formulas for amines are

```
H—N—H      H—N—R      R—N—R'     R—N—R'
   |          |          |          |
   H          H          H          R''
ammonia    primary    secondary   tertiary
            amine       amine      amine
```

Nitrogen group substituted chains should be numbered so that the carbon attached to the nitrogen has the lowest possible number. The following table lists other classes of nitrogen containing organic compounds.

Amides are also organic compounds containing nitrogen. The structure of an amide can be seen in the table below.

TABLE 18-4

Organic Compounds Containing Nitrogen

Compound	General Formula*	Example
Amines	R—NH$_2$	CH$_3$CH$_2$NH$_2$ ethanamine
Amides	R—C(=O)—NH$_2$	CH$_3$CONH$_2$ ethanamide
Amino acids	G—CH(NH$_2$)—COOH	CH$_3$CH(NH$_2$)COOH alanine (2-aminopropanoic acid)
Nitriles	R—C≡N	CH$_3$CH$_2$CH$_2$CN butanenitrile
Nitro compounds	R—NO$_2$	C$_6$H$_5$NO$_2$ nitrobenzene

*R represents any alkyl group such as —CH$_3$, methyl; CH$_3$CH$_2$—, ethyl and so on. G can represent a group made up of elements other than just carbon and hydrogen.

SECTION REVIEW

1. Name the following organic compounds.

   a. CH$_3$CH—CHCH$_2$CH$_3$
             | |
            CH$_3$ OH

   b. CH$_3$CH$_2$C(=O)CHCH$_3$
                       |
                      CH$_3$

c. CH₃CHCH=CH₂
　　　|
　　　CH₃

d. CH₃CH₂CH₂C(=O)H

e. 　　CH₃
　　　|
　　CH₃CCH₂CH₂CH₂OH
　　　|
　　　CH₃

f. 　　　CH₃
　　　　|
　　CH₂=CHCCH=CHCH₃
　　　　|
　　　　OH

2. Name the following organic compounds.

a. CH₃CH₂CHCH₂Cl
　　　　|
　　　　CH₃

b. 　CH₃
　　|
　CH₃C—CHCH₂Br
　　|　|
　　CH₃ CH₃

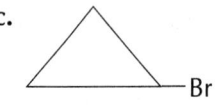

c. cyclopropane—Br

d. CH₃CH₂CHCH₂CH₃
　　　　|
　　　　Cl

e. 　CH₃
　　|
　CH₃CCH₂CH₃
　　|
　　OH

f. CH₃CH₂C=CHCH₃
　　　　|
　　　　Br

g. CH₃(CH₂)₂CH₂NH₂

h. H₂N—C(=O)—CH₂CH₃

3. Each of the following formulas can be written as two compounds with different functional groups. Write the structural formulas, name the compounds, and identify the functional groups.

a. C₂H₆O　　　b. C₃H₆O　　　c. C₅H₁₀

4. Draw structural formulas for the following.

a. ethanal
b. 2-butanone
c. 2-methyl-2-propanol
d. ethanoic acid
e. trimethanamine
f. 2-chlorobutane
g. 2-ethyl-3-methyl-1-butanol
h. cyclobutane
i. cyclohexanamine
j. 2-aminopentane
k. 1,4-nitrophenol
l. 1,3-nitrobenzoic acid
m. ethanenitrile
n. propenoic acid
o. 3,3-dimethylbutanoic acid
p. 2,5,5-trimethyl-4-heptone
q. 1,3-diiodobenzene
r. ethoxybenzene
s. 1-butanol
t. 2-ethyl-4-methylpentanal
u. 3-ethyl-2,4-dimethyl-3-hexanol
v. 5-chloro-3-ethyl-2-methylheptanoic acid
w. 7-bromo-2-naphthol
x. 4-bromobenzoic acid

The Chemistry of Life 19

19.1 MOLECULES OF LIFE

BIOMOLECULES

Twenty-one chemical elements have been found in living systems. These elements combine to form four groups of biomolecules: proteins, carbohydrates, lipids, and nucleic acids.

Proteins are polymers made of small monomer molecules linked together by amide groups. These monomer molecules are organic compounds called **amino acids.** A protein may contain 30 to several thousand amino acid units linked together. The sequence of the amino acids composing the protein determines the properties. Five amino acids can be arranged in 120 possible sequences. The chemical properties of a protein also depend upon the way in which the polymer chain is folded and coiled. The polar and nonpolar side chains help determine the characteristic twists and folds.

Organic molecules that contain the elements carbon, hydrogen, and oxygen in a ratio of about two hydrogen atoms and one oxygen atom for every carbon atom are called **carbohydrates.** They are important to living systems because they are used to provide energy and raw materials for cellular activity. They are also used to provide structure to plants (cellulose) and insects (chitin).

Monosaccharides are simple sugars that can link together to form polymers called polysaccharides. Cellulose is a polysaccharide that has a molecular mass in the millions. Plants store sugars in the form of starch, while animals form the polysaccharide glycogen. Carbohydrate storage provides the organism's energy reserves.

A biological substance that is more soluble in nonpolar organic solvents than in water is a **lipid.** Fats, oils, steroid hormones, and some vitamins are lipids.

Vegetable oils contain unsaturated fatty acids. Unsaturated fats contain double bonds and are generally liquids at room temperature. Animal fats are saturated and are usually solids at room temperature. Saturated fats contain only single bonds between the carbons.

Fats are esters formed from glycerol and three fatty acids. Fatty acids are long chain carboxylic acids having 12 to 20 carbon atoms in the chain.

Nucleic acids are vital to plants and animals. They control cell metabolism and transfer genetic information. Nucleic acids are polymers of **nucleotides.** A nucleotide has three parts: a nitrogen base, a sugar, and a phosphate group. The general structure of a nucleotide consists of a phosphate group bonded to a sugar (5 carbons) which is bonded to an organic base.

$$PO_4^{3-}-CH_2$$

a nucleotide

The five organic bases most often found in nucleotides are adenine, cytosine, guanine, thymine, and uracil.

Recall that the sequence of amino acids in a protein determines its properties. In the same way, the sequence of nucleotides determines the properties of the nucleic acid.

Two nucleic acids are present in the cells, ribonucleic acid (RNA) and deoxyribonucleic acid (DNA). Genetic information is transferred from one generation to the next by DNA. RNA aids in making chemicals such as enzymes.

SECTION REVIEW

1. What is the principal function of DNA in the organism?

2. A nucleotide is composed of what three substances?

3. Proteins are polymers of what substances?

4. Why are carbohydrates important to living systems?

5. What is the difference between a saturated and an unsaturated fat?

6. What term is used to describe a lipid that contains double bonds?

Chemical Reactions and Energy

20.1 ENERGY CHANGES IN CHEMICAL REACTIONS

MASS-ENERGY RELATIONSHIPS

When two moles of hydrogen gas react with one mole of oxygen gas to produce two moles of water vapor, heat is released.

$$2H_2(g) + O_2(g) \rightarrow 2H_2O(g) + 484 \text{ kJ}$$

The preceding reaction involves the formation of a compound from its elements. The energy involved is known as the heat of formation. Appendix B **Table B-12** lists the energies of formation per mole for some compounds. If the energy of formation of each reactant and product is known, a balanced chemical equation can be used to calculate the energy absorbed or released during a chemical reaction.

The difference between the sum of the energies of the products and the sum of the energies of the reactants is the energy absorbed (+) or released (−) by the reaction.

$$\Delta H°_{f(reaction)} = \sum \Delta H°_{f(products)} - \sum \Delta H°_{f(reactants)}$$

where $\sum$ stands for the sum.

EXAMPLE

How much energy is produced by the reaction of 16.0 grams of Fe_2O_3 with excess aluminum metal according to the equation:

$$Fe_2O_3(s) + 2Al(s) \rightarrow Al_2O_3(s) + 2Fe(s) + 852 \text{ kJ}$$

Solving Process:

Step 1. Begin with the balanced equation.

$$Fe_2O_3(s) + 2Al(s) \rightarrow Al_2O_3(s) + 2Fe(s) + 852 \text{ kJ}$$

Step 2. Convert grams of iron(III) oxide to moles.

$$\frac{16.0 \text{ g } Fe_2O_3}{} \left| \frac{1 \text{ mol } Fe_2O_3}{160 \text{ g } Fe_2O_3} \right.$$

Step 3. From the equation, determine the number of moles of reactant and the energy involved. Calculate the answer.

$$\frac{16.0 \text{ g Fe}_2\text{O}_3}{} \bigg| \frac{1 \text{ mol Fe}_2\text{O}_3}{160 \text{ g Fe}_2\text{O}_3} \bigg| \frac{852 \text{ kJ}}{1 \text{ mol Fe}_2\text{O}_3} = 85.2 \text{ kJ will be produced.}$$

PROBLEMS

1. A rocket fuel is prepared by reacting hydrazine and dinitrogen tetroxide according to the equation:

   $$2N_2H_4(l) + N_2O_4(l) \rightarrow 3N_2(g) + 4H_2O(g) + 2400 \text{ kJ}$$

   Calculate the heat released when 3200 grams of hydrazine are consumed in the rocket engine.

2. The dissociation of ammonia into its elements is an endothermic reaction, absorbing 92.2 kJ of energy according to the equation:

   $$2NH_3(g) + 92.2 \text{ kJ} \rightarrow 3H_2(g) + N_2(g)$$

   How much energy will be required to decompose 85.0 grams of ammonia?

SECTION REVIEW

1. When hydrogen peroxide is placed on a cut knee it decomposes into water and oxygen gas. How much energy will be released when 34.0 g of H_2O_2 decomposes according to the equation:

   $$2H_2O_2(l) \rightarrow 2H_2O(l) + O_2 + 200 \text{ kJ}$$

2. Manganese will react with hydrochloric acid to produce hydrogen gas according to the equation:

   $$Mn(s) + 2HCl(aq) \rightarrow MnCl_2(aq) + H_2(g) + 221 \text{ kJ}$$

   How much energy will be released when 5.494 g of manganese reacts completely?

3. How many kilojoules of energy will be needed to decompose 10.8 grams of N_2O_5 gas?

   $$2N_2O_5(g) + 110 \text{ kJ} \rightarrow 4NO_2(g) + O_2(g)$$

4. Tin metal can be extracted from its oxide according to the following reaction:

   $$SnO_2(s) + 4NO_2(g) + 2H_2O(l) + 192 \text{ kJ} \rightarrow Sn(s) + 4HNO_3(aq)$$

   How much energy will be required to extract 59.5 grams of tin?

5. Phosphorus burns in air to produce dense white clouds of P_4O_{10} gas. When this gas is dissolved in rain water, phosphoric acid is produced. How much energy is released when 14.2 g of P_4O_{10} reacts?

$$P_4O_{10}(g) + 6H_2O(l) \rightarrow 4H_3PO_4(aq) + 424 \text{ kJ}$$

20.2 MEASURING ENERGY CHANGES

MEASURING ENERGY CHANGES

The heat required to change the temperature of a substance depends upon the amount and nature of the substance as well as the extent of the temperature change. For example, one gram of water requires 4.18 joules of energy to cause a temperature change of one Celsius degree. It takes only 0.987 J to raise the temperature of 1 g of AlF_3 one Celsius degree.

Energy can be transferred between a system and its surroundings. The amount of energy transferred can be calculated from the relationship

$$\begin{pmatrix} \text{heat gained} \\ \text{or lost} \end{pmatrix} = \begin{pmatrix} \text{mass} \\ \text{in grams} \end{pmatrix} \begin{pmatrix} \text{change in} \\ \text{temperature} \end{pmatrix} \begin{pmatrix} \text{specific} \\ \text{heat} \end{pmatrix}$$

$$q = (m)(\Delta T)(C_p)$$

where q is the heat added (or removed), m is the mass of the substance, T is the change in temperature, and C_p is a property of the substance called its **specific heat**. The specific heat of a substance varies with the temperature. Specific heat values are given in **Table B-13** in Appendix B.

EXAMPLE

How much heat is required to raise the temperature of 68.0 g of AlF_3 from 25.0°C to 80.0°C?

Solving Process:
In addition to the temperature change and mass given in the statement of the problem we must consult **Table B-13** in Appendix B to obtain the specific heat of AlF_3, 0.8948 J/g · C°.

$$q = m(\Delta T)C_p$$
$$= 68.0 \text{ g} \times (80.0 - 25.0)°C \times \frac{0.8948 \text{ J}}{\text{g} \cdot °C} = 3350 \text{ J}$$

A calorimeter containing water is often used to measure the heat absorbed or released in a chemical reaction. The temperature change of the water is used to measure the amount of heat absorbed or released by the reaction. According to the law of conservation of energy, in an insulated system, any heat lost by one quantity of matter must be gained by another. Energy flows from the warmer material to the cooler material until the two reach the same temperature.

$$\text{heat lost} = \text{heat gained}$$
$$m(\Delta T)C_p = m(\Delta T)C_p$$

EXAMPLE

Suppose a piece of lead with a mass of 14.9 g at a temperature of 92.5°C is dropped into an insulated container of water. The mass of water is 165 g and its temperature before adding the lead is 20.0°C. What is the final temperature of the system? C_p lead = 0.1276 J/g · °C

Solving Process:
We know the heat lost equals the heat gained. Since the lead is at a higher temperature than the water, the lead will lose energy. The water will gain an equivalent amount of energy.

(a) The heat lost by the lead is

$$q = (m)(\Delta T)(C_p) = 14.9 \text{ g} \times (92.5°C - T_f) \times \frac{0.1276 \text{ J}}{\text{g} \cdot °C}$$

(b) The heat gained by the water is

$$q = (m)(\Delta T)(C_p) = 165 \text{ g} \times (T_f - 20.0°C) \times \frac{4.18 \text{ J}}{\text{g} \cdot °C}$$

(c) The heat gained must equal the heat lost.

$$165 \text{ g} \times (T_f - 20.0°C) \times \frac{4.18 \text{ J}}{\text{g} \cdot °C} = 14.9 \text{ g} \times (92.5°C - T_f) \times \frac{0.1276 \text{ J}}{\text{g} \cdot °C}$$

$$(T_f - 20.0°C) \times \frac{690. \text{ J}}{°C} = (92.5°C - T_f) \times \frac{1.90 \text{ J}}{°C}$$

$$\left(\frac{690. \text{ J}}{°C}\right)(T_f) - 13\ 800 \text{ J} = 176 \text{ J} - \left(\frac{1.90 \text{ J}}{°C}\right)(T_f)$$

$$\left(\frac{690. \text{ J}}{°C}\right)(T_f) + \left(\frac{1.90 \text{ J}}{°C}\right)(T_f) = 176 \text{ J} + 13\ 800 \text{ J}$$

$$\left(\frac{690. \text{ J}}{°C} + \frac{1.90 \text{ J}}{°C}\right)(T_f) = 14\ 000 \text{ J}$$

$$\left(\frac{692 \text{ J}}{°C}\right)(T_f) = 14\ 000 \text{ J}$$

$$T_f = 20.2°C$$

PROBLEMS

1. How much heat is required to raise the temperature of 789 g of acetic acid, CH_3COOH, from 25.0°C to 82.7°C?

2. How much heat is released when 432 g of water cools from 71.0°C to 18.0°C?

3. Compute the heat released when 42.8 g of calcium carbide, CaC_2, cools from 74.2°C to 11.5°C.

4. If a piece of gold (C_p = 0.129 J/g · °C) with mass 45.5 g and a temperature of 80.5°C is dropped into 192 g of water at 15.0°C, what is the final temperature of the system?

5. A piece of unknown metal with mass 14.9 is heated to 100.0°C and dropped into 75.0 g of water at 20.0°C. The final temperature of the system is 28.5°C. What is the specific heat of the metal?

SECTION REVIEW

Compute the energy changes associated with the following transitions using Table B-13.

1. 49.2 g acetic acid, CH_3COOH, is heated from 24.1°C to 67.3°C

2. 9.61 g ethanol, CH_3CH_2OH, is heated from 19.6°C to 75.0°C

3. 2.47 g sand, SiO_2, is heated from 17.1°C to 46.7°C

4. 31.9 g calcium sulfate, $CaSO_4$, is cooled from 83.2°C to 55.5°C

5. 63.6 g zinc sulfide, ZnS, is cooled from 95.5°C to 42.3°C

6. If a piece of silver (C_p = 0.2165 J/g · °C) with mass 14.16 g and a temperature of 133.5°C is dropped into 250.0 g of water at 17.20°C, what will be the final temperature of the system?

7. A piece of unknown metal with mass 17.19 g is heated to 100.00°C and dropped into 25.00 g of water at 24.50°C. The final temperature of the system is 30.05°C. What is the specific heat of the metal?

8. In order to make 4 cups of tea, 1.00 kg of water is heated from 22.0°C to 99.0°C. How much energy is required?

Nuclear Chemistry

21.1 TYPES OF RADIOACTIVITY

TYPES OF RADIATION

The reactions studied in preceding chapters involved alterations in the electronic structure of atoms. In chemical reactions, the atom's nucleus remains unchanged. In contrast, nuclear reactions change nuclei of atoms. The number of protons and/or neutrons in the nuclei may increase or decrease. One element may be converted into another element. Nuclear reactions are accompanied by a change in energy. The amount of energy involved is many times greater than the energy associated with chemical reactions.

Radioactive elements such as uranium, radium, and polonium have unstable nuclei. Particles are emitted from unstable nuclei as they undergo a process called **radioactive decay.** The decay process continues until a stable element is formed. Stable nuclei do not give off particles of radiation.

Radioactive elements like uranium, radium, and polonium occur naturally on Earth. Normally stable elements can be made radioactive in the laboratory by bombarding them with high speed neutrons or charged particles.

Naturally occurring radioactive material produces three types of radiation. Alpha and beta radiation are made up of particles. Gamma rays are high energy electomagnetic radiation.

Alpha particles (α) are positively charged helium nuclei, each consisting of 2 protons and 2 neutrons. Each particle can be represented by the symbol ^4_2He, in which the 2 represents the number of protons and the 4 represents the mass number.

Beta particles (β) are electrons represented by the symbol $^{\ \ 0}_{-1}e$. The atomic number of each particle is -1 and the mass number is zero. Electrons do not exist in the nucleus as such but are produced when a neutron decays to form a proton.

$$^1_0 n \rightarrow {}^1_1 H + {}^{\ \ 0}_{-1} e$$

When beta rays are emitted, the mass number of the nucleus remains the same, but the neutron/proton ratio is reduced.

Gamma rays (γ) possess neither mass nor charge but are high energy electromagnetic radiation, similar to X rays. Gamma rays are emitted when changes in the nucleus produce an excess of energy. Gamma radiation does not change the mass number or atomic number of the nucleus. The emission of excess energy brings the nucleus to a less excited, more stable state. Gamma rays travel at the speed of light.

Other types of radioactive particles can be emitted when nuclei are bombarded with charged particles or high-speed neutrons and made artificially radioactive. Examples of these particles include the following:

$^{1}_{1}H$ is a proton or hydrogen atom with $A = 1$ and $Z = 1$
$^{2}_{1}H$ is a deuteron or hydrogen isotope with $A = 2$ and $Z = 1$
$^{1}_{0}n$ is a neutron with $A = 1$ and $Z = 0$ (no electric charge)
$^{0}_{+1}e$ is a positron with $A = 0$ and $Z = 1$
$^{0}_{0}v$ is a neutrino with $A = 0$ and $Z = 0$

BALANCING NUCLEAR EQUATIONS

In balancing nuclear equations, two rules must be followed.

1. The sum of the mass numbers on the left side and the right side of the equation must be equal.

2. The sum of the electric charges on the left side and the right side of the equation must be equal.

Radioactive particles given off during nuclear reactions are included in these equations in order to balance them.

EXAMPLE

Complete the following nuclear equation.

$$^{208}_{84}Po \rightarrow ? + ^{4}_{2}He$$

Solving Process:
(a) Find the mass number of the unknown product. We know that the mass number is conserved in a nuclear reaction.

$$\text{mass no. of } 4 + \text{mass no. of } ? = 208$$
$$\text{mass no. of } ? = 208 - \text{mass no. of } 4$$
$$= 204$$

(b) Find the charge of the unknown product. We know that electric charge is conserved in a nuclear equation.

$$\text{charge of } 2 + \text{charge of } ? = 84$$
$$\text{charge of } ? = 84 - \text{charge of } 2$$
$$= 82$$

(c) Determine the identity of the unknown product and complete the nuclear equation. Turn to the periodic table and find which nuclide has an 82+ charge. This nuclide is lead, Pb. Thus, the completed nuclear equation is

$$^{208}_{84}Po \rightarrow ^{204}_{82}Pb + ^{4}_{2}He$$

PROBLEMS

1. Using the periodic table, write nuclear symbols for the isotopes.
   a. lead-208
   b. lead-210
   c. uranium-235
   d. carbon-14
   e. helium-5
   f. potassium-40
   g. lithium-8
   h. uranium-238

2. Complete and balance the following equations.
   a. $^{7}_{3}\text{Li} + ^{1}_{1}\text{H} \rightarrow ^{4}_{2}\text{He} + ?$
   b. $^{3}_{1}\text{H} + ^{2}_{1}\text{H} \rightarrow ? + ^{1}_{0}n$
   c. $^{14}_{6}\text{C} \rightarrow ^{14}_{7}\text{N} + ?$
   d. $^{9}_{4}\text{Be} + ^{4}_{2}\text{He} \rightarrow ^{12}_{6}\text{C} + ?$
   e. $^{14}_{7}\text{N} + ^{4}_{2}\text{He} \rightarrow ? + ^{0}_{+1}e$
   f. $^{26}_{12}\text{Mg} + ^{1}_{0}n \rightarrow ? + ^{0}_{+1}e$
   g. $^{59}_{27}\text{Co} + ^{2}_{1}\text{H} \rightarrow ? + ^{0}_{+1}e$

3. In a portion of the uranium decay series, lead-214 decays to bismuth-214 by beta emission. The bismuth-214 decays to polonium-214 by beta emission. The polonium-214 decays to lead-210 by alpha emission. Write balanced nuclear equations to represent these three steps.

HALF-LIFE

In a nuclear reaction, one element is changed into another element when there is a change in the number of protons in the nucleus. This process, called **transmutation,** can be natural or artificial. Transmutation continues until a stable element, whose nucleus is not radioactive, is produced.

TABLE 21-1
Half-Life and Decay Mode of Selected Nuclides

Nuclide	Half-Life	Decay Mode
$^{3}_{1}\text{H}$	12.26 years	β^-
$^{6}_{2}\text{He}$	0.797 seconds	β^-
$^{14}_{6}\text{C}$	5730 years	β^-
$^{19}_{8}\text{O}$	29.1 seconds	β^- and γ
$^{26}_{14}\text{Si}$	2.1 seconds	β^- and γ
$^{60}_{26}\text{Fe}$	3×10^5 years	β^-
$^{71}_{30}\text{Zn}$	2.4 minutes	β^- and γ
$^{84}_{34}\text{Se}$	3.2 minutes	β^-
$^{212}_{82}\text{Pb}$	10.6 hours	β^- and γ
$^{210}_{84}\text{Po}$	138.40 days	α
$^{227}_{92}\text{U}$	1.3 minutes	α and γ
$^{235}_{92}\text{U}$	7.1×10^8 years	α and γ
$^{238}_{92}\text{U}$	4.51×10^9 years	α and γ
$^{236}_{94}\text{Pu}$	2.85 years	α and γ
$^{242}_{94}\text{Pu}$	3.79×10^5 years	α

The time required for half of a sample of a radioactive isotope to decay is termed its **half-life.** Half-lives of some isotopes are only a fraction of a second. For others, the half-life may be millions or billions of years.

The half-life of one isotope of zinc, $^{71}_{30}Zn$, is 2.4 minutes. Suppose we begin with 10.0 g of this isotope. At the end of 2.4 minutes, 5.0 g $^{71}_{30}Zn$ would remain. The rest of the 10.0 g sample would have decayed to gallium. At the end of another 2.4 minutes, 2.5 g $^{71}_{30}Zn$ would remain. After the third 2.4 minutes, the original 10.0 g sample would contain 1.25 g of the zinc isotope. The other 8.75 g $^{71}_{30}Zn$ would have decayed to gallium.

EXAMPLE

Cobalt-60 is used in cancer radiation therapy. If you start with 4.516×10^8 atoms of $^{60}_{27}Co$, how much time will pass before the amount is reduced to 1.764×10^6 atoms? The half-life is 5.26 years.

Solving Process:
(a) Divide the original amount by the present amount to obtain a ratio of atoms.

$$\frac{4.516 \times 10^8 \text{ atoms}}{1.764 \times 10^6 \text{ atoms}} = \frac{256 \text{ original atoms}}{1 \text{ remaining atom}}$$

(b) Determine the number of half-lives, where n is the number of half-lives.

$$\tfrac{1}{2} \times 256 = 128$$
$$\tfrac{1}{2} \times 128 = 64$$
$$\tfrac{1}{2} \times 64 = 32$$
$$\tfrac{1}{2} \times 32 = 16$$
$$\tfrac{1}{2} \times 16 = 8$$
$$\tfrac{1}{2} \times 8 = 4$$
$$\tfrac{1}{2} \times 4 = 2$$
$$\tfrac{1}{2} \times 2 = 1$$
$$\tfrac{1}{2} \times \tfrac{1}{2} \times \tfrac{1}{2} \times \tfrac{1}{2} \times \tfrac{1}{2} \times \tfrac{1}{2} \times \tfrac{1}{2} \times \tfrac{1}{2} \times 256 = 1$$
$$= 8 \text{ half-lives}$$

(c) Calculate the amount of time that will pass.

$$\text{elapsed time} = \frac{5.26 \text{ y}}{\text{half-life}} \times 8 \text{ half-lives} = 42.1 \text{ years}$$

EXAMPLE

Strontium-90 is present in nuclear fallout. Because it is in the same family as calcium, it can be found in milk and later, bones. If you start with 1.94×10^{17} atoms of $^{90}_{38}Sr$, how many atoms will remain after 140.5 years? The half-life of $^{90}_{38}Sr$ is 28.1 years.

Solving Process:

$$\text{number of remaining atoms} = \text{number of original atoms} \times \tfrac{1}{2}^n$$

(a) Divide 140.5 years by 28.1 years to find the number of half-lives.

$$\frac{140.5 \text{ y}}{28.1 \text{ y/half-life}} = 5.00 \text{ half-lives}$$

(b) To determine the number of remaining atoms, multiply the original number by ½ for each half-life. For five half-lives ($n = 5$), you would multiply the original number by ½, five times.

$$(½)^n \times 1.94 \times 10^{17} \text{ atoms} =$$
$$½ \times ½ \times ½ \times ½ \times ½ \times 1.94 \times 10^{17} \text{ atoms} = 6.06 \times 10^{15} \text{ atoms}$$

Thus after 140.5 years, 6.06×10^{15} atoms of radioactive $^{90}_{38}\text{Sr}$ remain.

PROBLEMS

4. The half-life of $^{71}_{30}\text{Zn}$ is 2.4 minutes. How long will it take for 32 g of zinc-71 to decay to 2 g?

5. A radioactive tracer, sodium-24, is used to study circulatory problems. If you start with 5.85×10^{23} atoms, how many atoms will remain after 12.0 days? The half-life of $^{24}_{11}\text{Na}$ is 4.0 days.

6. Some patients with thyroid disorders receive radioactive iodine-131. The half-life of $^{131}_{53}\text{I}$ is 8.07 days. If you start with 7.73×10^{12} atoms, how much time will pass before the amount is reduced to 2.42×10^{11} atoms?

SECTION REVIEW

1. Complete the following nuclear equations. Indicate the new element formed during these reactions. Name the nuclear particle emitted.
   a. $^{22}_{11}\text{Na} \rightarrow ? + ^{0}_{-1}e$
   b. $^{66}_{29}\text{Cu} \rightarrow ? + ^{0}_{-1}e$
   c. $^{208}_{84}\text{Po} \rightarrow ? + ^{4}_{2}\text{He}$
   d. $^{27}_{14}\text{Si} \rightarrow ? + ^{0}_{+1}e$

2. Complete the following nuclear equations.
   a. $^{27}_{13}\text{Al} + ^{2}_{1}\text{H} \rightarrow ? + ^{4}_{2}\text{He}$
   b. $? + ^{1}_{0}n \rightarrow ^{42}_{19}\text{K} + ^{4}_{2}\text{He}$
   c. $^{63}_{29}\text{Cu} + ^{1}_{1}\text{H} \rightarrow ^{63}_{30}\text{Zn} + ?$
   d. $^{1}_{0}n + ? \rightarrow ^{136}_{53}\text{I} + ^{96}_{39}\text{Y} + 4^{1}_{0}n$

3. Batteries used in heart pacemakers contain plutonium-238. If your original sample contains 2.57×10^9 atoms of $^{238}_{94}\text{Pu}$, how much time will pass before the amount is reduced to 5.02×10^6 atoms? The half-life is 27.1 years.

4. Carbon-14 has a half-life of 5730 years and is used for radioactive dating. Assume we started with 2.18×10^{17} atoms of $^{14}_{6}\text{C}$ in a wood sample obtained from a wooden beam from an ancient tomb. There are 1.09×10^{17} atoms remaining. How old can we assume the wooden beam to be?

5. Promethium-147 has a half-life of 2.5 years and is used to paint luminous dials. If a sample originally contains 9.72×10^{23} atoms of $^{147}_{61}$Pm, how many atoms will remain after 10.0 years?

21.2 NUCLEAR REACTIONS AND ENERGY

NUCLEAR APPLICATIONS

Elements having atomic numbers greater than 92 are called the **transuranium elements.** The transuranium elements that have been synthesized were produced by converting lighter elements into heavier ones. This can be accomplished by neutron capture followed by beta emission and by bombarding elements with the nuclei of other elements.

Radiation with enough energy can penetrate living cells and disrupt their function. We are always exposed to some radiation from rocks, building materials, and as cosmic rays from space. This is called **background radiation**. Gamma rays are the most penetrating. Bacteria and fungi on foods can be destroyed by gamma radiation from cobalt-60.

Radioactive tracers are used to study reaction mechanisms. They can also be used to research how our bodies utilize certain substances. Tracers are used as an aid in a medical diagnosis. Naturally occurring radioactive nuclides can be used by archaeologists for dating artifacts.

A nuclear reaction in which two or more small nuclei combine to form one larger nucleus is called a **fusion reaction.** Fusion reactions occur at temperatures near one billion degrees Celsius. Today's nuclear reactors are fission reactors. **Fission** is the breaking apart of a very heavy nucleus into two parts. A nuclear reactor is a device for controlling nuclear fission. Reactors can be designed to produce energy for electric power generation plants or for propulsion units in ships and submarines.

SECTION REVIEW

1. What name is used to describe synthesized elements that have atomic numbers greater than 92?

2. How do scientists refer to natural radiation from rocks, building materials, and outer space?

3. What is nuclear fusion?

4. What word is used to describe the splitting of a heavy nucleus into two parts?

5. What device is constructed to contain and control a nuclear fission reaction?

Appendix A

SUPPLEMENT TO THE CHEMISTRY SKILL HANDBOOK, APPENDIX A, OF THE STUDENT BOOK

Chemistry is a physical science based on measurements. A chemist uses these measurements to form conclusions about the behavior of matter. The units of the measurement designate the quantity being measured. If scientists are to understand one another, units that are familiar to all scientists must be used. Standard units have been adopted so that scientists everywhere can communicate their findings.

THE INTERNATIONAL SYSTEM (SI)

During the past two centuries, many versions of the metric system have been used. One system, called the **International System of Units (SI),** was established by international agreement. SI is used commonly by scientists in all countries. The most common SI units used in chemistry are listed in **Table B-1** of Appendix B.

In the SI system there is one base unit for each category of measurement—mass, length, time, and so on. These base units are multiplied by factors of ten to form larger and smaller units. The factors are indicated by prefixes attached to the base units. **Table B-2** of Appendix B lists the SI prefixes. A kilometer, for example, is 1000 meters; a microgram is one millionth of a gram; a nanomole is one billionth of a mole.

Two situations that often confuse students are the measurements for mass and weight and temperature and heat. Mass and weight are different quantities and are not interchangeable in usage. **Mass** is a measure of the quantity of matter in an object and is measured in grams. **Weight** is a measure of gravitational attraction on an object and is measured in Newtons. **Temperature** is a measure of the kinetic energy of particles. While the standard unit of temperature is the kelvin (K), the size of the Celsius degree (C°) is equal to the kelvin.

$$K = °C + 273$$

Heat is a means of energy transfer and is measured in joules.

DERIVED UNITS

By combining basic SI units, we obtain measurement units used to express other quantities. Distance divided by time equals speed, m/s. If we multiply length by length, we get area, m^2. Length cubed equals volume, m^3.

Other derived units are given special names. The force that will cause a 1.00-kg mass to accelerate at 1.00 m/s^2 is defined as one newton, N. One pascal, Pa, is a pressure of one newton per square meter, N/m^2. Gas pressure is measured in pascals. Derived units are also used as labels in the factor label method of problem solving.

SIGNIFICANT DIGITS

The accuracy of the answer to a problem depends upon the accuracy of the numbers used to express each measurement. The **accuracy** of any measurement depends upon the instrument that is used and upon the observer. The digits in an answer that imply more accuracy than the measurements justify are not significant and should be dropped. The digits that remain truly indicate the accuracy of the original measurements. These remaining numerals are called significant digits. **Significant digits** consist of the definitely known digits plus one estimated digit.

Imagine that you have measured the length of a page in this book with a small ruler that is calibrated in tenths of a centimeter. You find that the edge of the page is between 27.6 and 27.7 cm. You estimate that the last digit is closer to 0.6. You record the measurement as 27.6 cm. You did not record the length as 27.6215 cm because you would be exceeding the accuracy of the ruler and your ability to estimate that number of decimal places. Since the last digit is estimated, it is said to be uncertain. Unless otherwise stated, the uncertainty in a measurement is assumed to be within ±1 in the last indicated digit. Therefore, the uncertainty of your measurement can be expressed as 27.6 ± 0.1 cm. The last digit is uncertain but it is part of the measurement and is a significant digit. The significant digits of a measurement consist of all known digits plus one estimated digit.

If five people measured the same page in this book using the same ruler and recorded the length as 27.6 cm, we would say that the measurement is precise. Precision refers to the reproducibility of identical measurements of a quantity on the same instrument. The accuracy is determined by comparison of the measured value to an accepted or true value. The ruler, if poorly made, may give precise measurements that are not accurate. Measurements are written using the correct number of significant digits in order to indicate precision.

The following rules are used to determine the number of significant digits in a recorded measurement.

1. Digits other than zero are always significant.

    56.1   3 significant digits

2. Zeros between nonzero digits are always significant.

    3.108   4 significant digits

3. Any final zero used after a decimal point is significant.

    4.320   4 significant digits

4. Zeros used solely for spacing the decimal point (place holders) are not significant.

    400   1 significant digit
    0.0026   2 significant digits

Not all numbers used in a calculation are measurements. Exact numbers, such as counted numbers or defined numbers, may be part of the calculation. How many students are present in your chemistry class? The answer is an exact number. It contains no uncertainty. Exact numbers are sometimes said to have an infinite number of significant digits. Definitions, such as 1 minute = 60 seconds, contain exact numbers and do not limit the number of significant digits used in a calculation.

EXAMPLE

Determine the number of significant digits and the uncertainty in the measurement 20.17 grams.

Solving Process:
Rules 1 and 2 indicate that there are 4 significant digits. The last digit is estimated and is uncertain. It occurs in the hundredth's place. The uncertainty is ±0.01 gram.

PROBLEM

1. Determine the number of significant digits and the uncertainty in each of the following.

   a. 6.751 g
   b. 0.157 kg
   c. 28.0 mL
   d. 2500 m
   e. 0.070 g
   f. 30.07 g
   g. 0.106 cm
   h. 0.0067 g
   i. 0.0230 cm^3
   j. 26.509 cm
   k. 54.52 cm^3
   l. 0.1209 m
   m. 2.690 g
   n. 43.07 cm
   o. 6 352 001 g

HANDLING NUMBERS IN SCIENCE

The least accurate measurement determines the accuracy of an answer in an addition or subtraction problem. The answer must be rounded off to the highest decimal place containing uncertainty. Use the following guidelines when rounding measurements.

1. If the eliminated digit is less than 5, do not change the preceding digit.

   Rounded to 3 digits   *Rounded to 2 digits*
   2.473 becomes 2.47   3.64 becomes 3.6

2. If the eliminated digit is 5 or more, add 1 to the preceding digit.

   Rounded to 3 digits   *Rounded to 2 digits*
   8.276 becomes 8.28   0.478 becomes 0.48

In the addition and subtraction examples below the answers must be rounded to the tenth's place. In each case the least accurate measurement is expressed to tenths.

Add		Subtract
50.23 g		28.75 cm
23.7 g		17.5 cm
14.678 g		11.25 cm
88.608 g		
88.6 g	**Answer**	11.3 cm

In multiplication and division, the answer should have the same number of significant digits as the factor having the least number of significant digits (the least precise measurement) in the problem.

If you are using a calculator to obtain your numerical answer, you must be very careful to observe significant digits. The calculator may give you an answer of eight or more digits. All of these digits may not be justified by your data. For example, in the problem 4.8070/1.23 the number of significant digits is five and three, respectively. The calculator answer may appear as 3.908 130 081, but rounding the calculator answer to the smaller number of significant digits (three) gives a final answer of 3.91.

PROBLEMS

Express each answer in the correct significant digits.

2. Add.
   a. 16.5 cm + 8 cm + 4.37 cm
   b. 13.25 g + 10.00 g + 9.6 g
   c. 2.36 m + 3.38 m + 0.355 m + 1.06 m
   d. 0.0853 g + 0.0547 g + 0.037 g + 0.00387 g

3. Subtract.
   a. 23.27 km − 12.058 km
   b. 13.57 g − 6.3 g
   c. 350.0 m − 200 m
   d. 27.68 cm − 14.369 cm

4. Multiply.
   a. 2.6 cm × 3.78 cm
   b. 6.54 m × 0.37 m
   c. 0.036 m × 0.02 m
   d. 3.08 km × 5.2 km
   e. 3.15 dm × 2.5 dm × 4.00 dm
   f. 35.7 cm × 0.78 cm × 2.3 cm

5. Divide.
   a. 35 cm^2 ÷ 0.62 cm
   b. 39 g ÷ 24.2 g
   c. 0.58 dm^3 ÷ 2.15 dm
   d. 40.8 m^2 ÷ 5.050 m
   e. 3.76 km ÷ 1.62 km
   f. 0.075 g ÷ 0.003 cm^3

SCIENTIFIC NOTATION

The average distance between the earth and the sun is 150 000 000 kilometers. This large number can be written as 1.5×10^8 kilometers. The diameter of atoms is about 0.000 000 02 centimeters. This small number can be written as 2×10^8 centimeters.

Both large and small numbers can be manipulated with ease in multiplication and division problems by putting them in scientific notation. In **scientific notation** the number is expressed in the form $M \times 10^n$, where $1 \leq M < 10$ and n is an integer.

Numbers written as powers of 10 can be used to indicate the number of significant digits. The total number of digits in the first portion of a value (M above) in scientific notation indicates the number of significant digits.

Number of Significant Digits	Power of Ten
2	1.5×10^5
3	1.50×10^5
4	1.500×10^5
5	1.5000×10^5

Let us review the addition, subtraction, multiplication, and division of values expressed in scientific notation.

To add or subtract numbers with exponents ($M10^n$), all exponents must be the same.

EXAMPLE

Find the sum of $(6.5 \times 10^2 \text{ g}) + (2.0 \times 10^3 \text{ g}) + (30.0 \times 10^3 \text{ g})$.

Solving Process:
Method 1: Using longhand calculations

$$\text{Change } 6.5 \times 10^2 \text{ to } M \times 10^3$$
$$6.5 \times 10^2 = 0.65 \times 10^3$$
$$(0.65 \times 10^3) + (2.0 \times 10^3) + (30.0 \times 10^3) = (0.65 + 2.0 + 30.0) \times 10^3$$
$$= 32.7 \times 10^3$$
$$= 3.27 \times 10^4 \text{ g}$$

Method 2: Using a calculator
Enter the M part of the number (6.5) into the calculator. Then instead of multiplying by 10^2, press the $\boxed{\text{EE}}$ or $\boxed{\text{EXP}}$ key followed by the value of the exponent. If the exponent is negative, change its sign by using the $\boxed{+/-}$ key.

The key stroke sequence for the above problem is

$$6.5 \boxed{\text{EE}} 2 + 2.0 \boxed{\text{EE}} 3 + 30.0 \boxed{\text{EE}} 3 = 3.27 \times 10^4 \text{ g}$$

For multiplication problems involving numbers with exponents ($M \times 10^n$), multiply the values of M and add the exponents. The exponents do not need to be alike as they do in addition and subtraction in order to do longhand calculations.

EXAMPLE

Find the product of $(4.0 \times 10^{-2}$ cm$)(3.0 \times 10^{-4}$ cm$)(2.0 \times 10^{1}$ cm$)$.

Solving Process:
Add the exponents: $-2 + (-4) + 1 = -5$
Multiply the values of M: $4.0 \times 3.0 \times 2.0 = 24$

$$(4.0 \times 10^{-2})(3.0 \times 10^{-4})(2.0 \times 10^{1}) = (4.0 \times 3.0 \times 2.0) \times 10^{-2-4+1}$$
$$= 24 \times 10^{-5} = 2.4 \times 10^{-4} \text{ cm}^3$$

Division is similar to multiplication except the exponents are subtracted instead of added. The exponents do not need to be the same. To divide exponential numbers ($M \times 10^n$), divide the values of M and subtract the exponent of the denominator from the exponent of the numerator.

EXAMPLE

Divide $(12.73 \times 10^{-6}$ g$)$ by $(4.6 \times 10^{2}$ cm$^3)$

Solving Process:
Subtract the exponents: $-6-(2) = -8$

Divide the values of M: $\dfrac{12.73}{4.6} = 2.8$

$$\dfrac{12.73 \times 10^{-6} \text{ g}}{4.6 \times 10^{2} \text{ cm}^3} = \dfrac{12.73}{4.6} \times 10^{-6-2} = 2.8 \times 10^{-8} \text{ g/cm}^3$$

EXAMPLE

$$\dfrac{(8.0 \times 10^{6} \text{ cm}^3)(4.0 \times 10^{3} \text{ kPa})(3.0 \times 10^{2} \text{ K})}{(3.0 \times 10^{4} \text{ kPa})(2.0 \times 10^{2} \text{ K})}$$

Solving Process:

$$= \dfrac{(8.0 \times 4.0 \times 3.0) \times 10^{6+3+2} \text{ cm}^3}{(3.0 \times 2.0) \times 10^{4+2}}$$

$$= \dfrac{96}{6.0} \times \dfrac{10^{11}}{10^{6}} = 16 \times 10^{11-6} \text{ cm}^3$$

$$= 16 \times 10^{5} = 1.6 \times 10^{6} \text{ cm}^3$$

PROBLEMS

6. Express the following in scientific notation.
   a. 0.000 03 cm
   b. 8 000 000 g
   c. 55 000 000 m
   d. 0.002 g
   e. 0.000 007 m
   f. 65 000 km

7. Do the following calculations using scientific notation.
   a. $(5.1 \times 10^{-4}$ cm$)(2.8 \times 10^{-3}$ cm$)$
   b. $(6.5 \times 10^{4}$ m$)(3.27 \times 10^{-5}$ m$)$
   c. $(4.00 \times 10^{2}$ g$) \div (2.000 \times 10^{2}$ cm$^3)$
   d. $\dfrac{(6.33 \times 10^{-7}\text{ km})(2.189 \times 10^{-3}\text{ km})}{(3.007 \times 10^{-8}\text{ km})}$
   e. $(7.072 \times 10^{5}$ cm$)(5.77 \times 10^{-3}$ cm$)(2.0 \times 10^{2}$ cm$)$
   f. $(7.5 \times 10^{5}$ g$) \div (2.5 \times 10^{2}$ g$)$
   g. $(9.000\,00 \times 10^{7}$ m$) \div (3.0000 \times 10^{3}$ s$)$
   h. $\dfrac{(4 \times 10^{5}\text{ m}^3)(345\text{ K})(2.008 \times 10^{2}\text{ kPa})}{(273\text{ K})(1.013\,25 \times 10^{2}\text{ kPa})}$

CONVERSION FACTORS

In **Table B-2** the values of the SI prefixes are described. Using these definitions and SI base units we can form conversion ratios to convert a given unit to any other related unit.

EXAMPLE

How many meters are in 175 cm?

Solving Process:
Table B-2 defines centi- as 1/100. Therefore there are 100 cm in 1 m.
Since 100 cm = 1 m, two ratios equal to 1 are possible.

$$\frac{100\text{ cm}}{1\text{ m}} \quad \text{or} \quad \frac{1\text{ m}}{100\text{ cm}} = 1$$

Since we wish to convert cm to m, we use the second ratio.

$$\text{number of meters} = 175\text{ cm} \times \frac{1\text{ m}}{100\text{ cm}} = 1.75\text{ m}$$

The centimeters divide out and the answer is given in meters. Since the multiplying ratio equals one, the quantity has not changed, merely the units in which it is expressed.

PROBLEMS

8. Convert.
   a. 0.75 kg to mg
   b. 1500 mm to km
   c. 1.00 day to seconds
   d. 0.52 kilometer to meters
   e. 65 grams to kilograms
   f. 750 micrograms to grams

PROBLEM SOLVING—FACTOR LABEL METHOD

The study of chemistry requires skill in handling units and solving problems. You can develop this skill in problem solving by practice. Essentially, successful problem solving requires that you look for a pattern.

Problems consist of three parts: a known beginning, a desired end, and a connecting path or conversion method. For any word problem, first select the information that is given or known. Then decide what information you must find. The connecting path comes from your general knowledge and the chemistry knowledge you acquire on a regular basis through study. This connecting path involves the use of conversion factors.

Consider the following problem. Ask yourself what is known, what is desired, and what is the connecting path.

EXAMPLE

An object is traveling at a speed of 7500 centimeters per second. Convert the value to kilometers per day.

Solving Process:
From the problem, the known value and the desired value can be written as ratios.

$$\frac{7500 \text{ centimeters}}{\text{second}} \quad \text{and} \quad \frac{? \text{ kilometers}}{\text{day}}$$

What relationships are known between centimeters and kilometers? Between seconds and days? Write them down.

$$100 \text{ cm} = 1 \text{ m} \quad 1000 \text{ m} = 1 \text{ km} \quad 60 \text{ s} = 1 \text{ min}$$
$$60 \text{ min} = 1 \text{ h} \quad 24 \text{ h} = 1 \text{ day}$$

Use these relationships as ratios in such a way that seconds, minutes, hours, centimeters, and meters divide out. If the units don't divide out, your answer will have unusual units such as second squared.

$$\frac{\text{km}}{\text{day}} = \frac{7500 \text{ cm}}{\text{s}} \left| \frac{60 \text{ s}}{1 \text{ min}} \right| \frac{60 \text{ min}}{\text{h}} \left| \frac{24 \text{ h}}{\text{day}} \right| \frac{1 \text{ m}}{100 \text{ cm}} \left| \frac{1 \text{ km}}{1000 \text{ m}} \right.$$

$$= 6480 \frac{\text{km}}{\text{day}} = 6500 \frac{\text{km}}{\text{day}}$$

Note that this example is for one chain of operations.

EXAMPLE

One edge of a copper cube is carefully measured and found to be 2.162 cm. An atom of copper has a volume of 8.785×10^{-3} nm^3. How many atoms of copper are contained in the cube?

Solving Process:
To develop your skill in solving problems, it is good practice to write down the given values, the desired quantity, and the relationships used to construct conversion factors.

Given: edge of cube = 2.162 centimeters (cm)
diameter of copper atom = 0.2560 nanometer (nm)

Desired quantity: number of copper atoms in cube

Relationships: 10^9 nm = 1 m
10^2 cm = 1 m
Volume of cube = $edge^3$

To relate the volume of a copper atom to the volume of the cube, length values must be in the same units.

$$\text{edge of cube} = \frac{2.162 \text{ cm}}{} \left| \frac{1 \text{ m}}{1 \times 10^2 \text{ cm}} \right| \frac{1 \times 10^9 \text{ nm}}{1 \text{ m}}$$
$$= 2.162 \times 10^7 \text{ nm}$$

$$\text{volume of cube} = edge^3 = (2.162 \times 10^7 \text{ nm})^3 = 1.011 \times 10^{22} \text{ nm}^3$$

$$\text{number of atoms in cube} = \frac{1.011 \times 10^{22} \text{ nm}^3}{\text{cube}} \left| \frac{1 \text{ atom}}{8.785 \times 10^{-3} \text{ nm}^3} \right.$$
$$= 1.151 \times 10^{24} \text{ atoms/cube}$$

PROBLEMS

9. The following information is given in a science supply catalog: 60 rubber stoppers = 500.0 grams = $4.89

   Each student in a class will need 4 stoppers. There are 24 students in the class. What mass of stoppers must be ordered and what will be the cost?

10. The speed of a skyrocket is measured and found to be 145.3 m/s. What is the rocket's speed in km/h?

11. The dimensions of an aquarium are found to be 76.7 cm, 114.5 cm, and 104.2 cm. What is its volume in m^3?

12. An aquarium filter will clean 275 mL of water per minute. How long will it take to filter 125 L of dirty water?

13. A light-year is the distance light can travel in one year. If the sun is 150 000 000 kilometers away, how many light years is the sun from the earth? Assume that light travels at a speed of 3.00×10^{10} cm/s.

GRAPHING

Throughout your study of chemistry you will be required to prepare graphs or interpret graphs of experimental data. Thus you should be familiar with the composition of a graph.

The data that you will be using involves two variables, dependent and independent. The quantity that is deliberately varied is the **independent variable.** The quantity that changes due to variation in the independent variable is the **dependent variable.** The independent variable is plotted on the horizontal axis. This axis is referred to as the **abscissa** or x axis. The dependent variable is plotted on the vertical axis. The vertical axis is referred to as the **ordinate** or y axis.

Graph titles should clearly state the purpose of the graph and include the dependent and independent variables. For example, **Figure 1** is titled The effect of temperature on the volume of a gas. Each axis should be labeled with the appropriate variable and units of measurement. For **Figure 1** the abscissa is labeled Temperature (K, C°), indicating that the scale is marked in both kelvins and Celsius degrees. The ordinate is labeled Volume (L), with the scale marked in liters. Each axis has equal intervals. The intervals are 0.5 L for the ordinate and 100°C or K for the abscissa.

FIGURE 1

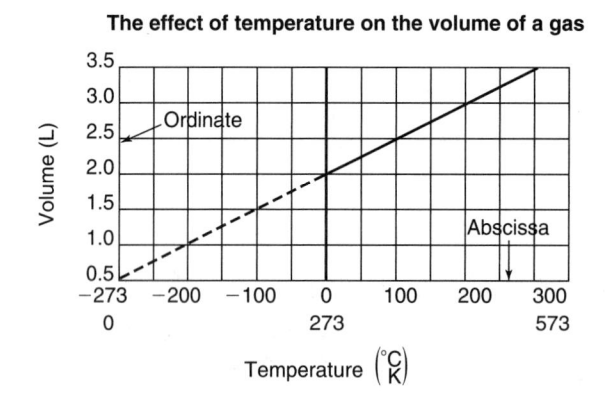

The effect of temperature on the volume of a gas

INTERPRETING GRAPHS

Sometimes it is necessary to find a value for a variable at a point along the graph that is not one of the original data points. For example, on **Figure 1** assume that we want to know the volume of a gas when the temperature is 75°C. The original data was not recorded at 75°C. In order to determine the volume of the gas at 75°C you must **interpolate,** or read from the graph between data points. By interpolating we can see that the volume of the gas is 2.3 L at 75°C.

If a value is needed that is beyond the limits of the graph you must extrapolate. Reading a graph beyond the limits of the experimentally determined data points is **extrapolation.** To determine the theoretical volume of a gas at −273°C we must extrapolate to find the answer, 0 L. You should be cautious when extrapolating data. The relationship between the variables may not remain the same beyond the limits of your investigation.

SECTION REVIEW

1. Determine the number of significant digits in each of the following.
   - **a.** 35 g
   - **b.** 3.57 m
   - **c.** 3.507 km
   - **d.** 0.035 kg
   - **e.** 0.246
   - **f.** 0.004 m^3
   - **g.** 24.068 kPa
   - **h.** 268 K
   - **i.** 20.040 80 g
   - **j.** 730 000 kg

Perform the following calculations and express your answer to the proper number of significant digits.

2. (5.14 cm) (6.742 × 10^2 cm)

3. (2.8 × 10^3 g) ÷ (6.86 × 10^2 cm^3)

4. $\dfrac{(6.88 \times 10^2 \text{ m}^3)(2.14 \times 10^2 \text{ K})}{(3.8 \times 10^2 \text{ K})}$

5. (7.500 00 cm) (2.040 × 10^3 cm) (3.0 × 10^2 cm)

6. (6.0 × 10^{-3} m) ÷ (3 × 10^{-4} s)

7. $\dfrac{(5 \times 10^3 \text{ cm}^3)(8 \times 10^2 \text{ kPa})}{(4.5 \times 10^2 \text{ kPa})}$

8. Convert.
   - **a.** 3.50 m to cm
   - **b.** 65 g to kg
   - **c.** 0.52 km to mm
   - **d.** 8.14 dm^3 to cm^3

9. Write the correct units to the answer for the following problem.

$$\text{lab} \times \frac{\text{lump}}{\text{bog}} \times \frac{\text{bang}}{\text{lump}} \times \frac{\text{bam}}{\text{bog}} \times \frac{\text{bog}^2}{\text{bang}} \times \frac{\text{mess}}{\text{bam}}$$

10. A sign in a town gives the speed limit at 50 km/h. What is this speed in centimeters per second?

FIGURE 2

The effects of temperature and pressure on the percent yield of NH_3

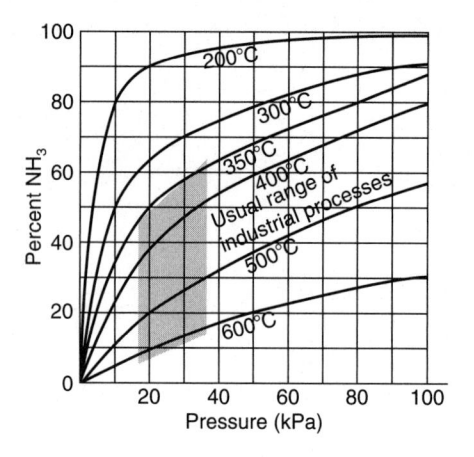

11. What is the title of the graph?

12. What variable is plotted along the abscissa?

13. What variable is plotted along the ordinate?

14. In what units is pressure measured?

15. What is the interval for each block along the *y* axis?

16. At 70 kPa and 600°C, what is the percent yield of NH_3?

17. Predict the percent yield of NH_3 at 120 kPa and 200°C.

18. Considering the usual range of industrial processes, what is the maximum yield that can be expected?

19. In order to obtain at least a 90% yield, in what temperature range would NH_3 be produced (pressure not to exceed 100 kPa)?

Appendix B

DATA TABLES

TABLE B-1
SI Base Units

Quantity	Name	Symbol
Length	meter	m
Mass	kilogram	kg
Time	second	s
Electric current	ampere	A
Thermodynamic temperature	kelvin	K
Amount of substance	mole	mol
Luminous intensity	candela	cd

TABLE B-2
SI Prefixes

Prefix	Symbol	Meaning	Multiplier (Numerical)	Multiplier (Exponential)
Greater than 1				
tera	T	trillion	**1 000 000 000 000	10^{12}
giga	G	billion	1 000 000 000	10^{9}
mega	M	million	1 000 000	10^{6}
*kilo	k	thousand	1 000	10^{3}
hecto	h	hundred	100	10^{2}
deka	da	ten	10	10^{1}
Less than 1				
*deci	d	tenth	0.1	10^{-1}
*centi	c	hundredth	0.01	10^{-2}
*milli	m	thousandth	0.001	10^{-3}
*micro	μ	millionth	0.000 001	10^{-6}
*nano	n	billionth	0.000 000 001	10^{-9}
pico	p	trillionth	0.000 000 000 001	10^{-12}
femto	f	quadrillionth	0.000 000 000 000 001	10^{-15}
atto	a	quintillionth	0.000 000 000 000 000 001	10^{-18}

*These prefixes are commonly used in this book and should be memorized.
**Spaces are used to group digits in long numbers. In some countries, a comma indicates a decimal point. Therefore, commas will not be used.

TABLE B-3
Greek Alphabet

Greek letter	Greek name	English equivalent	Greek letter	Greek name	English equivalent
A α	alpha	ä	N ν	nu	n
B β	beta	b	Ξ ξ	xi	ks
Γ γ	gamma	g	O ο	omicron	o
Δ δ	delta	d	Π π	pi	p
E ε	epsilon	e	P ρ	rho	r
Z ζ	zeta	z	Σ σ	sigma	s
H η	eta	ā	T τ	tau	t
Θ θ	theta	th	Υ υ	upsilon	ü, $\overline{oo}$
I ι	iota	ē	Φ φ	phi	f
K κ	kappa	k	X χ	chi	h
Λ λ	lambda	l	Ψ ψ	psi	ps
M μ	mu	m	Ω ω	omega	ō

TABLE B-4
Common Physical Constants

Absolute Zero = $-273.15°C$ = 0 K
Atmospheric pressure (standard): 1 atm = 1.013 25 Pa = 760 mm Hg
Avogadro constant: N_0 = 6.022 17 × 10^{23} per mole
Charge of the electron: e = $-1.602\ 19 \times 10^{19}$ coulomb
Faraday constant: F = 96 486.7 C/mol e^-
Ideal gas constant: R = 8.314 51 J/mol · K
Heat of fusion of ice: 334 J/g
Heat of vaporization of water: 2260 J/g
Mass of electron: m_e = 9.109 53 × 10^{-31} kg = 5.49 × 10^{-4} u
Mass of neutron: m_n = 1.675 495 × 10^{-27} kg = 1.008 67 u
Mass of proton: m_p = 1.673 265 × 10^{-27} kg = 1.007 28 u
Molar gas volume: 22.413 6 dm^3 (STP)
Planck constant: h = 6.626 08 × 10^{-34} J/Hz (J · s)
Speed of light in vacuum: c = 2.997 925 × 10^8 m/s

TABLE B-5
Symbols and Abbreviations

α = rays from radioactive materials, helium nuclei	K_b = ionization constant (base)
β = rays from radioactive materials, electrons	K_{eq} = equilibrium constant
	K_{sp} = solubility product constant
γ = rays from radioactive materials, high-energy quanta	kg = kilogram
	M = molarity
Δ = change in	m = mass, molality
γ = wavelength	m = meter *(length)*
ν = frequency	mol = mole *(amount)*
Π = osmotic pressure	min = minute *(time)*
A = ampere *(electric current)*	N = newton *(force)*
Bq = becquerel *(nuclear disintegration)*	N_A = Avogadro constant
°C = Celsius degree *(temperature)*	n = number of moles
C = coulomb *(quantity of electricity)*	P = pressure, power
c = speed of light	Pa = pascal *(pressure)*
cd = candela *(luminous intensity)*	$\boldsymbol{p}$ = momentum
C_p = specific heat	q = heat
D = density	R = *gas constant*
E = energy, electromotive force	S = entropy
F = force, Faraday	Sv = sievert *(absorbed radiation)*
G = free energy	s = second *(time)*
g = gram *(mass)*	T = temperature
H = enthalpy *(heat)*	U = internal energy
Hz = hertz *(frequency)*	u = atomic mass unit
h = Planck's constant	V = volume
h = hour *(time)*	V = volt *(electromotive force)*
J = joule *(energy)*	v = velocity
K = kelvin *(temperature)*	W = watt *(power)*
K_a = ionization constant (acid)	w = work
	x = mole fraction

TABLE B-6
Oxidation Numbers of Monatomic Ions

1+	2+	3+
cesium, Cs^+	barium, Ba^{2+}	aluminum, Al^{3+}
copper(I), Cu^+	beryllium, Be^{2+}	antimony(III), Sb^{3+}
hydrogen, H^+	cadmium, Cd^{2+}	bismuth(III), Bi^{3+}
indium(I), In^+	calcium, Ca^{2+}	boron, B^{3+}
lithium, Li^+	chromium(II), Cr^{2+}	cerium(III), Ce^{3+}
potassium, K^+	cobalt(II), Co^{2+}	cobalt(III), Co^{3+}
rubidium, Rb^+	copper(II), Cu^{2+}	chromium(III), Cr^{3+}
silver, Ag^+	iridium(II), Ir^{2+}	gallium(III), Ga^{3+}
sodium, Na^+	iron(II), Fe^{2+}	indium(III), In^{3+}
thallium(I), Tl^+	lead(II), Pb^{2+}	iridium(III), Ir^{3+}
	magnesium, Mg^{2+}	iron(III), Fe^{3+}
	manganese(II), Mn^{2+}	phosphorus(III), P^{3+}
	mercury(II), Hg^{2+}	rhodium(III), Rh^{3+}
	nickel(II), Ni^{2+}	thallium(III), Tl^{3+}
	platinum(II), Pt^{2+}	titanium(III), Ti^{3+}
	strontium, Sr^{2+}	uranium(III), U^{3+}
	tin(II), Sn^{2+}	vanadium(III), V^{3+}
	titanium(II), Ti^{2+}	
	tungsten(II), W^{2+}	
	vanadium(II), V^{2+}	
	zinc, Zn^{2+}	
	zirconium(II), Zr^{2+}	

4+		5+
cerium(IV), Ce^{4+}	titanium(IV), Ti^{4+}	antimony(V), Sb^{5+}
germanium(IV), Ge^{4+}	tin(IV), Sn^{4+}	bismuth(V), Bi^{5+}
iridium(IV), Ir^{4+}	tungsten(IV), W^{4+}	phosphorus(V), P^{5+}
lead(IV), Pb^{4+}	uranium(IV), U^{4+}	tungsten(V), W^{5+}
platinum(IV), Pt^{4+}	vanadium(IV), V^{4+}	uranium(V), U^{5+}
thorium(IV), Th^{4+}	zirconium(IV), Zr^{4+}	vanadium(V), V^{5+}

1−	2−	3−	4−
bromide, Br^-	oxide, O^{2-}	nitride, N^{3-}	carbide, C^{4-}
chloride, Cl^-	selenide, Se^{2-}	phosphide, P^{3-}	
fluoride, F^-	sulfide^{2-}		
hydride, H^-			
iodide, I^-			

TABLE B-7
Charges of Common Polyatomic Ions

1+	2+
ammonium, NH_4^+	mercury(I), Hg_2^{2+}

1−	2−
acetate, CH_3COO^-	carbonate, CO_3^{2-}
amide, NH_2^-	chromate, CrO_4^{2-}
azide, N_3^-	dichromate, $Cr_2O_7^{2-}$
benzoate, $C_6H_5COO^-$	hexachloroplatinate(IV), $PtCl_6^{2-}$
bromate, BrO_3^-	hexafluorosilicate, SiF_6^{2-}
chlorate, ClO_3^-	molybdate, MoO_4^{2-}
cyanide, CN^-	oxalate, $C_2O_4^{2-}$
formate, $HCOO^-$	peroxide, O_2^{2-}
hydroxide, OH^-	peroxydisulfate, $S_2O_8^{2-}$
hypochlorite, ClO^-	selenate, SeO_4^{2-}
hypophosphite, $H_2PO_2^-$	silicate, SiO_3^{2-}
iodate, IO_3^-	sulfate, SO_4^{2-}
metaphosphate, PO_3^-	sulfite, SO_3^{2-}
nitrate, NO_3^-	tartrate, $C_4H_4O_6^{2-}$
nitrite, NO_2^-	tellurate, TeO_4^{2-}
perchlorate, ClO_4^-	tetraborate, $B_4O_7^{2-}$
periodate, IO_4^-	thiosulfate, $S_2O_3^{2-}$
permanganate, MnO_4^-	tungstate, WO_4^{2-}
peroxyborate, BO_3^-	
thiocyanate, SCN^-	
vanadate, VO_3^-	

3−
arsenate, AsO_4^{3-}
citrate, $C_6H_5O_7^{3-}$
hexacyanoferrate(III), $Fe(CN)_6^{3-}$
phosphate, PO_4^{3-}

4−
hexacyanoferrate(II), $Fe(CN)_6^{4-}$
diphosphate, $P_2O_7^{4-}$

TABLE B-8
Electronegativities

H 2.1																	He —
Li 1.0	Be 1.5											B 2.0	C 2.5	N 3.0	O 3.5	F 4.0	Ne —
Na 0.9	Mg 1.2											Al 1.5	Si 1.8	P 2.1	S 2.5	Cl 3.0	Ar —
K 0.8	Ca 1.0	Sc 1.3	Ti 1.5	V 1.6	Cr 1.6	Mn 1.5	Fe 1.8	Co 1.8	Ni 1.8	Cu 1.9	Zn 1.6	Ga 1.6	Ge 1.8	As 2.0	Se 2.4	Br 2.8	Kr —
Rb 0.8	Sr 1.0	Y 1.2	Zr 1.4	Nb 1.6	Mo 1.8	Tc 1.9	Ru 2.2	Rh 2.2	Pd 2.2	Ag 1.9	Cd 1.7	In 1.7	Sn 1.8	Sb 1.9	Te 2.1	I 2.5	Xe —
Cs 0.7	Ba 0.9	La 1.1	Hf 1.3	Ta 1.5	W 1.7	Re 1.9	Os 2.2	Ir 2.2	Pt 2.2	Au 2.4	Hg 1.9	Tl 1.8	Pb 1.9	Bi 1.9	Po 2.0	At 2.2	Rn —
Fr 0.7	Ra 0.9	Ac 1.1															

Ce 1.1	Pr 1.1	Nd 1.1	Pm 1.2	Sm 1.2	Eu 1.1	Gd 1.2	Tb 1.2	Dy 1.2	Ho 1.2	Er 1.2	Tm 1.2	Yb 1.2	Lu 1.3
Th 1.3	Pa 1.5	U 1.7	Np 1.3	Pu 1.3	Am 1.3	Cm 1.3	Bk 1.3	Cf 1.3	Es 1.3	Fm 1.3	Md 1.3	No 1.5	

TABLE B-9
Vapor Pressure of Water

Temperature (°C)	Pressure (kPa)	Temperature (°C)	Pressure (kPa)
0	0.6	26	3.4
5	0.9	27	3.6
8	1.1	28	3.8
10	1.2	29	4.0
12	1.4	30	4.2
14	1.6	35	5.6
16	1.8	40	7.4
18	2.1	50	12.3
20	2.3	60	19.9
21	2.5	70	31.2
22	2.6	80	47.3
23	2.8	90	70.1
24	3.0	100	101.3
25	3.2		

TABLE B-10
Solubility Rules*

You will be working with water solutions, and it is helpful to have a few rules concerning what substances are soluble in water. The more common rules are listed below.

1. All common salts of the Group 1 elements and ammonium ion are soluble.

2. All common acetates and nitrates are soluble.

3. All binary compounds of Group 17 elements (other than F) with metals are soluble except those of silver, mercury(I), and lead.

4. All sulfates are soluble except those of barium, strontium, lead, calcium, silver, and mercury(I).

5. Except for those in Rule 1, carbonates, hydroxides, oxides, sulfides, and phosphates are insoluble.

*A substance is considered soluble if more than 3 g of the substance dissolve in 100 cm^3 of water.

TABLE B-11
Standard Reduction Potentials
(at 25°C, 101.325 kPa, 1*M*)

Half-Reaction	E° (Volts)	Half-Reaction	E° (Volts)
$Li^+ + e^- \longrightarrow Li$	−3.040	$AgCl + e^- \longrightarrow Ag + Cl^-$	0.22
$K^+ + e^- \longrightarrow K$	−2.924	$Hg_2Cl_2 + 2e^- \longrightarrow 2Hg + 2Cl^-$	0.27
$Cs^+ + e^- \longrightarrow Cs$	−2.92	$UO_2^{2+} + 4H^+ + 2e^- \longrightarrow U^{4+} + 2H_2O$	0.27
$Ba^{2+} + 2e^- \longrightarrow Ba$	−2.92	$Cu^{2+} + 2e^- \longrightarrow Cu$	0.340
$Ca^{2+} + 2e^- \longrightarrow Ca$	−2.84	$Fe(CN)_6^{3-} + e^- \longrightarrow Fe(CN)_6^{4-}$	0.36
$Na^+ + e^- \longrightarrow Na$	−2.713	$Cu^+ + e^- \longrightarrow Cu$	0.520
$Am^{3+} + 3e^- \longrightarrow Am$	−2.38	$I_2 + 2e^- \longrightarrow 2I^-$	0.5355
$Mg^{2+} + 2e^- \longrightarrow Mg$	−2.356	$Hg_2SO_4 + 2e^- \longrightarrow 2Hg + SO_4^{2-}$	0.62
$Ce^{3+} + 3e^- \longrightarrow Ce$	−2.34	$2HgCl_2 + 2e^- \longrightarrow Hg_2Cl_2 + 2Cl^-$	0.63
$H_2 + 2e^- \longrightarrow 2H^-$	−2.25	$O_2 + 2H^+ + 2e^- \longrightarrow H_2O_2$	0.695
$Pu^{3+} + 3e^- \longrightarrow Pu$	−2.03	$Fe^{3+} + e^- \longrightarrow Fe^{2+}$	0.771
$Be^{2+} + 2e^- \longrightarrow Be$	−1.97	$Hg_2^{2+} + 2e^- \longrightarrow 2Hg$	0.7960
$Al^{3+} + 3e^- \longrightarrow Al$	−1.676	$Ag^+ + e^- \longrightarrow Ag$	0.7991
$SiF_6^{2-} + 4e^- \longrightarrow Si + 6F^-$	−1.20	$NO_3^- + 2H^+ + e^- \longrightarrow NO_2 + H_2O$	0.80
$Mn^{2+} + 2e^- \longrightarrow Mn$	−1.18	$O_2 + 4H^+(10^{-7}M) + 4e^- \longrightarrow 2H_2O$	0.82
$OCN^- + H_2O + 2e^- \longrightarrow CN^- + 2OH^-$	−0.97	$Hg^{2+} + 2e^- \longrightarrow Hg$	0.8535
$Cr^{2+} + 2e^- \longrightarrow Cr$	−0.91	$ClO^- + H_2O + 2e^- \longrightarrow Cl^- + 2OH^-$	0.90
$2H_2O + 2e^- \longrightarrow H_2 + 2OH^-$	−0.828	$2Hg^{2+} + 2e^- \longrightarrow Hg_2^{2+}$	0.9110
$Zn^{2+} + 2e^- \longrightarrow Zn$	−0.7626	$NO_3^- + 3H^+ + 2e^- \longrightarrow HNO_2 + H_2O$	0.957
$Ga^{3+} + 3e^- \longrightarrow Ga$	−0.529	$NO_3^- + 4H^+ + 3e^- \longrightarrow NO(g) + 2H_2O$	0.96
$U^{4+} + e^- \longrightarrow U^{3+}$	−0.52	$Pd^{2+} + 2e^- \longrightarrow Pd$	0.99
$H_3PO_3 + 2H^+ + 2e^- \longrightarrow H_3PO_2 + H_2O$	−0.50	$Br_2 + 2e^- \longrightarrow 2Br^-$	1.0652
$2CO_2 + 2H^+ + 2e^- \longrightarrow H_2C_2O_4$	−0.475	$MnO_2 + 4H^+ + 2e^- \longrightarrow Mn^{2+} + 2H_2O$	1.23
$NO_2^- + H_2O + e^- \longrightarrow NO + 2OH^-$	−0.46	$O_2 + 4H^+ + 4e^- \longrightarrow 2H_2O$	1.229
$Fe^{2+} + 2e^- \longrightarrow Fe$	−0.44	$2HNO_2 + 4H^+ + 4e^- \longrightarrow N_2O + 3H_2O$	1.27
$Eu^{3+} + 3e^- \longrightarrow Eu$	−0.43	$Cl_2 + 2e^- \longrightarrow 2Cl^-$	1.35828
$Cr^{3+} + e^- \longrightarrow Cr^{2+}$	−0.424	$Au^{3+} + 2e^- \longrightarrow Au^+$	1.36
$2H^+(10^{-7}M) + 2e^- \longrightarrow H_2$	−0.414	$Cr_2O_7^{2-} + 14H^+ + 6e^- \longrightarrow 2Cr^{3+} + 7H_2O$	1.36
$Cd^{2+} + 2e^- \longrightarrow Cd$	−0.4025	$PbO_2 + 4H^+ + 2e^- \longrightarrow Pb^{2+} + 2H_2O$	1.46
$PbSO_4 + 2e^- \longrightarrow Pb + SO_4^{2-}$	−0.3505	$2ClO_3^- + 12H^+ + 10e^- \longrightarrow Cl_2 + 6H_2O$	1.47
$Co^{2+} + 2e^- \longrightarrow Co$	−0.277	$HClO + H^+ + 2e^- \longrightarrow Cl^- + H_2O$	1.49
$Ni^{2+} + 2e^- \longrightarrow Ni$	−0.257	$MnO_4^- + 8H^+ + 5e^- \longrightarrow Mn^{2+} + 4H_2O$	1.51
$Sn^{2+} + 2e^- \longrightarrow Sn$	−0.1316	$Au^{3+} + 3e^- \longrightarrow Au$	1.52
$Pb^{2+} + 2e^- \longrightarrow Pb$	−0.1251	$MnO_4^- + 4H^+ + 3e^- \longrightarrow MnO_2 + 2H_2O$	1.70
$AgCN + e^- \longrightarrow Ag + CN^-$	0.02	$H_2O_2 + 2H^+ + 2e^- \longrightarrow 2H_2O$	1.763
$2H^+ + 2e^- \longrightarrow H_2$	0.000	$Co^{3+} + e^- \longrightarrow Co^{2+}$	1.92
$UO_2^{2+} + e^- \longrightarrow UO_2^+$	0.06	$S_2O_8^{2-} + 2e^- \longrightarrow 2SO_4^{2-}$	1.96
$S + 2H^+ + 2e^- \longrightarrow H_2S$	0.14	$O_3 + 2H^+ + 2e^- \longrightarrow O_2 + H_2O$	2.075
$Sn^{4+} + 2e^- \longrightarrow Sn^{2+}$	0.154	$F_2 + 2e^- \longrightarrow 2F^-$	2.87
$SO_4^{2-} + 4H^+ + 2e^- \longrightarrow SO_2(aq) + 2H_2O$	0.158	$F_2 + 2H^+ + 2e^- \longrightarrow 2HF$	3.053
$Cu^{2+} + e^- \longrightarrow Cu^+$	0.159		

TABLE B-12
Heat of Formation (25°C, 100.000 kPa)

ΔH_f° in kJ/mol
(concentration of aqueous solutions is 1M)

Substance	ΔH_f°	Substance	ΔH_f°
Ag(s)	0	H_2O(g)	−241.818
Ag_2SO_4(aq)	−698	H_2O_2(l)	−186
Al(s)	0	H_3PO_4(aq)	−1279.0
Al_2O_3(s)	−1675.7	H_2SO_4(l)	−814
Br_2(g)	30.9	H_2SO_4(aq)	−909.27
Br_2(l)	0	KBr(s)	−393.798
CH_4(g)	−74.81	K_2SO_4(aq)	−1409
C_2H_4(g)	52.26	Mg(s)	0
C_2H_6(g)	−84.7	Mg_3N_2(s)	−461
C_4H_{10}(g)	−125	$Mg(NO_3)_2$(aq)	−875
CO_2(g)	−393.509	$Mg(OH)_2$(s)	−925
Ca(s)	0	N_2(g)	0
$CaCl_2$(aq)	−878	NH_3(g)	−46.11
CaO(s)	−635	NH_4Cl(aq)	−300
$Ca(OH)_2$(s)	−986.09	NH_4NO_3(s)	−366
Cl_2(g)	0	NO(g)	90.25
Cu(s)	0	NO_2(g)	33.18
$Cu(NO_3)_2$(aq)	−350	N_2O(g)	82.05
$CuSO_4$(aq)	−679	NaCl(s)	−411.153
Fe(s)	0	NaCl(aq)	−446
Fe_2O_3(s)	−824.2	$NaNO_3$(aq)	−447.48
H(g)	217.965	NaOH(aq)	−427
H_2(g)	0	Na_2SO_4(aq)	−1387.08
HBr(g)	−36.40	O_2(g)	0
HCl(g)	−92.307	P_4O_{10}(s)	−2984.0
HCl(aq)	−167.159	Zn(s)	0
HNO_2(aq)	−119	$Zn(NO_3)_2$(aq)	−569
HNO_3(aq)	−207	$Zn(OH)_2$(s)	−642
H_2O(l)	−285.830		

TABLE B-13
Specific Heat Values (in J/g · C°)

Substance	C_p	Substance	C_p	Substance	C_p	Substance	C_p
Al	0.9025	$C_6H_5CH_3$	1.80	H_2O(l)	4.18	Na_2CO_3	1.0595
AlF_3	0.8948	CCl_3CCl_3	0.728	H_2O(g)	2.02	PCl_3	0.874
As	0.3289	chalk	0.920	ICl	0.661	SiC	0.6699
Au	0.12905	CH_3COCH_3	2.18	In(s)	0.2407	SiO_2	0.7395
BeO	1.020	CH_3CH_2OH	2.4194	In(l)	0.216	Sn	0.2274
CaC_2	0.9785	CH_3COOH	2.05	K_2CO_3	0.904	steel(s)	0.4494
$CaSO_4$	0.7320	Fe	0.4494	kerosene	2.09	steel(l)	0.719
CCl_4	0.85651	glass	0.753	$LiNO_3$	1.21	Ti	0.5226
C_6H_6	1.74	He	5.1931	$MgCO_3$	0.8957	$TiCl_4$	0.76535
C_6H_{14}	2.26	HI	0.22795	$Mg(OH)_2$	1.321	ZnS	0.469
C_6H_5Br	0.989	H_2O(s)	2.06	$MgSO_4$	0.8015		

TABLE B-14
Atomic Masses

Element	Symbol	Atomic number	Atomic mass	Element	Symbol	Atomic number	Atomic mass
Actinium	Ac	89	227.027 8*	Iron	Fe	26	55.847
Aluminum	Al	13	26.981 539	Krypton	Kr	36	83.80
Americium	Am	95	243.061 4*	Lanthanum	La	57	38.905 5
Antimony	Sb	51	121.757	Lawrencium	Lr	103	260.105 4*
Argon	Ar	18	39.948	Lead	Pb	82	207.2
Arsenic	As	33	74.921 59	Lithium	Li	3	6.941
Astatine	At	85	209.987 1*	Lutetium	Lu	71	174.967
Barium	Ba	56	137.327	Magnesium	Mg	12	24.305 0
Berkelium	Bk	97	247.070 3*	Manganese	Mn	25	54.938 05
Beryllium	Be	4	9.012 182	Meiterium	Mt	109	266*
Bismuth	Bi	83	208.980 37	Mendelevium	Md	101	258.098 6*
Bohrium	Bh	107	262*	Mercury	Hg	80	200.59
Boron	B	5	10.811	Molybdenum	Mo	42	95.94
Bromine	Br	35	79.904	Neodymium	Nd	60	144.24
Cadmium	Cd	48	112.411	Neon	Ne	10	20.179 7
Calcium	Ca	20	40.078	Neptunium	Np	93	237.048 2
Californium	Cf	98	251.079 6*	Nickel	Ni	28	58.693 4
Carbon	C	6	12.011	Niobium	Nb	41	92.906 38
Cerium	Ce	58	140.115	Nitrogen	N	7	14.006 74
Cesium	Cs	55	132.905 43	Nobelium	No	102	259.100 9*
Chlorine	Cl	17	35.452 7	Osmium	Os	76	190.2
Chromium	Cr	24	51.996 1	Oxygen	O	8	15.999 4
Cobalt	Co	27	58.933 20	Palladium	Pd	46	106.42
Copper	Cu	29	63.546	Phosphorus	P	15	30.973 762
Curium	Cm	96	247.070 3*	Platinum	Pt	78	195.08
Dubnium	Db	105	262*	Plutonium	Pu	94	244.064 2*
Dysprosium	Dy	66	162.50	Polonium	Po	84	208.982 4*
Einsteinium	Es	99	252.082 8*	Potassium	K	19	39.098 3
Erbium	Er	68	167.26	Praseodymium	Pr	59	140.907 65
Europium	Eu	63	151.965	Promethium	Pm	61	144.912 8*
Fermium	Fm	100	257.095 1*	Protactinium	Pa	91	231.035 88
Fluorine	F	9	18.998 403 2	Radium	Ra	88	226.025 4
Francium	Fr	87	223.019 7*	Radon	Rn	86	222.017 6*
Gadolinium	Gd	64	157.25	Rhenium	Re	75	186.207
Gallium	Ga	31	69.723	Rhodium	Rh	45	102.905 50
Germanium	Ge	32	72.61	Rubidium	Rb	37	85.467 8
Gold	Au	79	196.966 54	Ruthenium	Ru	44	101.07
Hafnium	Hf	72	178.49	Rutherfordium	Rf	104	261*
Hassium	Hs	108	265*	Samarium	Sm	62	150.36
Helium	He	2	4.002 602	Scandium	Sc	21	44955 910
Holmium	Ho	67	164.930 32	Seaborgium	Sg	106	263*
Hydrogen	H	1	1.007 94	Selenium	Se	34	78.96
Indium	In	49	114.82	Silicon	Si	14	28.085 5
Iodine	I	53	126.904 47	Silver	Ag	47	107.868 2
Iridium	Ir	77	192.22	Sodium	Na	11	22.989 768

Element	Symbol	Atomic number	Atomic mass	Element	Symbol	Atomic number	Atomic mass
Strontium	Sr	38	87.62	Tungsten	W	74	183.85
Sulfur	S	16	32.066	Uub	Uub	112	
Tantalum	Ta	73	180.947 9	Uun	Uun	110	
Technetium	Tc	43	97.907 2*	Uuu	Uuu	111	
Tellurium	Te	52	127.60	Uranium	U	92	238.028 9
Terbium	Tb	65	158.925 34	Vanadium	V	23	50.941 5
Thallium	Tl	81	204.383 3	Xenon	Xe	54	131.29
Thorium	Th	90	232.038 1	Ytterbium	Yb	70	173.04
Thulium	Tm	69	168.934 21	Yttrium	Y	39	88.905 85
Tin	Sn	50	118.710	Zinc	Zn	30	65.39
Titanium	Ti	22	47.88	Zirconium	Zr	40	91.224

*The mass of the isotope with the longest known half-life.